TAKING CHARGE

Strategic Leadership in the Middle Game

Stephen A. Stumpf
Thomas P. Mullen
New York University

Prentice Hall, Englewood Cliffs, NJ 07632

Library of Congress Cataloging-in-Publication Data

Stumpf, Stephen A.
  Taking charge: strategic leadership in the middle game / Stephen A. Stumpf,
Thomas P. Mullen.
    p.   cm.
  Includes index.
  ISBN 0-13-851999-4
  1. Middle managers.   2. Industrial management.   I. Mullen, Thomas P., (date) II. Title.
HD38.2.S8   1992   91-15065
658.4'3—dc20   CIP

Editorial/production supervision, interior design,
  and page makeup: *June Sanns*
Acquisitions editor: *John Willig*
Copy editor: *Linda B. Pawelchak*
Cover designer: *Lundgren Graphics*
Prepress buyer: *Mary McCartney*
Manufacturing buyer: *Susan Brunke*
Editorial assistant: *Maureen Dianna*

© 1992 by Stephen A. Stumpf and Thomas P. Mullen

Published by Prentice-Hall, Inc.
A Simon & Schuster Company
Englewood Cliffs, New Jersey 07632

The publisher offers discounts on this book when ordered
in bulk quantities. For more information, write:
  Special Sales/College Marketing
  Prentice-Hall, Inc.
  College Technical and Reference Division
  Englewood Cliffs, NJ 07632

Printed in the United States of America

10 9 8 7 6 5 4 3 2 1

ISBN 0-13-851999-4

PRENTICE-HALL INTERNATIONAL (UK) LIMITED, *London*
PRENTICE-HALL OF AUSTRALIA PTY. LIMITED, *Sydney*
PRENTICE-HALL CANADA INC., *Toronto*
PRENTICE-HALL HISPANOAMERICANA, S.A., *Mexico*
PRENTICE-HALL OF INDIA PRIVATE LIMITED, *New Delhi*
PRENTICE-HALL OF JAPAN, INC., *Tokyo*
SIMON & SCHUSTER ASIA PTE. LTD., *Singapore*
EDITORA PRENTICE-HALL DO BRASIL LTDA., *Rio de Janeiro*

Dedicated to our parents,
Richard and Jacqueline Stumpf
and Benjamin and Catherine Mullen,
for their encouragement,
patience,
and most of all,
for their love.

Contents

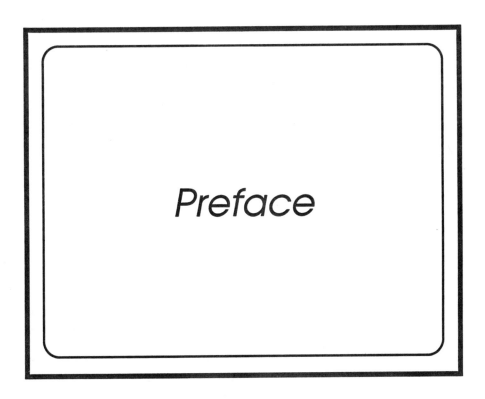

Preface

A book, like a business, needs to have a purpose—a mission. Ours is to inspire middle-level managers to challenge their leadership abilities and to empower those who take this challenge to meet it. Leadership in work organizations in the decade ahead will be more demanding, more complex, and more frustrating than it has ever been before. It has the potential to be more creative, more energizing, and more meaningful, particularly for those who are willing to embrace the many changes taking place in the economy, society, and themselves as they reach the middle levels of organizations.

In our view, the role of managers in strategic leadership is to: (1) understand several key concepts about strategy, planning, and organizational processes, (2) identify the mission, vision, goals, and objectives of their business unit, (3) assess their skills and personal preferences for leading others, and (4) enhance their capacity for strategic leadership through applying the concepts proposed, practicing the skills identified, and pursuing work opportunities and other career options that can develop their strategic thinking. The organization's role in this process is to balance the traditions of the past with its vision of the future.

Taking Charge: Strategic Leadership in the Middle Game is for managers and students of management who are seeking new ideas, concepts, and skills that they can apply to their work situations. It is for the serious manager, the person who is actively seeking ways to improve the organization as well as him or herself. *Taking Charge* is not a book of quick fixes and formulas; we offer no magic words that can quickly transform an average employee to a charismatic leader. What we do is provide a series of frameworks that can alter the way managers think about issues, help them to define things in ways that are more understandable and acceptable to others, and begin a development process that can lead to new skill proficiencies.

Taking Charge is written for a general audience of managers, leaving the technical detail of its research underpinnings to footnotes and academic journal articles. Our research began 10 years ago and has involved several thousand managers at nearly every level of the organizational hierarchy. In many ways, this book is theirs, as we have learned from them how to fulfill the role of middle manager more effectively and develop skills that will enable them to be more successful senior managers.

The size of this undertaking is indicated by the large number of managers involved as well as a team of colleagues who worked with us in gaining access to corporations, collecting and analyzing data, and disseminating the results. Expressions of gratitude must start with those who have had the greatest effect on our thinking: Dale Zand, Robert Longman, Joel DeLuca, and Henry Mintzberg. These individuals have provided new and insightful ways to understand strategic leadership. Others have influenced us through our interactions and business activities with them, including Susan Berger, Sabra Brock, Susan DeLuca, Anne Hayden, Robert Kaplan, Dorothy Kramer, David Kreischer, Richard Lepsinger, Pat Martocci, Ed Mills, F. Anthony Orbe, Bob Powell, Milt Reisman, Lorna Simon, Barbara Stahl, Richard Straus, Candace Ulrich, Steve Wall, Randy White, Trish Williams, Bill Wingate, and numerous other colleagues and associates who have provided us with the opportunity to learn and grow. Still others who have contributed to this book are part of a team, known as the Management Simulation Projects Group at New York University, who worked together in the development and use of many of the concepts presented in *Taking Charge:* Catherine Ahern, Maria Arnone, Debra Barrows, Hrach Bedrosian, Roger Dunbar, Jane Dutton, Richard Green, Susan Heinbuch, Mary McBride, Mabel Miguel, Sidney Nachman, and Monica Shay.

A particular thank you needs to go to John Willig and June Sanns, both at Prentice-Hall. John for his belief in the ideas contained in the book and his support throughout the project; and June for her ever cheerful but determined approach to editing. We thank you both.

Most importantly, we appreciate the support of our families who both encouraged us and tolerated us during the weekends and late nights of writing and editing. To Maria and Eugene and Nancy, Katie, and Samatha, our heartfelt thanks.

S.A.S.
T.P.M.

PART ONE
THE MIDDLE

CHAPTER ONE
The Middle Game

CHAPTER TWO
The Middle Manager

CHAPTER ONE
The Middle Game

Strategic leadership—the critical inspiration and direction needed to accomplish an organization's mission—is essential to every enterprise. Concepts and theories of strategic leadership are widely written about; prescriptions for executives to follow in running their organizations have made several books best sellers. If we know so much about strategic leadership, why is it that many managers continually struggle to improve the effectiveness of the parts of the organization for which they are responsible?

One answer is that common knowledge is not necessarily common practice. *Doing* something differently is much harder than *thinking* about doing it differently. Many people have watched inspirational leaders excite an audience; observing their style and skills often gives one some knowledge of how they inspire others, but it rarely gives one the ability to be an inspirational leader. Turning knowledge into practice is a human challenge.

We believe that there is an additional reason why managers are continuously struggling to improve the effectiveness of their businesses. They struggle because the bulk of their efforts each day is spent in trying to manage their businesses during the middle game—that ordinary and common period of conflict and competition that exists after organizations have been functioning for some time. However, most of the business advice provided assumes that resources can be made available to pursue new or additional areas of business that are most attractive. In that case, the tasks are to identify the potential industry and business segments in which one wants to compete, do market research, conduct competitive analyses, evaluate this information in light of organizational strengths and the current business situation, and then make the best choice. The organization has implicitly agreed to provide resources for the venture subject to a compelling proposal.

When one has the opportunity to start a new venture, or enter a new line of business, the ideas and advice available on business strategy and entrepreneurship can be quite useful. But, how does this information help managers in organizations who are attending to significant existing business activity during periods of contracting resource availability? A common challenge for managers today is to accomplish more next year, with fewer resources, and by using systems, equipment, and people that are entrenched in yesterday's way of doing business.

A CHESS MATCH

The game of chess is a useful metaphor to consider with respect to strategic leadership. The phrase *middle game* is commonly used to describe a portion of a chess match. Although there are well-known and detailed descriptions of strategies for the opening game and the endgame in chess, it is the middle game that is the least understood, yet the most complex. Experts frequently recommend that a beginning chess player learn the different strategies for the opening game and then deploy resources against the selected strategy for as long as is viable given the competitive response. If one can develop and sustain an advantage, the middle game may be quite structured and short. This is sometimes taken to an extreme in chess books by extending the opening-game strategy well into the middle game, as if there were no difference between the two periods of play. This is similar to an emerging business following an opening-game strategy into the middle game just because that opening-game strategy was successful when there was relatively little competition and limited customer awareness of its products and services.

Chess experts also encourage players to develop technique around their endgame. This is the period in the game when there are only a few pieces left on the board. By knowing specific combinations and patterns of play with one's favorite pieces, checkmate can be achieved. In contrast to the wide variety of approaches to the opening game, the endgame involves a depth of knowledge with respect to a simplified situation. It is the depth of understanding in the endgame that often leads endgame specialists to victory.

Unlike chess players, who can learn the game in small chunks and logical progression, managers are commonly immersed into the middle game without the benefits or experience of playing many games from start to finish. In fact, one might argue that the middle game is 90 percent of an organization's life cycle. Many managers do not experience an opening game or an endgame until after they have had business unit or functional area responsibilities for years. Even when they do get the opportunity to experience the opening game or an endgame, experts in the areas of entrepreneurship or mergers and acquisitions are frequently involved, or the task is directed by a manager more seasoned with such activities.

The time spent and number of managers involved in the start-up and shutdown of a business, product line, plant, or distribution channel are minor compared to the time spent and number of managers involved in providing that day-to-day inspiration and direction to their part of the enterprise. It is providing this inspiration and direction that we refer to as "strategic leadership in the middle" for a business unit or functional area. This inspiration and direction is essential during the middle game, and it is the middle-level manager who must provide it.

THE MIDDLE GAME

A number of factors exist that make the middle game the most difficult to play (in both chess and business). Consider the following middle-game attributes:

1. Many of one's resources are deployed—they are in play. At the start of most corporate ventures, resources are being amassed (corporate funds, venture capital, personnel). Decisions are approached through a logical analysis, including likely return on investments; critical path analysis of what needs to be done first, second, third; and so on. Choices involve expending the resources in one way versus another where the resources are not yet committed. This is not the situation in the middle game because the decisions of the opening game have developed the business in some specific ways that are difficult to change, at least in the short run of a year or two. One must manage a business with financial and human commitments that restrict one's freedom to pursue alternative strategies. In all likelihood, some of the logical analyses performed that led to the current business situation were based on flawed data, or the situation changed after the analysis was completed such that the inferences based on the analysis are flawed. In either case, one cannot just start over.

Redeploying resources is often more difficult than deploying them originally because people's jobs, egos, and values are now part of the fabric of the organization, and many people may be wedded to the existing systems and ways of doing things. Changing what someone is doing, or what someone believes is best to do, is much more difficult than providing options to someone who is not yet committed to a course of action and letting that person choose. Managers often know this intuitively, as witnessed by their investment of tremendous time and energy in selecting people, choosing the product line and product features, and targeting the customer groups. Once these choices are made, the task shifts to the more difficult ones of developing new skills in the people already employed, altering production processes and product attributes, and changing employee and customer behaviors. These developmental changes typically reflect the desire on the part of managers to adjust actions in the middle game to shifts in the economy, to competitor actions and reactions, to labor market conditions, to technological shortcomings or advances, and/or to changes in the legal and regulatory systems that monitor the enterprise's activities.

2. In the middle game, there are few recurring sequences of moves that lead to victory. One frequently does battle for position, with the hope that positioning can provide some advantage. It is particularly difficult to teach managers how to position their units (and themselves) so as to increase their chances of success. In chess, this skill often evolves over years of playing the game. It is through seeing hundreds of middle games that one develops a sense for which patterns of play are incrementally better than other patterns. It is through managing hundreds of days that one has the opportunity to develop a sense for which patterns of people, issues, and events are incrementally better than other patterns. Chess players have a distinct advantage over managers: Their game has a fixed board, there are a limited number of chess pieces that move only in specific ways, and most importantly, chess is played against a single other person whose approach can be analyzed and partially understood based on past actions. Managers cannot easily develop the same degree of useful intuition as chess players do because managerial situations are frequently changing, managers deal with a large number of different people, and competition is unpredictable.

3. During the middle game, the match is at a peak of complexity. Because there are many pieces actively deployed on the board, the relationships among them are more complex than at other times in the game. There are so many possibilities during the middle game that no number of books or examples can cover them all. The possible moves in the game exceed human information-processing abilities. The challenge for managers easily exceeds that for the chess player. The number of people vying for attention, resources, and the manager's time is overwhelming. These others can be subordinates who may have similar goals as the manager with respect to the prosperity of the enterprise, or they could be other stakeholders such as customers, regulators, union members, or the press who often have different goals and different definitions of what makes the enterprise successful.

STRATEGIC LEADERSHIP IN THE MIDDLE GAME

To the extent that the chess metaphor reflects the situation that managers face, the middle game is a period of particular difficulty. There are the challenges of redeploying resources (not just deploying them), the lack of recurring sequences of activity to learn from so as to improve one's analytical or intuitive responses to situations, and the complexity created by changing relationships with many different stakeholders. There is also the possibility that there will not be an endgame during the manager's tenure in the position. This phenomenon of organic systems such as business and social organizations is untrue for most living systems or competitive events. If managers know when the endgame will occur, either in terms of time or configuration, then they can adjust their thinking to strategies for the endgame. Some organizations may even choose to rush into the endgame by eliminating parts of the business in various swaps, trades, or shutdowns so as to hasten the endgame's arrival when they perceive a competitive advantage from doing so. By not knowing when the endgame will occur, managers are forced to manage in the middle game for extended periods of time.

Strategic leadership in the middle involves providing the inspiration and direction to accomplish the organization's mission during this difficult time. Since the organization's mission is not always known by middle managers, they are sometimes confronted with not knowing how senior executives define business success. This creates an additional demand on managers in the middle game: Become intimate with the organization's mission—it may well define the rules of the game.

If the organization's mission is known (or knowable), energy can be directed towards developing and implementing strategy. Developing strategy is often the thrust of the opening game. If the strategy is well thought through based on logical analyses, the middle game can be devoted to strategy implementation and flawless execution. Right? Probably not.

DELIBERATE AND EMERGENT STRATEGIES

Strategic leadership involves the complex and collective process of strategy-making—of crafting strategies.[1] Strategy-making, much like a craft, involves a certain amount of planning for the future while simultaneously learning from past and on-going actions. Although business planners attempt to make the strategy-making process synonymous with creating the five-year business plan, managers quickly ignore any plans that do not reflect the current situation as they experience it. As a military expert once said, "no plan survives contact with the enemy." Developing a logical plan of where we want to be and how we want to get there says little about the perils experienced along the way.

Interestingly, many managers enjoy dealing with the perils just as people enjoy watching Indiana Jones or James Bond deal with adversity. Goal accomplishment is important for one's resume; the managerial process is important for one's vitality. Managers want to be involved in strategy-making, not just with planning. They want to be involved throughout the middle game, often up to the endgame. Their involvement results in most deliberate strategies being altered over time as emergent events suggest a shift in approach. This process, depicted in Figure 1–1, suggests that strategy-making is as much a flow as it is an event.[2]

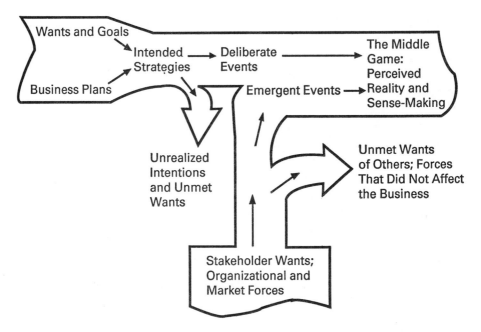

FIGURE 1-1 The Merging of Intended and Emergent Events
in the Strategy-Making Process

Source: Figure adapted from J. Waters and H. Mintzberg, "Of Strategies, Deliberate and Emergent," *Strategic Management Journal,* 1985, 6(3), 257–72. Reprinted by permission of John Wiley & Sons, Ltd., Sussex, England.

This "river" model identifies two streams of thoughts and behaviors that merge to create the reality managers perceive and work within each day. The stream at the top-left moving across the figure carries some combination of the wants and goals of the managers and the strategies articulated in the business plan. Based on managers' wants and goals and the business plan, managers develop intended business strategies on how to accomplish these goals. But not all of these intentions lead to behaviors. Some intentions remain unrealized possibilities that fall by the wayside; other intentions become the deliberate strategies that managers enact.

The stream at the bottom-center moving upward carries with it the wants and goals of the stakeholders in a business as well as various organizational and exogenous market forces that might affect the organization. Stakeholders include the individuals, groups, and organizations that have some stake in what occurs in the business. Organizational and market forces include the internal and external labor markets, economic conditions, governmental pressures on business practices, human resource policies, and so forth. Collectively, the wants and goals of these stakeholders along with the organizational and exogenous market forces influence managers' thoughts and motivation to implement the deliberate strategies. Although not all stakeholder and market forces have a direct impact on business strategies, possibly due to unmet wants and behaviors, their effects are sizable—and at times controlling. The result is that managers experience life at the point where the two streams merge as they manage their organizations. What they experience and attempt to comprehend are their deliberate actions mixed in among many emergent events. Business strategies are meant to change and evolve over time as they come in contact with the environment. Strategic leadership in the middle game is mastering the process, the journey, not just arriving at the destination.

"One is never able to step into the same river twice."

Heraclitus

MANAGEMENT AS A CHESS GAME?

Is management like a chess game? For some, maybe. For most, probably not. But management and chess games do have a few interesting things in common. Both frequently involve competition and conflict that occur within a set of rules, roles, and procedures. Both involve strategic thinking, a mission, goals, and actions. Both involve players who are interested in winning, generally by following the rules that define the event. Both can be amusing while simultaneously capturing one's full and serious attention. Both have a middle game.

Of course, management is more than a chess game. The rewards and penalties are real. Motivation is derived from more than the desire for intrinsic rewards. There are no breaks in the action when the competition stops so that managers can rethink a strategy or plan. It is not possible to stop the stream of ideas, issues, and events that are flowing into the river, forcing managers to continuously deal with differences among their personal wants and goals, their business's plan for itself over the next several years, and the various stakeholder wants and market forces. As Mintzberg has suggested, management may be best thought of as a craft—a blending of science and art, thought and action, control and discovery, structure and flexibility.

THE MIDDLE MANAGER IN THE MIDDLE GAME

Who is managing the middle game? It is not the senior executives as one might initially think. Our observations of the middle-manager and executive levels of many firms suggest that the executives monitor the middle game through periodic business reviews and MIS reports, while middle-level managers handle and control the business. It is the middle managers who are expected to have mastered the business, to really know how the business works. It is the middle managers who are actively diagnosing strategic issues, examining business results, probing for more information, making employment decisions, directing efforts to solve problems, and supervising others. They are in touch with the business. They are at its core. It is only at budget approval time or when the monitoring of a business unit or functional area indicates deviations from the forecasted results that senior executives exert their influence. But even then, senior executives rarely involve themselves in managing specific business issues directly. Executives' attention has become increasingly directed to their external stakeholders—members of their boards of directors, stockholders, consumer interest groups, environmentalists, conservationists, regulators, the press, and government agencies—leaving the management of the business to the middle-level managers, supervisors, and workers.

One should **not** interpret this as a criticism of the executive ranks. It is a descriptive statement that reflects the external pressures coming to bear on today's senior executives. The decades ahead are likely to be sufficiently turbulent and convoluted to require the more senior levels of management in the enterprise to be more outwardly directed than inwardly attentive in their activities. What is critical is that middle managers understand the need and the opportunity that this creates for them to assume the responsibility for the strategic leadership of their business units and functional areas. Middle managers may continue to receive senior executive guidance and input during the opening game (defining the mission, strategy formulation for the enterprise as a whole, portfolio management with respect to one's line of business) and the endgame (divestitures, plant shutdowns, bankruptcies, takeovers). But for the middle game, executive attention is already scarce. Our focus in this book is on these middle managers in the middle game. The key attributes of the middle game are summa-

⊃ Many of the unit's resources are deployed—some are not recoverable.

⊃ Many courses of action are no longer viable, given the resources that are already deployed.

⊃ Energy has shifted from choosing what the business wants to accomplish to molding things into what the business can get accomplished.

⊃ History is an unreliable predictor of the future since there are few recurring sequences of events.

⊃ The complexity of the business situation and the attentional demands on the manager's time are beyond human information-processing capabilities.

⊃ Managers (not the founders or entrepreneurs) are held accountable for middle-game results.

⊃ Deliberate strategies are altered by emergent events—managers do not have complete control over the business.

⊃ An endgame that would define success has not yet been considered.

FIGURE 1–2 **Attributes of the Middle Game**

rized in Figure 1–2. Who are these middle managers, how are their roles changing, and is strategic leadership for them something different than it is for the executive ranks? These are the topics of the next chapter.

NOTES

[1]See H. Mintzberg, *Mintzberg on Management.* (New York: The Free Press, 1989), pp. 25–42.

[2]Adapted from J. Waters, and H. Mintzberg. "Of Strategies, Deliberate and Emergent." *Strategic Management Journal,* 1985, 6(3), 257–72.

CHAPTER TWO
The Middle Manager

Just as "Who are those guys?" was asked in the western classic *Butch Cassidy and the Sundance Kid*, we ask, "Who are the middle managers?" Middle managers are individuals in the middle of the organizational hierarchy—people who are typically thought of as having responsibility for implementing strategy. They are the agents for both executives and workers—bringing the organization's mission, vision, and objectives to the workers and the workers' mission, vision, and objectives to the executives. As intermediaries and go-betweens, they serve both the executive ranks and the worker ranks.

The middle-manager rank came under attack in the 1980s, to the point that many middle managers thought their jobs were threatened. This situation has persisted and became even more widespread as we entered the last decade of the century. Since the executive ranks were encouraged to get in touch with their customers and workforce, and "downsizing" became a corporate slogan, little was left for many middle managers to do except prepare their resumes. Competitive pressures from foreign manufacturers or deregulation has led such organizations as Honeywell, General Motors, General Electric, Eastman Kodak, AT&T, The Sun Company, and Mobil Oil to drastically reduce their costs. The resulting downsizing meant reducing the number of levels of hierarchy and thinning managerial ranks.[1] This trend, in combination with additional demands being placed on the executive ranks from external constituencies, have created new roles and placed additional responsibilities for strategic leadership on those managers who remain. As a result, middle managers need to develop a broader, longer-term perspective and new skills to meet these challenges and fulfill new roles.

Do middle managers need to be strategic leaders in today's organizations? We address this question by examining some basic ideas of how organizations are structured, how the business environment has changed, and the implications these changes are likely to have on middle managers over the next decade.

ORGANIZATIONAL HIERARCHIES: AGENDAS AND STRUCTURES

Three easily observable levels of hierarchy generally operate within an organization: the executive level, the manager level, and the worker level. Individuals at the executive level have the responsibility for the development and management of the **organizational agenda.** Organizational agendas are comprised of issues that affect the enterprise as a whole—its profitability, its status in financial markets, board of director approvals, and government regulations. Positions at this level include the chief executive officer, the president, the chief operating officer, executive vice-presidents, managing partners, and senior vice-presidents.

The next level, the managers, includes a broad band of individuals in the middle levels of the organization who are held responsible for implementing the agenda developed by members of the executive group. They do so by developing and implementing **business level** or **subunit agendas** for these activities over which they have direct **operating** responsibility. Business and subunit agendas often include issues such as capacity planning, choice of geographic and consumer market areas, new product development, design and use of control systems (e.g., MIS and accounting practices), and the like. Business units can be broken down into additional, distinct subunits, and involve managers' supervising one of three areas in an organization: Line activities, which involve the basic production or manufacture of the goods or services offered to prospective buyers; technical functions, such as engineering, accounting, marketing, and information systems; and, support functions, such as legal, public relations, and human resources. These middle managers frequently have positions as division managers, vice-presidents and assistant vice-presidents, directors, plant managers, and operations managers.

Below the manager level is the third major group of employees. These individuals may be first-line supervisors of line employees or nonsupervisory technical and support personnel. These people—the workers—have primary responsibility for implementing the business level agenda. Workers accomplish this by developing and managing **functional agendas**—agendas comprised of issues relating to the day-to-day functioning of the firm. Functional agendas should support the business level agenda.

The image often used to capture these three levels of organizational structure is a pyramid—executives on top, managers in the middle, workers at the base. One retail organization, Nordstrom, has made an interesting statement to its employees by turning the pyramid so that it sits on its apex, as illustrated in Figure 2–1.[2] The message: Executives support managers, manag-

FIGURE 2–1 Nordstrom's Organizational Chart

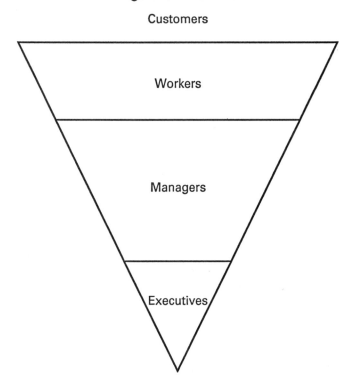

Customers

Workers

Managers

Executives

ers support workers, and workers represent the entire organization to its stakeholders—particularly customers who interact with the workers and thereby directly affect the accomplishment of organizational and business level agendas.

Thinking of organization structures as hierarchies, can unintentionally imply a series of linear events between hierarchical levels for building agendas within organizations: Executives determine the organizational level agenda, managers take the organizational agenda and build business agendas to support the organizational agenda, workers develop functional agendas to support the business agendas. Power and authority for determining agendas are retained largely by the top of the organization where the emphasis tends to be on recognizing and fulfilling the organizational agenda. This process of nesting agendas within each other is presented graphically in Figure 2–2.

FIGURE 2–2 Alignment of Agendas of Different Units and Subunits within the Executives' Organizational Agenda

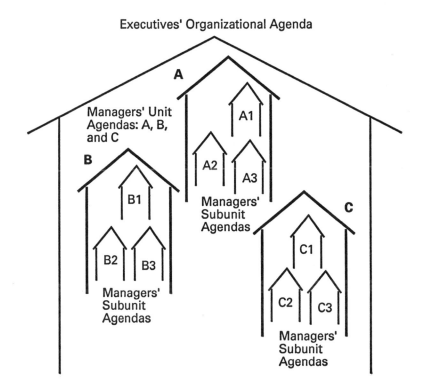

If all the nested agendas are nicely aligned, organizations might function in much the way textbooks describe them. Some organizations probably do, and these are frequently the organizations that are most heavily criticized for a lack of flexibility and innovation. For example, bureaucratic organizations create rules and procedures to align many of the different agendas. The objective is a highly efficient organization as suggested by the aligned arrows in Figure 2–2. Yet, what most employees experience is not a neat alignment of agendas, but a variety of partially aligned agendas as suggested in Figure 2–3. This latter arrangement reflects an environment with many points of friction among agendas. At times heated conflict may occur that can lead to the withdrawal or removal of key managers and/or revisions in the organization's structure, rules, and procedures.

Aligning agendas and managing the misalignments are two of the challenges of strategic leadership in the middle game.

FIGURE 2–3 **Misalignment of Agendas of Different Units and Subunits within the Executives' Organizational Agenda**

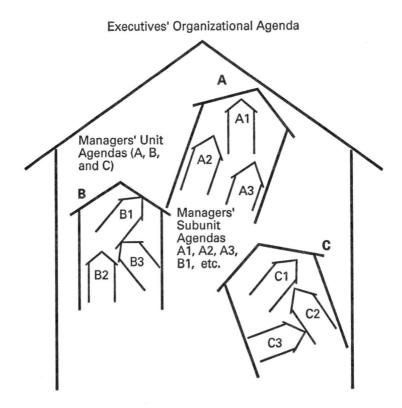

Individuals at all levels in an organization must build and manage agendas that recognize and value the emergent aspect of issues as well as deliberate efforts to resolve them. The misaligned arrows in Figure 2–3 exist in the middle game—and various players are already accountable for action on many agenda items. Managers have sufficiently full agendas, and increasing their responsibilities is not often feasible. What makes the situation even more demanding is that agendas are not static; they are frequently adjusted as priorities change. Emergent events alter deliberate agendas by redirecting people's attention to different issues in the organization and environment.

In addition, the changing, nested agendas create a turbulence within the organization's structure. The agenda arrows shown in Figure 2–3 keep rubbing up against each other—sometimes merging, frequently with substantial friction, often ricocheting off each other, sometimes leaving substantial dents before moving off in a new direction and colliding with a different agenda. If we consider the three levels of nested arrows to be the agendas of the executive, manager, and worker ranks, we can observe the following:

1. Executive agendas are the heaviest and most solid. They take a lot of hits but shift only slightly because many of the hits counteract each other. It is only when repeated bumps occur from within the same general area that we see the organizational agenda shift in direction. Otherwise, the agenda simply vibrates, fiercely at times, but the forces are sufficiently balanced to sustain a direction.

2. Manager agendas take hits from internal and external forces in much the same way as executive agendas; they vibrate a great deal and get redirected on occasion. But manager agendas also do some bumping of their own as suggested in Figure 2–4. They challenge executive agendas. This may feel a bit like being in a bumper car at an amusement park where you are both bumping and being bumped. The bumps come from different directions at short time intervals. After 10 minutes of driving a bumper car, it is often difficult to walk straight. One feels a bit battered. Yet we expect managers to think straight both during and after the collision of their agendas with the agendas of others.

The excitement and mechanics of bumper cars should not be ignored. Many managers find it exciting to have their agenda bounced around. The line of people waiting to get into the action is

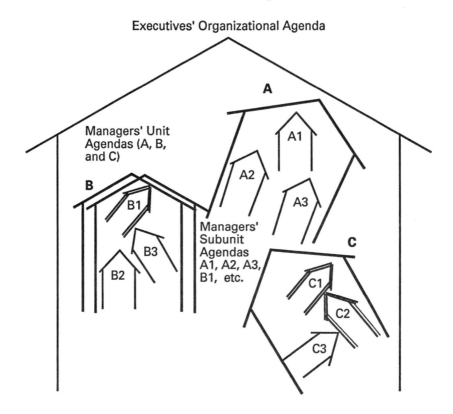

Executives' Organizational Agenda

FIGURE 2–4 **Misalignment and Shifting of Agendas of Different Units and Subunits within the Executives' Organizational Agenda**

quite long for both the bumper car ride and careers in management. Apparently the battering that occurs is part of the excitement.

The mechanics of what occurs in bumper cars—forces, counterforces, glancing blows, head-on collisions, teaming up to amass several separate forces going in the same direction—are akin to managers' merging their deliberate agendas. It is possible for individual managers to affect executive agendas—through building up significant energy in a particular direction by being very focused on what is wanted, by getting several other managers' agendas to align with their agenda, or by getting many of the workers' agendas to be supportive of their agenda. As with bumper cars, this is easier to say than to do.

Less frequently, there are windows of opportunity for a bumper car to move from one end of the arena to the other without much contact with other cars. Middle managers have similar opportunities to create momentum for their agendas. This sometimes occurs through the process of redefining a portion of their activities. Redefinition may involve shifting from an adaptive frame of reference to an innovative one, or from an operations focus to a marketing focus. We discuss these possibilities in greater detail in Chapter 9—Creativity Counts.

3. Worker agendas bump up against managers' agendas as well as other workers' agendas. As such, the dominant effect may be one of being bounced around. But the bumps have less force because there is little opportunity or resources for an individual worker to develop a head of steam before another bump occurs. This should not imply that workers have no power. On the contrary, as a group their numbers and functions define the business. During most middle games, they create tremendous stability in the organization. There are too many workers to replace quickly, and key technologies, services, products, markets, and manufacturing processes are integrated into the workers' jobs. But workers may feel powerless in spite of their strengths. Their agendas frequently get ignored or altered with little explanation.

A summary of these dynamics across the three levels of agendas is provided in Figure 2–5. Individuals at each level contribute to the tension that exists across the three levels of agendas. This may occur without their realizing it because they are focusing much of their mental and physical energy on building and managing their own agendas.

FIGURE 2–5 The Dynamics Present Across the Hierarchy of Agendas

AGENDAS	DYNAMICS PRESENT
Organizational Level	Wants to Provide Direction
	Seeks Alignment of Subordinate Agendas
Business Level	Wants to Share Insights Gained through Experience
	Seeks Flexibility and Influence Upward
	Seeks Alignment and Control Downward
Operating and Functional Level	Wants to Share Insights Gained through Interface with Customers
	Seeks Influence Upward
	Seeks Stable Structure and Processes

THE CHANGING ENVIRONMENT OF MIDDLE MANAGERS

Defining key aspects of the current environment and understanding how this environment developed and how it continues to evolve lay the foundation for understanding the changing role of the middle manager. Analysis of the automobile and life insurance industries provides useful illustrations.

Following the initial development of the car, the automobile industry has gone through three major phases: growth, consolidation, and internationalization. During the growth phase, there were a number of manufacturers who were building automobiles of various makes and models. This changed as the manufacturing technology for autos became more sophisticated and the capital required to build facilities to produce cars at a competitive price increased. At this point, the industry started to consolidate. What evolved over several decades was an industry dominated by a few, large competitors. One reason the auto industry became an oligopoly was that three firms achieved such overwhelming economies of scale through mass production that the capital required to compete in this business drove out the smaller firms. As a result, barriers to entry became significant; few other organizations were prepared to risk the capital.

To increase profits and achieve stability, the major players within the auto industry focused on operational considerations. In terms of organization structures, hierarchy was king. Organizational agendas were set by the senior executives to be executed by workers under the direction of managers. Managers were not to have agendas of their own, and workers were to be closely controlled through supervision and the use of expensive manufacturing technology which defined each worker's role on the shop floor.

Somewhat different events resulted in a similar operational focus in the life insurance industry. The two major evolutionary phases have been regulated growth and deregulated diversification. Initially, a relatively small number of insurance companies were serving a large number of customers within broadly defined market segments in a regulated, stable environment. Large insurance organizations emphasized mass distribution networks and stable operating environments—the efficient handling and execution of many similar, small transactions.

In these two industries, as well as numerous others, organizations were driven by operational concerns and, as a result, developed significant operational expertise. Once the operational concerns were under control, there was an agenda shift to selling what the company had to offer. Inventories or unused capacity were expensive to maintain. First produce efficiently, then sell. There was little emphasis on identifying, developing, and marketing what the customer wanted.

During the consolidation phase in the auto industry and the regulated growth phase in the insurance industry, organizational agendas carried with them a particular set of rules for the middle game. Organizations that were operationally driven wanted their environments to be stable. So they created stability in the ways that they defined their business and markets.

Some industries tried to create stability through controlling technology, others through continually increasing capital requirements for equipment and inventories, still others by restricting distribution systems, and some by furthering regulatory constraints. These and other considerations created barriers to entry that provided for more stability. Organizations in numerous industries from securities firms to utility companies prospered for decades by seeking and enacting such environments.

The rules in this middle-game environment focused managers' attention on minimizing uncertainty and risk. Agenda items increasing uncertainty and risk were ignored or given low priority. Managers were directed towards activities that maximized the use of existing assets and reduced variable costs—such as matching capacity to clearly defined present needs and efficiently using existing operational capabilities.

This strong focus on operations aligned the agendas of managers and workers with the executive agenda and provided clear guidance to executives on how to handle deviations (see Figure 2–2). If managers bumped too hard (e.g., Figure 2–4), they were encouraged to leave the game. If workers bumped too hard against the manager's agenda, they were asked to leave the game.[3]

The middle game was simplified for managers during this era because of a restriction in the number of viable agenda items for them to consider. Since this benefited managers, it made it easy for them to go along with the organizational agenda created by their executives. The primary agenda items for managers were focused on: maintaining stability and minimizing change. Manager energies were directed towards enacting the intended agendas and strategy—to the point of building dams to redirect or prevent the emergent stream of agenda items and goals from mixing with the intended agendas.

This environment persisted in the American auto industry until internationalization occurred. In the life insurance industry, it persisted until deregulation was forced upon it. And in many other industries, market forces have had an increasingly more direct impact on how organizations conduct their businesses. In the process, executive agendas are being altered and the role of the middle manager is being redefined.

Stronger Market Forces

A number of market forces gathered tremendous strength in the last two decades. As shown in Figure 2–6, the causes of change can be captured in four general categories—*internationalization,* involving the creation of the global factory and global markets; *deregulation,* involving the lowering of national and international barriers to entry; *consumer awareness,* involving an increasingly more sophisticated and discerning buyer; and *technicalization,* involving the widespread access to specialized technologies by organizations outside of the traditional industry participants.

FIGURE 2–6 Four Strong Market Forces That Create Change

MARKET FORCE	⇨	CHANGE DYNAMIC	⇨	RESULTING ENVIRONMENT
Internationalization	⇨	Global Factory and Global Markets	⇨	Greater Turbulence
				Greater Uncertainty
				Greater Complexity
Deregulation	⇨	Reduction of Barriers to Entry	⇨	Greater Rates of Change
				Greater Ambiguity
Consumer Awareness	⇨	Sophisticated and Discerning Buyers	⇨	Decreased Stability in Structures, Markets, and the Workforce
Technicalization	⇨	Access to Specialized Technologies	⇨	Decreased Utility of Rules and Procedures
				Decreased Utility of History to Predict Future Events

Each of these market forces has had the effect of opening the marketplace to more competitors. In the automobile industry, lower wage rates and improvements in quality control have enabled foreign manufacturers to become major players in the U.S. marketplace. In the U.S. life insurance industry, a loosening of regulatory constraints has allowed noninsurance firms to participate in most aspects of the business except underwriting. In the electronics industry, increased consumer awareness has led to an overwhelming willingness on the part of the American consumer to purchase products made outside the United States. In the steel industry, new technologies have led to steel being produced by new players both inside and outside the United States in new, superefficient micromills, at a lower cost per ton than many of the traditional U.S. competitors charge.

New, more accessible technologies have also led to a variety of industries experiencing new and unlikely competitors. For example, institutions such as New York University (NYU) have become participants in the utility business. NYU currently produces a significant portion of its own electricity and sells the excess capacity back to the local utility, Con Edison. In these industries and many others, a more sophisticated marketplace has led the purchasers of goods and services to consider a global set of suppliers and a significantly broader set of product/service characteristics prior to making a purchase decision.

The environment in such organizations can be characterized by high turbulence, rapid technological change, and new and unpredictable competitors. The effect of this environment has been to shift the attention of many organizations away from efforts to maintain stability and operationally driven agendas to adapting to change and adopting agendas within the contexts of these emergent market forces. The rules of the middle game in change-oriented, market-driven organizations direct managers to accept and accommodate increasing levels of both ambiguity and risk. Executives foster this acceptance while attempting to control it by requiring a broader set of skills from their managers—skills that in many instances have previously been required primarily at the executive level. Organizational agendas indicative of a market-driven focus include: investing in new technologies to maintain existing market share, creating products for new or emerging markets, building capacity to meet anticipated demand, and actively seeking ways to leverage existing strengths and take advantage of new opportunities.

A key challenge for organizations as they experience these market forces has been to recognize and develop effective responses while not losing their existing operational expertise.

IMPLICATIONS FOR MANAGERS

As executives in the 1980s began to press forward with a more flexible, market-driven approach, substantial changes also took place in the direction executives established for managers. Managers had previously been expected to execute against a specific organizational agenda established at the executive level; now managers were expected to operate within a broader, more flexible agenda established by the executive level, often with the participation of managers and workers. Managers today must balance their traditional responsibilities for **efficiency**—doing things right—with **effectiveness**—doing the right things.[4] The rapid rate of organizational and environmental change places demands on managers to **embrace change;** to ignore or resist change can be fatal. In order for managers to achieve a productive balance among these three responsibilities, they must alter their perspectives of their roles, responsibilities, and positions. Figure 2–7 shows the necessary balance among these three responsibilities as an equilateral triangle on its apex emphasizing the pivotal role that embracing change plays in balancing between efficiency and effectiveness. The changes in managerial perspectives necessary to achieve this balance are discussed below and summarized in Figure 2–8.

FIGURE 2–7 Balancing Efficiency, Effectiveness, and Embracing Change

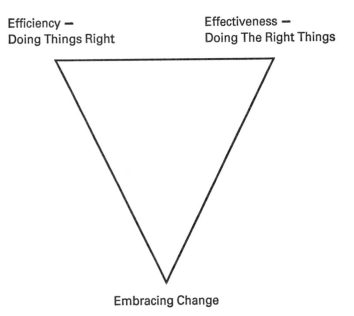

Efficiency — Doing Things Right

Effectiveness — Doing The Right Things

Embracing Change

1970s and 1980s		1990s
EFFICIENCY—DOING THINGS RIGHT		
Use existing policies, procedures, structures, and systems	and	Create new policies, procedures, structures, and systems
Focus on rules, requirements, and duties	and	Focus on commitment, enthusiasm, and empowerment
Produce efficiently and sell what is produced	and	Efficiently produce what will sell
EFFECTIVENESS—DOING THE RIGHT THINGS		
Develop agendas within a narrow, stable executive agenda	and	Develop agendas within a broad, shifting executive agenda
Focus on the deliberate agendas established by executives	and	Focus on deliberate and emergent agendas established with executives and workers
Focus on existing market demand and what is the same in the marketplace	and	Focus on emerging market demand and what is changing in the marketplace
Develop operationally driven agendas that focus on maintaining stability	and	Develop operationally driven agendas that focus on incorporating change
Accept reality	and	Define reality
EMBRACING CHANGE		
Exhibit adaptive behaviors	and	Exhibit a range of behaviors from adaptive to creative and innovative
Strive for clarity, control, and stability	and	Tolerate ambiguity and frequent changes in activities
Analyze activities to quantify and reduce risks	and	Seek risks and opportunities to influence the future

FIGURE 2–8 Managerial Perspectives Needed to Be Successful in the Middle Game

Efficiency—Doing Things Right

Efficiency has often meant that someone analyzes a situation or task and determines the most timely and cost-effective way in which the task should be done. Time and motion studies typify this view of efficiency. The outcome of such research and analysis has been policies, procedures, organizational structures, and systems that, if followed, would lead to optimum results (i.e., maximum efficiency). The meaning of efficiency for managers has been to ensure the appropriate enactment of these policies, procedures, structures, and systems through rules, requirements, and the clear specification of job duties. Efficiency for managers in the middle game over the next decade is likely to mean something more. The additional meanings of efficiency are likely to include the on-going creation of new policies, procedures, structures, and systems as they are needed to reflect the changing conditions of the business and the workforce. For example, reward systems may need to be modified frequently in order to respond to changing market conditions if the most productive workers are to be retained. The focus on rules, requirements, and job duties is expanding to encompass the development of commitment, enthusiasm, and empowerment of one's subordinates. Managers and workers must be able to respond to unpredictable events in their work environment efficiently—not just execute routine tasks efficiently. If they lack commitment, enthusiasm, or empowerment, they are not likely to respond by "doing things right" in a timely manner.

Efficiency also means considering and responding to customer wants before designing production systems. This suggests that manufacturing technologies will need to be flexible enough to efficiently produce what is wanted in real time. The "Just in Time" production approach is an example of this shift in perspective. The use of inventories to stock goods as a buffer for fluctuations in demand is no longer viewed as an efficient use of organizational resources by many companies.

Effectiveness—Doing the Right Things

Although many companies have been able to establish their organizational agendas with considerable clarity and precision at the executive level in the past, rapid changes in market conditions have led some of these executives to be less clear and precise about what they want. Executives in many organizations now define the organizational agenda in broad, general terms.[5] Because of the breadth of these organizational agendas, managers are being asked to develop specific agendas for their areas of activity. When the organizational agendas under which managers operate are broadly defined, managers can respond to a broad range of possibilities. This allows managers to exercise greater discretion in determining their agendas; it also provides less guidance as to what appropriate agenda items might be. In order to use this discretion efficiently and cope with the ambiguity of being provided little direction, managers need to alter their perspective of what effectiveness means to them as strategic leaders.

"Doing the right things" is likely to go beyond looking to the organization for its deliberate strategy and market objectives. It is now necessary to consider the emergent agendas of the executive, manager, and worker levels and to incorporate these with an understanding of the changes in the marketplace (i.e., changes in what different stakeholders want). This implies that the leadership dynamic will not only seek stability and predictability but will also attempt to incorporate changes into agendas and actions as a need emerges. The idea that there is a reality "out there" that needs to be understood will become a misleading concept. There will be many realities out there, including the reality that managers themselves define and develop—how they see and articulate business issues.

Embracing Change

Developing a perspective to embrace change is the third area that managers must address in the decade ahead. As the apex of the triangle in Figure 2–7, its instability is apparent—too much focus on efficiency and the triangle falls to the left; too much focus on effectiveness and the triangle falls to the right. A "new orientation" with the triangle resting on one of its sides might appear more comfortable to some managers. Our premise is that the marketplace changes taking place in the 1990s will not accommodate a "comfortable" view of managing in the middle game. What the environment will demand is a willingness to manage tension and embrace change. As a Citibank executive recently noted about the role of tension in strategy,

> There's tension architected into the organization and we need to manage it carefully. We need to manage the inherent tension between the local and the national perspective; between customization to meet customer needs and standardization to deliver across a broad customer base; between raw entrepreneurship gone awry, and focus and discipline; between function and geography; between pricing models and local market conditions; and between customer benefit, franchise building, and shareholder value.[6]

Efficiency and effectiveness will rest on the ability of managers to embrace change. Being adaptive will no longer be enough. Managers will sometimes need to be innovative—those creative acts of uninhibited self-expression often permitted in primary school but later expunged from our thinking through subsequent educational and on-the-job experiences will need to be relearned. The press for clarity, control, and stability will **not** result in clarity, control, and stability. It may result in frustration, anger, and depression. If one accepts this premise, then a management perspective and climate that values (or at least tolerates) ambiguity and allows things to be done in many different ways needs to be created and supported. This may well start with an extension of efforts from analyzing activities to quantify and reduce risks to also seeking risks and opportunities that can influence the business's future in the years to come.

MEETING THE LEADERSHIP CHALLENGE

Organizational level agendas, as illustrated in many of today's corporate mission statements, may fail to provide adequate direction. They allow for many different agenda items to be proposed and many possible courses of action to be considered. The greater the variety of products, services, market segments, geographic regions, and distribution systems being offered, used, or serviced by the organization, the more likely this is to be true. Clarity, to the extent that it is desired, is the responsibility of managers in developing their business level agendas. It is at this level that agendas can help managers to determine priorities that balance efficiency, effectiveness, and change.

As we and others have suggested, the business conditions in the future are likely to require that executives become increasingly occupied with addressing the needs of external stakeholders such as regulators and stockholders. This shift in their attention, coupled with the greater complexity and uncertainty in the marketplace, has pushed the manager into a more prominent and sophisticated role. Executives are recognizing that it is their managers who must absorb, accommodate, and respond to the increased pressures from suppliers, buyers, distributors, and internal stakeholders (e.g., other functional areas, career concerns of employees, etc.). It is the manager who is closer to both the operations and the customer; it is the manager who is positioned to respond to changes during the middle game. Developing and empowering the middle manager to meet the challenges emerging from these sources will enable organizations to meet the challenges posed by employees, customers, competitors, and by the environment.

Part Two of *Taking Charge: Strategic Leadership in the Middle Game* focuses on defining and discussing how ideas of business strategy and planning can be useful to managers in the middle game. We start in Chapter Three by exploring the value of business planning techniques and stakeholder analyses as a way of assessing the business environment. With this as a foundation, Chapter Four focuses on a small set of planning concepts that we have observed to be of most value to managers in their day-to-day dealings in the middle-game environment.

Part Three moves from concepts of strategic leadership to managers' capacity to think strategically, strategic management skills, personal style, and techniques that can be used by managers to enhance their efficiency, effectiveness, and ability to embrace change throughout each business day. In Chapter Five, we propose a way to think about worker, business, and organizational level agendas that can be integrated into one's day-to-day activities. Chapter Six explores the unique skills required by managers to be effective as leaders in the middle game. Strategic leadership is not just thinking about things in new ways; it is also becoming a craftsperson through the identification, learning, and practice of new skills. Chapter Seven examines the effects of managerial preferences in searching for and using information on their personal style and action orientation. Techniques for "working the system" that reflect the concepts presented in Part Two along with the strategic management skills and personal style dimensions discussed in Part Three, are the focus of Chapter Eight.

Part Four identifies ways in which managers can develop greater capacity for strategic leadership through practicing the concepts and skills that they have learned. Chapter Nine identifies ways for managers to tap their creativity, thereby overcoming some of the common barriers to change. Chapter Ten identifies ways for managers to develop their strategic leadership concepts, skills, and style through both educational and on-the-job experiences.

ENDNOTES

[1]*Business Week,* September 12, 1988, p. 44–49.

[2]See T. Peters, *Thriving on Chaos.* (New York: Harper and Row, 1987, p. 445).

[3]An interesting aside is the role of unions in workers' responses to the forced alignment of agendas and the success of recent ideas stressing worker involvement in reaction to this alignment. Unions served to protect the workers when upper level agendas threatened workers' livelihood. Worker involvement has helped to alleviate this tension. At the organizational level, the use of strong

frames of reference such as the "family" metaphor or the "school" metaphor as an organizational tool to force alignment of agendas has helped to ensure alignment of agendas.

[4]P. F. Drucker, *The Effective Executive.* (New York: Harper and Row, 1967).

[5]One notable exception to this trend are financial goals such as short-term revenue and income objectives—objectives established as part of the organization's measurement system to report its successes to external stakeholders such as stockholders, regulators, the IRS, and the government.

[6]Comments made by a senior Citibank executive at a management conference; reprinted in *OneBank U.S.,* published by the USCBG, Citibank, May 1990.

PART TWO
STRATEGIC LEADERSHIP

CHAPTER THREE
Assessing the Environment

CHAPTER FOUR
Planning: From Concepts to Practice

CHAPTER THREE
Assessing the Environment

One reason often given by managers for not taking a broader, longer-term perspective is, "I cannot be more strategic because my boss is not more strategic." Although this statement may reflect the day-to-day pressure of business, it can also be an indication of a lack of commitment to business planning or a lack of planning expertise in the organization.

Historically, planning has been done at the top of the organization. To assist executives in this function, many organizations hired professional planners in the 1970s. By the mid-1980s, *Business Week* and other periodicals announced the demise of the professional planner.[1] Their articles chronicled the laying off or reassignment of professional planners from corporate staff positions to other positions that involved assisting line managers in planning for their units. Executives retained responsibility for portfolio level plans, and business unit managers became responsible for the plans of their units. Unfortunately, this transition was rarely accompanied by management development efforts aimed at strategic planning.

Some managers were ready to add the role of planner to their jobs. Managers with relevant education, previous experience in designing business plans, or an intuitive ability to think about threats and opportunities using a long-term perspective could incorporate planning into their activities. Other managers could not do so for a number of reasons: They did not know how to develop a business plan; they were not recognized and rewarded for doing so; or they did not believe such planning was important or appropriate. As a result, there is enormous variance in the level of planning expertise among managers. There is also significant variance in the perceived value of strategic planning within organizations.

THE ORIGINS OF PLANNING

Planning has been part of organizations for more than a century. Frederick Taylor introduced planning in the late 1880s as a way to better manage the tasks performed by individual workers. Over several decades, these early planning efforts created what has become known as *scientific management*. Using principles that he developed, Taylor applied a planned approach to the execution of routine tasks. He suggested that if you divide a job up into discrete parts and examine the execution of each part, you can develop ways to shorten the time necessary to accomplish the entire job, reduce the training required to develop competent workers to perform each task, and increase the quality of the product produced.

In the 1920s, the development of formalized policies and procedures for the execution of routine activities by workers was extended to include the establishment of norms and standards for a variety of tasks throughout the organization. Time and motion studies were used as a way to refine and apply principles of scientific management. By the 1940s, the concept of designing plans to improve productivity had been extended again, this time beyond the worker level to managers and their work units. Management by objectives (MBO), originally developed to motivate employees to become interested in their work, brought planning responsibilities to middle managers within organizations.

In the 1950s, a new generation of planning ideas emerged in business organizations that paralleled the growth of business schools. These ideas were based on the techniques used to train managers on the use of planning in the military, and they became part of the post-war industrialization of America. Operations research, a management approach initiated by the British and adopted by the Americans in response to new, complex problems during World War II, found its way into business shortly after the war. Principles of warfare planning were refined and applied by managers in the planning and execution of activities in their business organizations. Project-planning techniques such as PERT (Program Evaluation and Review Technique) developed by the U.S. Navy with Lockheed and Booz, Allen, and Hamilton and the CPM (Critical Path Method) developed by DuPont are two well-known examples of operations research techniques developed during this time.

Planning continued to grow in importance and applicability during the 1960s and 1970s. Just as scientific management applied planning to individually performed tasks, and MBO and PERT applied it to managerial tasks and large capital projects, portfolio management and other planning frameworks applied planning to corporations and their decisions to grow through merger and acquisition activities. As these techniques became more commonly used, they were often supported by a professional planning staff (i.e., people who specialized in planning, often through obtaining advanced education that focused on strategic planning models and techniques). As the use of planning techniques expanded, there was a growing belief that planning as a management tool would improve organizational decision-making and profitability.

Through the 1960s, what was then referred to as business planning was primarily focused on operations. As Peter Drucker has noted, managerial emphasis was on efficiency—doing things right. PERT and CPM are examples of using planning technology to improve project management efficiency. There was relatively little emphasis on determining whether or not those things being done right were the right things to do. Strategic planning extended the role of business planning to include effectiveness—doing the right things. This change was due to increased competition in the marketplace and wider dissemination and use of management concepts and theories. Strategic leadership extends the concepts of strategic planning to include implementation—doing the right things in efficient ways while responding to changing conditions.[2]

ORGANIZATIONAL LIFE CYCLES

As strategic planning began to play a greater role in how many organizations were being managed, the life cycle model for understanding and predicting organizational performance gained popularity. Just as there are product life cycles, there are also organizational life cycles. Organizations, units, and subunits within organizations may also go through stages of growth, maturity, and decline (and in some instances, extinction).

For some organizations, these stages occur in relatively quick succession. Companies producing personal computers such as Apple and Compaq are examples of organizations that made the transition from growth to maturity quickly. For other organizations, movement from one stage to another occurs over extended periods of time. The more stable environments of the 1950s and 1960s allowed a number of well-established organizations to enter into the mature stage and remain there for more than a decade. The auto industry is one example where this occurred. The oligopoly in this industry emerged in the 1950s and was sustained through the late 1970s. The U.S. auto industry moved from maturity to the early stages of decline in the 1980s. More recently, renewal has become the dominant focus of the U.S. auto manufacturers. Different events have caused a similar transition in the steel industry.

Some large, established organizations have used organizational life cycle concepts as a planning tool for organizational renewal efforts. Their business units have typically gone through development or start-up activities, and periods of rapid growth to a state of maturity when growth has slowed or stopped altogether. As business units approach maturity, an assessment is made regarding the efficacy of investing more resources into the business. Executives and managers must decide whether renewal, maintenance, or decline is most appropriate for the business. Techniques have been suggested for prolonging the life of a mature business or managing it in a way that will encourage the design of strategies for continued growth. Intrapreneurship and quality circles are two examples of such practices. The life cycle model, including renewal as a way to extend the life cycle, is presented in Figure 3–1.

Organizations often try to maintain and extend their mature businesses while simultaneously investing in parts of the organization that are new ventures entering into the growth stage. The goal of many organizations is to have the mature and renewed parts of the organization contribute to the prosperity of the entire organization. Strategies to accomplish these goals include improving production efficiencies, penetrating new markets at home and abroad, and integrating operations either forward to buyers or backward to suppliers. One organization that has successfully adopted some of these strategies is Anheuser Busch. It has grown through aggressive marketing both domestically and internationally and through improving production and distribution efficiencies into what many consider to be a mature company in a mature industry—the beer

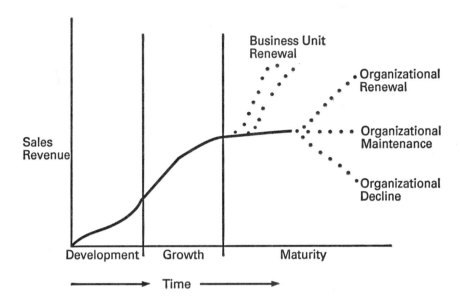

FIGURE 3–1 **Organizational Life Cycle**

industry. Other strategies for renewal include developing new products for new markets and building capacity to meet changing demands. Many of the tobacco companies have taken this latter approach through launching low tar and menthol cigarettes.

Just as executives can enhance the performance of their organization through application of life cycle concepts and strategies for renewal, business unit managers can also find these concepts useful. Each manager's unit, as well as the subunits, may be in an identifiable life cycle stage. The unit and the subunits may be in the same life cycle stage, or they may not. Managers may find their subunits populated by individuals who hold a particular perspective about their future that is not consistent with what the executive level or other significant stakeholders expect. For example, a subunit may perceive itself to be in a growth phase regarding the services it provides to the organization, while others see it as being in a mature or declining phase. Expected resources are not likely to be forthcoming unless this perceptual difference is resolved.

THE PLAN VERSUS PLANNING

During the late 1960s, the focus of strategic planning was on formulating the one, right strategy. Executives and managers within organizations attempted to enact through their planning process the same stability that characterized their industries in earlier decades. A dominant image for the senior executive during this time might have been "leader as organizational architect."

With the strengthening of market forces during the 1970s that affected a business's performance, including the emergence of stronger and more diverse competitors, the focus shifted from designing the best plan to execute against to embracing a planning process. This suggests a shift from viewing planning as a procedure with an outcome called the plan to an emphasis on the planning process itself. Leadership roles today include **pathfinder** and **orchestra conductor** responsibilities as well as those of an architect. As several CEOs said to a recently retired colleague, "The process of strategic planning is important, while the plan is not."[3]

The implications of this are significant. The business plan tends to be a linear, often static document that specifies the preferred activities for the organization to pursue over the next several years. A plan is a blueprint that is intended to define future activities. In practice, each plan is based on assumptions about the external and internal environments that may not be valid for more than a few months. As the rate of change in the environment increases, fewer and fewer of these assumptions are likely to be true over time. This can result in a plan that is of little use as a blueprint for action. However, the plan may still have value to managers who have developed their ability to embrace change.

Apart from the plan itself, the planning process can be dynamic and responsive. It initially involves information collecting, exploration of the environments, diagnosis of issues, analysis, and the suggestion of a deliberate strategy. When managers view planning as a process, they can recognize and value the emergent events that affect the design intentions. This is done by incorporating environmental changes into the plan through planning iterations that do not end with the production of a formal plan document. Continually reviewing the deliberate strategy and incorporating emergent events allow managers to embrace changes that they were not able to predict or otherwise incorporate into the plan. The strategy that results from this interaction has been called the *realized strategy*: the strategy that is actually pursued but may not be identifiable until after it is enacted.[4]

Organizations derive several benefits from fostering an ideology of planning as a process. These benefits include:

1. continually realigning managers' perceptions of marketplace dynamics with actual marketplace events,

2. developing a common framework for analyzing new and emergent information about the industry and the business,

3. fostering an attitude of responsiveness to new information,

4. ensuring a market-driven orientation in managers who may have been previously driven by operational considerations,

5. building a base from which managers can both adapt to and anticipate change,

6. providing a rallying point for the organization,

7. encouraging each manager to adjust individual self-interests to be consistent with the interests of the organization.[5]

Planning as a process recognizes and values the need for a planning document and the deliberate strategy proposed therein. However, it does not presuppose that the deliberate strategy is a blueprint for action. A plan can be a set of guidelines, milestones, or common ways of thinking about and discussing key issues. The development of the plan can result in new and deeper understandings of the business and the environment. The plan does not necessarily identify how to do things right or all of the right things to do. Rather it is a platform of knowledge from which emergent events can be identified and informed management decisions can be made.

Strategic planning as a process places a premium on those managers who have a greater tolerance for ambiguity, an ability to diagnose emergent events, and a willingness to embrace change. These attributes, in large part, were not needed by managers operating in the more stable environments of the past. It is within the context of valuing both the plan and the planning process that managers need to examine their environment.

A STAKEHOLDERS' FRAMEWORK FOR ASSESSING THE ENVIRONMENT

The assessment of the environment for managers dealing with on-going business activities (i.e., managing within the middle game) includes identifying issues and diagnosing trends outside of and within the organization. Issues tend to be problems or opportunities that have some immediacy and have come to the attention of managers. Trends are patterns of events that have existed over time that are likely to persist; trends are sometimes difficult to identify without active reflection, some theory building, and statistical analyses.

We approach the assessment of issues and trends in the business environment through a discussion of stakeholders. Stakeholders include individuals, groups, and organizations who have a stake in what occurs in a business. In most instances, stakeholders have needs and wants of their own that can translate into issues and trends. It is the stakeholders' issues and trends that affect a manager's business that need to be recognized and addressed as part of the middle game.

Stakeholder Analysis

In analyzing the environment and identifying stakeholders, it is important to identify the level or focus of the analysis. Is the analysis focused on the portfolio of business activity, a particular business, or a function within a business? An executive's unit of analysis is most frequently the portfolio level. Executives are concerned with the whole organization, all of its businesses, and all of its stakeholders. Decisions made at this level address such questions as, "Which businesses should we pursue or divest? Is our current mix of businesses appropriate for our desired level of risk, growth, and resources to invest?"

A manager's level of analysis is typically the business unit, a line of business, or a business department. Managers primarily focus on their unit, the subunits within the unit, and those segments of the external and internal environments with which their unit interfaces. Decisions made at this level address such questions as, "Within our business, who are our target markets? What is our competitive advantage? What are our critical success factors?"

Workers' primary interests are with functional issues or specific tasks or projects to be completed. They attend to those portions of the external and internal environments with which they interact. Decisions made at this level address such questions as, "What should I be doing differently? Is the quality of my work acceptable to others who must use it? How can I be more effective and be recognized for my contribution?"

Each of the three levels in the organization has primary and secondary external and internal stakeholders. These stakeholders create a manager's environment. Figure 3–2 presents a graphic representation of a manager's possible stakeholders.[6]

The primary external stakeholders for many managers are their customers, buyers and suppliers, competitors, regulators, owners, and the various other organizations affiliated with the business through strategic alliances, joint ventures, and trading partnerships. In addition to these primary external stakeholders, there are secondary external stakeholders who frequently initiate

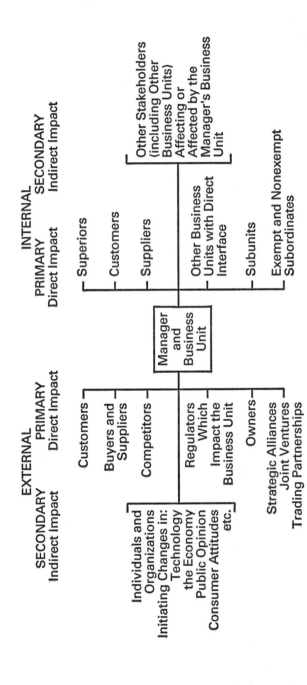

FIGURE 3-2 **Stakeholder Analysis for Managers**

actions that can indirectly influence a business unit and can result in changes in technology, in the economy, in public opinion, in consumer attitudes, and/or in the broader sociopolitical arena.

The primary internal stakeholders are defined and determined by the position a manager holds within the organization. They include a manager's superior, internal customers, internal suppliers, other business units that directly interface with a manager's business unit, the unit's subunits, and subordinates. Secondary internal stakeholders are others in the organization who affect or are affected by the actions of the manager's unit. These might include staff departments such as legal, public affairs, human resources, building services, and so forth.

An assessment of the external environment through a review of external stakeholders will be discussed first. An analysis of the internal environment through a review of internal stakeholders follows.

Assessing the External Environment

Although the external stakeholders for executives, managers, and workers overlap, the nature of the relationship varies by level in the organization, by industry, and by the size of the organization. For example, executives and managers may be dealing with the same customer segments or groups. One difference in the relationship managers and executives may have with this stakeholder group is that managers generally have regular contact with a subset of the organization's total customer base to discuss operational matters, while executives have less frequent contact with these customers and tend to interact with them on an exception basis.

The importance and extent of contact with various external stakeholders for each of these levels within the organization can also vary by industry. In many manufacturing firms, the workers have little or no contact with customers. The workers may need information regarding customer relations to be transmitted to them from managers who have more regular contact with customers. In retailing organizations such as Macy's and Nordstrom, the workers have the primary contacts with the organization's customers. The managers and executives need information regarding customer relations to be transmitted to them from their workers.

The importance and extent of contact with various stakeholders also varies by the size of the organization. The smaller the organization, the more likely it is that it will be necessary for managers to directly address the needs of a wider variety of stakeholders. For example, in community and regional banks, managers are likely to be involved with a diverse group of customers. As a result, managers have a broader spectrum of external stakeholder groups, in this case, more types of customers who probably require different services. In money center banks, managers are often deeply involved with a particular aspect of the organization and only address the needs of a specific group of customers. These managers have fewer types of external stakeholders, in this case fewer types of customers, that they must address directly.

The nature of managers' relationships with other external stakeholders, such as suppliers, buyers, and regulators, also varies by their level in the organization, the industry, and the size of their organization. In the case of competitors, managers in small firms with a limited product line generally have fewer competitors than managers in larger firms with a broader product line. Managers lower in the organization with responsibility over a smaller set of activities have fewer competitors than managers higher in the organization with a broader set of activities. Similarly, managers in such specialized industries as fasteners for roofing materials have fewer competitors than managers in an industry such as Paris night clubs.

Analysis of these competitors, regardless of size, level, or industry, should include a profile of each competitor or type of competitor, an assessment of the competitors' current strategy, an analysis of what drives each competitor, and assumptions about the industry. This last area, assumptions about the industry, includes such items as industry growth rate, the current state and expected changes in the competitive environment, the mix and number of competitors, cyclical trends, number and diversity of markets, and resource availability.

Not withstanding current trends to the contrary, the role of executives in dealing with competitors and many other stakeholders continues to be characterized as that of the figurehead for the corporation as a whole. This places pressure on managers to take a stronger role in identifying key stakeholders, identifying the trends and issues emerging from these stakeholders, and then responding to these trends and issues. It also places a greater emphasis on the manager's role as a conduit to the executive ranks, passing along information about and from these stakeholders.

Primary External Stakeholders. Michael Porter, among others, has greatly expanded the framework for assessing the external environment through a thorough look at how competitive forces shape a business within an industry.[7] The emphasis goes beyond an analysis of traditional competitors and current industry dynamics. Primary external stakeholders to be considered include customers (the end customer or user of one's product and service as well as intermediary buyers), suppliers (including suppliers of raw material, capital, labor), competitors, regulators, and various strategic alliances such as joint ventures, licensing agreements, and the like. Each of these stakeholders can affect a business unit as well as the structure of the industry in which it competes.

Porter and his colleagues also stress that a careful analysis of five forces emanating from these stakeholders is critical in understanding a business's competitive position. The five forces are: (1) the bargaining power of suppliers, (2) the bargaining power of buyers and customers, (3) the threat of new entrants into a line of business, (4) the threat of substitute products and services, and (5) the rivalry that exists among the current competitors. Understanding these forces can help an organization shift from a position based on the current environment to one that influences the environment and anticipates future environments.

Porter's work is most usefully applied to line activities, rather than staff activities, because the external environment has greater direct impact on line activities. The internal environment, which is not as thoroughly addressed in the strategy literature, has relatively greater impact on staff activities.

Secondary External Stakeholders. Beyond the identification of the primary external stakeholders and the trends and issues emerging from these groups, managers need to analyze trends and issues emerging from secondary external stakeholders that are affecting their unit currently or may affect their unit in the future. Information developed by market research organizations, and emergent economic and demographic trends, can frequently provide an information base from which to identify and develop future competitive advantages in the marketplace.

In the 1980s, changes in the demographic profile of the American workforce lead to the rapid growth of a national child care industry with companies such as Kindercare and La Petite Academy emerging as leaders in this area. In a more recent instance, developments in the electronics industry have been borrowed by the pharmaceuticals industry to improve the efficiency of testing new drug compounds. Similarly, recent research in operations management conducted at universities has provided better models for managers from many industries to use when seeking to improve the efficiency of their factories.

What emerges from the assessment of the external environment is a profile of a unit's primary and secondary stakeholders. Once these stakeholders are identified, they should be examined in terms of what their stake in the business unit is, and what trends and issues emerge as a result of their actions. For example, customers have a stake in the firm's products. Changes in consumer preferences reflect one way in which their collective behaviors can affect a business. Businesses can also be affected by changes in the financial condition of a particular supplier or a change in the profile of the supplier's industry. Changes in competitors could include alterations in the number or mix of competitors or the identification of potential new competitors. With regulators, there could be changes in current regulatory constraints or the identification of emergent regulatory trends. In the case of other external relationships, changes could include the refinement of existing relationships or the development of new relationships. Similar trends and issues can be identified through an analysis of secondary external stakeholders.

In its broadest implications, an assessment of the external environment also provides a basis for measuring the present and future attractiveness of the industry within which a manager's unit competes. This is achieved through a review of the industry conditions and incorporating this review into the analysis of external stakeholders' actions and preferences.

Assessing the Internal Environment

Analysis of the internal environment begins with an identification of internal stakeholders. Internal stakeholders can include the board of directors, executives, managers, workers, and unions. Although these categories of stakeholders are similar for executives, managers and workers, as with external stakeholders, the nature of the relationship varies, primarily as a function of where a manager is located in the organization. Managers lower in the organization may be directly affected by a single executive and indirectly affected by other executives. Managers higher in the organization may still have one direct superior, but there are frequently many relationships between a higher-level manager and members of the executive committee. The larger the organization and the higher the level of the manager, the more numerous and complex are the internal stakeholder relationships.

In large organizations, there are frequently more levels of hierarchy which need to be considered when determining primary and secondary internal stakeholders. Differing dynamics in a given organization determine which groups represent a business unit's primary internal stakeholders. Secondary internal stakeholders are other stakeholders, including other business units, that affect or are affected by a manager's unit.

Primary Internal Stakeholders. For each level within the organization, primary internal stakeholder relationships include a manager's superior, the manager's internal suppliers and customers, other units that directly interface with the manager's unit, and a manager's subunits and subordinates.

The quality of the relationship with each of these internal stakeholders is frequently based on the on-going rapport developed between the manager and stakeholder and the degree and appropriateness of the direction being set by these stakeholders. Executives and direct superiors are generally a manager's most critical stakeholders. In determining the degree of direction from this group, the mission statement of the organization (or unit above the manager) is one starting point. An organizational mission statement is a description of why a particular organization exists.

Problems arise in organizations when the degree of clarity regarding direction is based on lack of interest or attention, rather than intent. An insufficient level of direction could indicate a lack of planning expertise or a lack of commitment to planning within the organization or within units of the organization. If there is a lack of definition and managers believe further definition is critical to success, they need to work towards helping their executives more clearly define the business proposition.

Secondary Internal Stakeholders. There are often other units within the organization that are indirectly affected by the actions of a particular business unit or whose actions may indirectly impact the business unit. These secondary stakeholders may not be of immediate importance, but they can be a valuable source of information regarding emergent organizational trends. For example, efforts to enter new markets by one business unit may ultimately signal a corporate-wide initiative. Similarly, efforts directed at expense management or control of headcount may initially surface within a particular business unit but may be subsequently applied throughout the organization. Identifying these and other secondary trends can enable a manager to redirect the unit's activities in such a way as to be consistent with emergent events.

What should surface from an analysis of the internal environment is an understanding of who the primary and secondary internal stakeholders are. Once identified, issues and trends emerging from these internal stakeholders should be defined. In the case of superiors, this may be a need to increase sales or cut expenses. In the case of customers, it may be a need to make products or services more in line with what is being offered in the external marketplace. In the case of suppliers, it may be to increase prices so that they reflect both the direct and indirect costs of the supplier. In the case of other business units, it may be to establish strategic alliances that would enable both units to make better use of their resources. In the case of subunits, it might be pressure for more resources or the need to clarify the unit's agenda. In the case of exempt and nonexempt employees, it might be a change in current working conditions or a recognition that wages are below market. Similar issues and trends emerge from an examination of secondary internal stakeholders.

Not every issue or trend identified, either externally or internally, needs to be addressed. Some can be ignored. Ironically, what frequently emerges from an environmental assessment is a realization that the business unit does not really know what its external stakeholders want from it. What also emerges is a recognition that many internal stakeholders do not know what they want, or they want so many things that the information is relatively useless. These understandings can trigger activities such as intelligence-gathering activities about external stakeholders and the formation of task forces to foster better understanding among internal stakeholders.

Ultimately, the information developed as a result of managers' environmental assessments of external and internal stakeholders provides the basis for the development of a mission for the business unit, a vision statement, and goals and objectives that enable the unit to implement the mission. Combined, these are the building blocks of strategic leadership.

SETTING DIRECTION

With the help of a stakeholder analysis, executives and managers seek to provide direction for the organization's or business unit's activities. Figure 3–3 shows different degrees of direction that executives can establish for managers through an organizational mission statement. This figure shows a continuum from nondirectional to highly focused. Although managers may place their

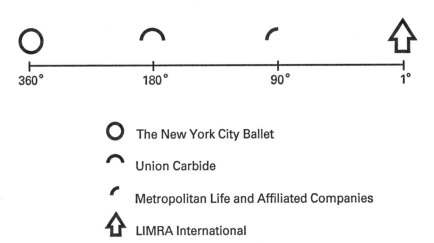

FIGURE 3–3 **Degrees of Direction That Executives Can Establish for Managers**

organization anywhere along the continuum, four representative points are discussed.

The first point, signified by a circle, represents an organization where little or no direction is being set by the executive ranks. This may occur by intent or because of a lack of understanding of the role of expressing the organization's mission to internal stakeholders. Universities are sometimes characterized by such global mission statements. One reason for a nondirectional mission statement within universities may be related to the concept of academic freedom. By denying little, no academic freedom is lost. The efficacy of this approach depends on the executives' values and the nature of the stakeholders in the educational process. As university administrators (the executives) recognize that demographic trends are influencing the size and nature of the applicant pool, and as administrators become more aware that universities are operating in a competitive marketplace, some direction may be desirable via the development of more focused mission statements. Organizations such as the PEW Foundation have been encouraging this through funding efforts that foster strategic leadership practices in individual schools and departments within universities. The PEW Foundation is not interested in funding knowledge generation and dissemination per se, but knowledge generation and dissemination in specific areas.

An organization that operates at this broad end of the continuum is The New York City Ballet. Its mission is to "use the classical tradition as a springboard to innovation."[8] By denying little, this organization is able to maximize its artistic freedom.

A second point on the continuum, the semicircle or 180-degree figure, indicates a broadly defined but identifiable direction set at the executive level. A semicircle is representative of the degree of direction provided by many large, diversified organizations. Consider the mission statement from Union Carbide from the late 1980s:

> Union Carbide exists to provide its shareholders with maximum value in the long term from all the resources available to it. Each Carbide business must strive to be among the best in its field. The principal role of the corporate entity is to create an enabling environment in which each of its businesses can be more successful than it could be independently.[9]

The executives at Union Carbide are providing definition regarding their responsiveness to one key stakeholder—the shareholder. They make a broad statement regarding quality, and they define the working relationship between the corporate entity and its various businesses. This mission statement allows for substantial diversity in the activities of its managers, while still providing some guidance and implicitly denying some activities. Yet the responsibility for defining customer segments, products and services offered, distribution systems used, and geographic regions served is implicitly left to the levels below.

The third point along the continuum is representative of an organization that has fairly defined areas of focus—in this instance a 90-degree arc is used. An example of such a mission statement is that created by Metropolitan Life and Affiliated Companies.

> The mission of Metropolitan Life and its family of companies is to provide our customers with high-quality, innovative and cost-effective insurance and other financial products and services. The objective of each Met Life business is to grow and to be the best in its field, while balancing the interests of customers, employees and the community.

The focus of the Met's mission statement is on insurance first and on other financial products and services second. The instruction to each business is growth and quality. This mission statement defines quality as "the best," not "among the best." There is no attempt to define the relationship between the corporate entity and the business lines. This suggests that the relationship between executives and managers may be close and that the organization may be more centralized. It also implies that the executives within this organization are willing and interested in providing substantial direction to the managers. Finally, there is a recognition of a broader set of values through the balancing of the interests of customers, employees, and the community. Most corporations include community values as part of a broader corporate statement. In Union Carbide's case, they have a specific section labeled *values*.

Aspects of Met Life's mission statement that give greater definition and guidance to managers than Union Carbide's mission statement are its definition of an industry, its guidance to grow, and its goal to be the best. There are fewer opportunities to select from once you have defined the industry, and you know you must continually grow and ultimately be the best, rather than provide maximum long-term value to shareholders.

The last point on the continuum is signified by an arrow. As we discussed in Chapter Two, this type of mission would be expected in organizations that are operating in stable environments and have clear, focused lines of business. Today, because of volatile market conditions, such mission statements are generally found in firms with a single product, operating in a single geographic region, with a single distribution system or single market segment orientation. An example of such an organization is LIMRA International. LIMRA states:

> Consistent with the highest standard of conduct and public responsibility, the mission of LIMRA is to support and enhance the marketing function of its member companies through industry-supported research, products and services.

Unlike the other mission statements discussed, this mission narrowly defines the customer, "the marketing function of member companies," and what LIMRA will provide the customer, "industry-supported research, products and services." Because LIMRA is a trade association for the life insurance industry, the focus of its mission enables LIMRA managers to direct their attention to those activities that are supported by one key internal stakeholder—the marketing function of their member organizations.

Although our discussion until now has focused on the degree of direction being set at the executive level, the same points need to be made for all the internal stakeholders with whom a manager's unit interfaces. Within most units in an organization, there are varying degrees of specificity regarding direction, and a general lack of mission statements to provide some of that direction. As a

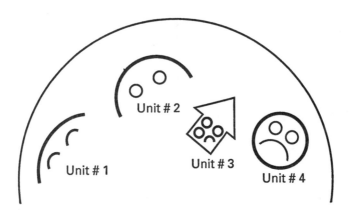

FIGURE 3-4 Different Levels of Direction Established
          by Middle Managers

result, there are varying degrees of clarity concerning what it is that a manager's internal stakeholders want.[10] Figure 3–4 provides a tongue-in-cheek example of many organizations today.

The executive level direction shown in Figure 3–4 is 180 degrees. This suggests that there is a broad arena within which individual managers can define their unit's mission. Within this example there are four units. Unit #1 has a more narrowly defined direction for its activities than Unit #2 or Unit #4. The subunits within it are similarly directed, and very much in line with the unit overall.

Unit #2 has a fairly broad sense of direction for itself, as noted by the semicircle. The subunits within Unit #2 are generally without direction, as characterized by the circles. In the best of situations, these subunits may be perceived by others in the organization as available to service the needs of anyone who requests assistance. In the worst case, these subunits are perceived as doing lots of things they should not be doing, thereby using the organization's resources inefficiently and ineffectively.

Unit #3 has a clear, narrowly defined direction. Unfortunately, the subunits within it are not aware of this clarity, or are not managing their activities consistent with the business unit's focus. This could be the result of poor communications, disagreement as to the appropriate direction, and/or poor monitoring systems to detect the activities that are off-strategy.

Unit #4 is without direction. Two of the three subunits within it share a similar lack of focus. The third subunit has developed direction for itself, but within a context of little or no direction. As the image suggests, this may not be a comfortable situation for the managers involved.

Identifying the presence of various business units' mission statements in organizations and analyzing their components and the level of specificity in these statements can provide managers with a vehicle for assessing the wants and needs of internal stakeholders. If one of Unit #1's primary stakeholders was Unit #4, it would be very difficult to meet the needs of this particular stakeholder because Unit #4 apparently does not have a clear direction and does not know what it wants. If on the other hand, Unit #3 was a primary stakeholder of Unit #2, it would be easier to meet its needs, because Unit #3 has a discernible focus.

Such mapping provides an indication of the amount of freedom managers have in defining the mission for their units. The amount of discretion available to managers lower in the organization is largely determined by the amount of direction from those units above the manager. In the absence of direction from above, there is the potential for the subunit within Unit #4 that has some direction to establish significant momentum for further defining its role and to influence the direction of Unit #4 as a whole. In other instances, the process of identifying the level of direction from above can uncover very specific agendas that have not been adequately communicated or understood. This might be the reason why many of the subunits within Unit #3 lack direction.

Although the discussion up to this point may imply that we are recommending that all businesses create precise degrees of direction, this is not the case. There are no right or wrong configurations per se; rather, some configurations may be more effective for some managers and in some situations. The appropriate configuration and degree of direction need to be determined by the executives and managers based on their understanding of their personal preferences, the business profit and loss dynamics, industry dynamics, and the internal workings of the organization. For example, art organizations for the most part, are founded on the idea of artistic freedom. Once members have demonstrated their abilities to perform, they are often allowed to pursue whatever ideas they select. Union Carbide, given the role that the executives have defined for themselves, has placed few constraints on the businesses in their organization. Metropolitan Life has provided substantial direction and, as a result, has set more precise expectations regarding the activities of its managers. LIMRA has provided even more precise direction for its managers through a narrow definition of its customers and what it is willing to provide to these customers.

Examining several concepts that have helped the managers in these organizations to develop a planning process that has led to a sense of mission is the topic to which we now turn.

E N D N O T E S

[1]*"The New Breed of Strategic Planner." Business Week,* Sept. 17, 1984, 62–68.

[2]P. F. Drucker, *The Effective Executive.* (New York: Harper and Row, 1967).

[3]James P. Bruce, *The Intuitive Pragmatists: Conversations with CEOs.* (Greensboro, NC: Center for Creative Leadership, 1987), p. 26.

[4]See H. Mintzberg, "Crafting Strategy." *Harvard Business Review,* July–August, 1987.

[5]W. Guth, and I. Macmillan, "Strategy Implementation versus Middle Management Self-Interest." *Strategic Management Journal,* 1986, 7(4), 313–27.

[6]The reason we have taken the approach of using stakeholders as the primary conceptual tool for identifying current and future issues and trends is that this approach has been more appropriate than traditional approaches for capturing the dynamics of the middle game. Using a stakeholder approach is specific enough to incorporate many of the existing techniques and sensitivities for analyzing today's external marketplace, while being broad enough to capture many of the internal, organizational complexities that managers face. Stakeholder analysis was developed by J. S. Armstrong, "Social Irresponsibility in Management," *Journal of Business Research,* 1977, 5 (Sept.), 185–213.

[7]Michael Porter, "How Competitive Forces Shape Strategy." *Harvard Business Review,* March–April, 1979, 137–45.

[8]*"Counting the Stars that Shone on City Ballet." The New York Times,* November, 1989, p. 12.

[9]*Our Mission, Our Values, Actions, and Goals,* Union Carbide publication, 1987.

[10]We are not arguing that every unit in every organization should have a mission statement, although many managers would find it helpful. We are arguing that many managers have not yet thought through, with the members of their unit, who their stakeholders are and what those stakeholders want. Nor have they identified a strategic agenda within that context. A mission statement is a widely used and easily understood tool for beginning the process of setting direction.

CHAPTER FOUR
Planning: From Concepts to Practice

Organizations are increasingly trying to develop a **strategic perspective** in their managers. Developing a strategic perspective involves new learning for most managers. In the last chapter, we discussed the importance of assessing the environment in and during the middle game and the evolving agendas within this environment that are consistent with organizational and stakeholder agendas. Chapter Four focuses on creating agendas, building momentum for the implementation of parts of these agendas, and learning to value change. Organizations such as Metropolitan Life, Citicorp, GTE, The New York Stock Exchange, Imperial Life Assurance, Data General, and others have allocated substantial resources to this effort. Understanding the steps necessary to develop a strategic perspective, and the shift in values that must accompany it, is the foundation from which managers become strategic leaders in their businesses.[1]

Inherent in building momentum for the implementation of strategy is the belief that strategy is not solely the domain of executives. Questions such as "What businesses is my unit really in?" and "Where do we want to go as a unit?" are necessary elements in developing a strategic perspective. However, there continues to be some confusion about these and other concepts for many managers today. This confusion adds to the frustration of the manager grappling with strategy and therefore limits the usefulness of strategy as a management tool.

The basic concepts of strategy have often been separated into two categories, planning and implementing. Broadly speaking, *planning* is the process of identifying and documenting beliefs about key stakeholders and the direction for the business. *Implementing* is the process of acting on and refining these understandings each day. Implicit within implementing is the need for all concerned to realize that much of what is discussed and decided upon during planning may change as assumptions are tested, new information emerges, and executives and managers change, or change their preferences. In most organizations, the need for on-going adjustment is not communicated sufficiently to those involved, yet it is critical to a manager's motivation and ability to adapt to change.

Although planning and implementing are frequently discussed separately, they need to be taking place simultaneously. Figure 4–1 shows that at various points in time, planning plays a more central role than implementing, but generally the opposite

FIGURE 4–1 Shifts in Focus from Planning to Implementing across a Fiscal Year

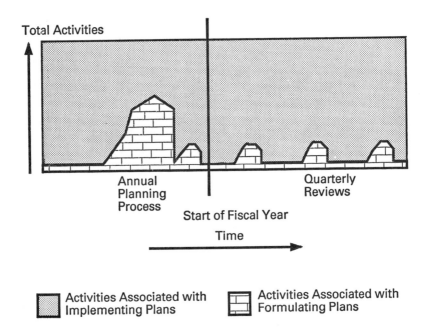

relationships exist: Managers spend 90 percent of their total activities implementing strategy.

The simultaneity of and interaction between planning and implementing provide an opportunity for learning. To the extent that managers are learning during the complex, convoluted experiences that are often responses to changing situations, they can improve their strategic leadership.

DYNAMIC PLANNING

Planning has traditionally been a periodic event, treated as a discrete activity within the work environment. The result of this event is known as the **deliberate strategy** or **strategic plan.** In most cases, the development of a strategic plan involves managers and their direct reports. Many managers have discounted strategic planning as a "necessary exercise" because of their belief that the plan will not be executed. They are looking for a **definitive** blueprint for action. When the blueprint is approved but not fully acted upon, they lose heart in the plan.

Implicit in the blueprint perspective of planning is that the analysis that went into the plan led to the "right answer." Maybe it did. But maybe there is more than one right answer. What about a second right answer? Or a third right answer? The power of planning is in continually asking the questions to stimulate thinking about many possible right answers. The usefulness of the various right answers depends on the condition of the business and the environment within which it operates. In businesses experiencing little growth in stable environments, the first right answer may be a useful guide for action. In businesses experiencing rapid growth in turbulent environments, the first right answer may be of less direct use. As changes occur in the environment, new right answers emerge. In competitive situations, others often accept and imitate the first right answers—thereby collectively reducing the efficacy of anyone pursuing that right answer for long.

Economists call this phenomenon the law of supply and demand. The first right answer leads to an increase in supply (everyone wanted to produce an electronic calculator). If many firms stop their strategic thinking with this right answer, the market will soon be flooded with calculators. Many did. It was. Prices fell. Firms left the market. The second and third and fourth right answers led some firms to continually improve, specialize, and redesign their calculators. Because of the rapid growth and turbulence in the industry, the strategic plan was not a blueprint. It might better have been thought of as a sketch on a scrap of paper or directional markings in the sand before a storm.

The possibility of more than one right answer should not lead one to conclude that planning is of less or little value in turbulent times. Rather, the nature of the benefits of planning vary as a function of the degrees of change taking place. When the rates of change are low, the value of a plan includes its attention to detail; its logic; the identification of proven relationships among elements; and its ability to draw on known principles of economics, science, engineering, and business. The blueprint created through the planning process can be very valuable.

As the rates of change increase, the value of planning changes, not in magnitude but in kind. Figure 4–2 suggests that with increased rates of change, the value of the plan shifts from that of a blueprint to that of providing the game plan—the intended approach that may need to be revised after play begins and competitors have responded to the plan.

As the rates of change increase further, the benefits of the plan are contained in the milestones it has created. How one reaches the milestones is not as relevant as reaching them. In the most turbulent times, plans provide a common language and way of thinking about the business. The plan provides the questions, not the answers. For business units experiencing such high rates of change, planning is useful for developing a conceptual framework within

FIGURE 4–2 The Nature of Planning in Environments with Different Rates of Change

Business Units Experiencing Low Rates of Change: Planning as Manuevering			Business Units Experiencing High Rates of Change: Planning as Learning
Planning Creates a Blueprint	Planning Creates a Game Plan	Planning Creates Periodic Milestones	Planning Allows for the Development of a Common Language and Context in Which Additional Planning Can Be Done

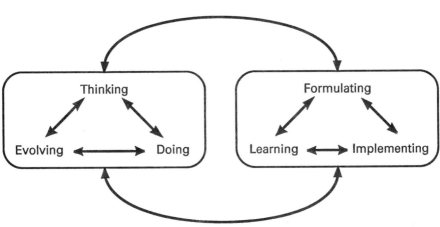

FIGURE 4–3 **Planning as a Discovery Process**

which to identify and interpret information that might otherwise go unnoticed or be interpreted from a more parochial point of view. In effect, planning and implementing for these managers become a discovery process that provides a common context within which to manage their business as it evolves.[2] This relationship is illustrated in Figure 4–3.

The planning field includes many labels such as mission, vision, objectives and goals, strategic action plans, tactics, and so forth. These labels help managers to highlight key questions, and it is through articulating these questions and developing many possible right answers that strategic plans evolve. It is when managers realize that most right answers are really BAATMs (best answers at the moment) that their capacity for strategic leadership increases. Given this greater capacity, the challenge is to more fully use it to improve the management of the business unit. We believe it is possible to do this by becoming more familiar with the questions of strategy so as to ask them more often to generate additional BAATMs that evolve into second and third right answers over time. The key "leading" questions associated with planning and their labels and intent are illustrated in Figure 4–4 and described below.

FIGURE 4–4 **Formulating Strategy**

What is our reason for being?—MISSION
Where do we want to go?—VISION
What do we want to accomplish?—OBJECTIVES AND GOALS
How will we achieve our objectives and goals?—STRATEGIC ACTIONS

By leading questions, we mean those questions that managers can and should ask as they participate in planning and implementing strategy. Of course, leading questions have "following" questions—these often require more information and input from others in order to be answered. The following questions tend to emerge out of exploring the answers to the leading questions.

WHAT IS OUR REASON FOR BEING?—MISSION

Most managers label the answer to this question their *mission statement*. Mission statements address our basic need for definition: "If an organization does not stand for something, does not represent some comprehensible theme or orientation, it lacks definition in the minds of the public as well as in the minds of its members, and this can undermine it externally and internally."[3]

For many organizations, the past two decades were a time when the mission statement, represented by the organizational arc, was expanding into a semicircle or an even broader configuration. This occurred as a portfolio of businesses was incorporated under one overall umbrella (the 180-degree arc to full-circle approach). The 1990s are a time when the organizational arc is growing smaller as numerous companies seek to divest themselves of businesses that are not contributing to the profits of the organization. These divestitures and downsizing activities are in large part due to the failure of many acquisitions and new ventures to live up to expectations (i.e., they don't meet the plan). It is also due, in large part, to economic globalization. As new markets open, as some companies seek to have a world-wide presence, and as other companies seek to protect themselves from global competitors, many organizations have been forced to conserve their resources in order to be competitive in their core businesses.

Developing the Mission Statement for a Business

A mission statement can serve the same function for a business unit as it does for the organization. One approach to developing a mission statement is to assess key market forces and industry dynamics and to identify the critical internal and external stakeholders along with what each set of stakeholders wants. A review of this information can help managers determine their "reason for being" within the broader organization. Line of business stakeholder analyses need to be sufficiently comprehensive and detailed so as not to overlook any key stakeholders or any of their significant wants. Such analyses can be equally valuable for understanding and providing direction within staff departments—staff departments serve the wants of a number of internal stakeholders. The mission statement for staff departments should reflect these internal stakeholder wants.

A critical element in developing a mission statement is to define the industry or business areas in which one chooses to compete. Industries tend to define themselves along specific dimensions, and businesses within an industry position themselves along these dimensions. For example, schools of dentistry as business units within universities tend to compete along two dimensions— teaching and research. Figure 4–5 shows how three dental schools chose to compete in the late 1980s as perceived by the dean (manager) at the time.[4]

FIGURE 4–5 Positioning of Three Dental Schools
along the Research and Teaching
Dimensions Relevant to the Educational Industry

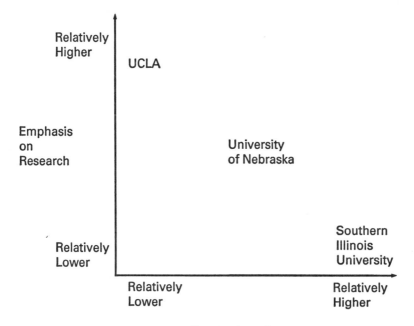

Realizing that stiff regional and national competition existed, Southern Illinois University's School of Dental Medicine sought to position itself competitively through excellence in teaching, with relatively less emphasis on research. The University of Nebraska Medical Center's College of Dentistry, recognizing that it serviced the needs of eight other states, positioned itself with a moderate focus on both education and research and emphasized geographic concerns. In contrast, the UCLA's School of Dentistry positioned itself as primarily striving for excellence in research. Its mission statement reads,

> As UCLA continues to strive towards becoming the highest quality 'research university'—a true center where teachers demonstrate excellence in scholarship, professional training, and creative activity—the most important consideration must be the quality of its faculty.

Excellence in teaching and research are two primary objectives for the higher educational industry (which is a trillion dollar industry). Possible dimensions that may influence the choice of mission for different educational institutions include whether the school is public or private, a university or a college, and in a rural or urban setting, as well as the level of degrees offered (e.g., bachelors, masters, doctorates). Note that some of these dimensions are under the control of the executives and managers in the middle game; others are determined at the opening game and may not be easily changed.

Each industry has specific dimensions that define its being— often in terms of customers served, products offered, distribution channels used, and the technologies employed. Managers must develop a clear sense of the industry's structure along these dimensions in order to define their particular mission. All too often the mission of one firm within an industry is articulated in the same way as that for many other firms within the industry. Over time, this leads to an oversupply of goods and services in specific business areas and the subsequent maturation and decline of many business enterprises within the industry. Much to our disappointment, this is likely to be the situation by the year 2000 for business schools around the country—oversupply followed by the decline and failure of many.

An important component of a business unit's mission is that it demonstrate its relationship and its contribution to both external and internal stakeholders, including the parent organization. To not do so runs the risk of the business unit's contribution to the organization being ignored or misunderstood. Documenting the relationship can also be useful internally to the members of the unit. It encourages them to recognize their responsibility to the larger entity. One dental school with which we are familiar was failing to serve the needs of several critical internal stakeholders. The school was perceived by the university to be nonessential to its overall mission. The dental school was eventually closed.

Nested Mission Statements. One way to conceptualize the relationship between a business unit and the larger organization is to think of mission statements as potentially nesting one within the other. A manager's mission statement, in most instances, would nest within the mission statements of the larger organization. A visual image of both nested and unnested missions is presented in Figure 4–6.

For reasons previously discussed, the executive level agenda in the 1990s for most organizations is likely to fall somewhere between a 90-degree and a 180-degree arc.[5] In Figure 4–6, Unit A's mission and the mission of each of its subunits nest within the broader organizational mission. In contrast, Unit B's mission nests partly outside of the organizational mission; Subunit B1 is partly

FIGURE 4–6 "Umbrella" Map of the Mission Statements for the Organization, Two Units, and Three Subunits within Each Unit

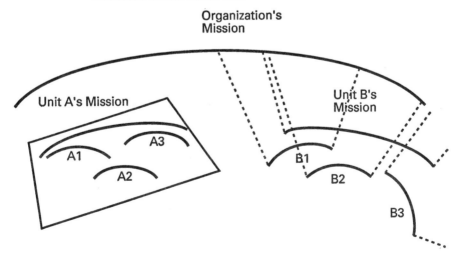

outside of the Unit B's mission but still within the organization's mission. Also note that there is some overlap between Subunits B1 and B2. This could represent redundant activities, or alternatively, it could indicate that the portion of Subunit B1's activities that do not fall under Unit B could be transferred to some other unit. Subunit B3 is outside of the organization's mission entirely.

Given the position of Subunit B3, the organization and Unit B could do several things if they choose to resolve the inconsistency. They could have the unit and subunit align more closely, discontinuing those activities that do not nest in the higher-level mission statement. They could adjust the higher-level mission to incorporate the additional activities of Subunit B3. They could sell Subunit B3. Or, if they choose not to resolve the inconsistency, they could ignore it for the time being. Certainly each possibility has different implications for the allocation of resources to the unit, as well as the way in which the unit is likely to be perceived within the larger organization.

Figure 4–7 illustrates an organization that has changed its organizational mission to incorporate Unit B and Subunit B3. Since it did not actually broaden its mission, much of Unit A's activities now fall outside of the larger organizational agenda. This figure graphically displays what sometimes happens when a new CEO takes charge, or there is a shift in which units are politically favored

FIGURE 4–7 "Umbrella" Map of the Mission Statements for the Organization, Two Units, and Three Areas within Each Unit

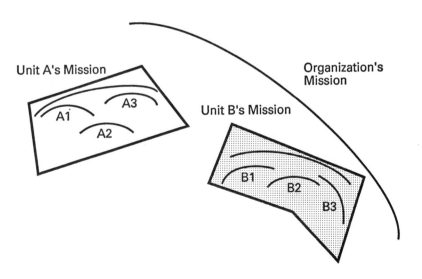

within the organization. It can also reflect changes in technology, labor supply, and other external market conditions. For example, the word-processing equipment industry experienced dramatic changes once personal computers were made available to the professional and administrative staff. Many companies shifted their attention and resources to other areas of endeavor as a result of the advances in personal computer technology.

To make this argument more concrete, consider the mission statements from the late 1980s of three successively smaller units within a financial services company:

> *Investments Area:* The mission of our investment units it to provide outstanding investment management and advisory services to our customers, primarily (our internal) businesses and subsidiaries.
>
> *Department* (within the Investments Area): The mission of the department is (1) to serve our customers by being the best full-line organization in our industry, (2) to have the capability of investing and managing up to 50 percent of the company's investable funds in a variety of investments, and (3) to provide a full range of (departmental) services on a profitable basis both in support of our investment activities and for sale outside the Company.
>
> *Territory* (within the Department): The mission of the territory is (1) to provide our customers with investments of the quality, characteristics, and quantities that would assist in positioning them to excel in their line of business, (2) to provide our clients with a level of service in furnishing their financial needs so that (our company) becomes their primary funding source, and (3) to provide an environment that encourages teamwork as well as individual excellence, where satisfying our customers' and clients' needs is both challenging and rewarding.

Do these mission statements nest from a broad to a more narrow scope of operation? In part yes, but not completely. Three differences among them can be noted: the emphasis on being the best, the definition of the customer, and the attention given to the work-group climate. The idea of being the best was not present in the territory's statement. This suggests that this may not have been a primary focus for this unit. Or, if it was a primary focus, the message was not being communicated to its employees by way of the mission statement.

The definition of customer varies among the mission statements, or the customer was not specifically mentioned. This suggests that there may be a lack of awareness, or confusion, or possibly disagreement within the three levels as to who the primary customers are.

The territory's mission statement also mentions a work environment that encourages teamwork as well as excellence. This suggests that this unit articulates its concern for its people more aggressively than the broader units of which it is a part.

Do mission statements that do not neatly nest one within the other represent poor management? Not necessarily. For some organizations, a subunit mission that does not nest within the unit's mission may reflect an effective adaptation to changes in the environment. Nor do overlapping mission statements of two different business units necessarily indicate ineffective management. This type of organizational redundancy may be an attempt by the executive level to change the way a business unit does business. If the executive level does not like the way product development is being done in one area, it may choose to introduce an internal competitor who also has responsibility for product development.

Citibank pursued such a strategy for nearly two decades. Multiple Citibank businesses competed by offering comparable products to the same customer segments. Was it effective? Profitability and market performance of these competing lines of business in the early 1980s suggests that it was. This approach did have a price tag that many other financial institutions were not willing to fund. However, it provided many managers within Citibank with the opportunity to demonstrate their skills, develop personally, and learn how to run a business. In 1988, Citibank reorganized to reduce the redundancy and capitalize on what it had learned. It was now ready to consolidate its activities, leverage its strengths, and build only those businesses that had the most promise for the 1990s.

Mission statements, like all uses of language, reflect and shape how individuals define reality—in this case their business unit. The greater the clarity and direction provided by a mission statement, particularly when one is coping with an uncertain environment, the more likely that the mission will affect thoughts and behaviors. However, rigid adherence to a mission in a rapidly changing environment can be as problematic for a business unit as having no sense of mission at all. In most cases, misalignment, overlap, or lack of clarity costs money and diffuses the energy of the business unit and the larger organization. Imprecise nesting, when it occurs, should be with intent rather than through neglect.

Mission Statements and Values. Many organizations incorporate a description of the values and ethical principles to which the business's managers subscribe into their mission statements. These principles generally include statements of how customers and employees should be treated and a description of a set of beliefs about the quality of the products and services offered. For example, the Union Carbide mission statement mentioned earlier was followed by these statements:

> As we achieve this mission, we will comply with the laws of the countries in which we do business, and, we will adhere to the highest standards of business integrity and ethics. In fulfilling this mission, we will emphasize quality in all that we do. This will require the best efforts of all Carbide people. Union Carbide will provide services and value for our customers and challenging and rewarding careers for employees; and we carry out our social responsibility by making significant contributions to the well being of the communities in which we live and work.[6]

This statement was then followed by further descriptions of selected values.

In some organizations, the answers to the question of corporate mission, as well as the first right answers to questions of vision, objectives and goals, and strategy are available. In others, these statements may not be available, or there may be more useful second or third right answers that are yet to be discovered. For managers in functionally organized firms, the **organizational responses** to these questions from the executive level and from other internal stakeholders are critical because the activities across functions need to be intimately linked. In organizations where business lines dominate, the direction provided by the organization becomes less critical as independent action by individual business units is generally accepted and appropriate. In both cases, stakeholders must be acknowledged and their needs must be recognized and addressed. What differs is the nature of the relationship with the stakeholders by the respective functional area or line of business managers.

Developing a statement of a unit's mission, as well as addressing the questions that follow, can be a useful tool for building a team spirit and defining a common agenda for a business unit. Involving more people from the business unit, rather than fewer, generally leads to greater awareness and acceptance of the unit's mission. Sharing the unit's mission with its primary stakeholders can also assist in energizing people to work towards the realization of the mission.

WHERE DO WE WANT TO GO AS A BUSINESS—VISION

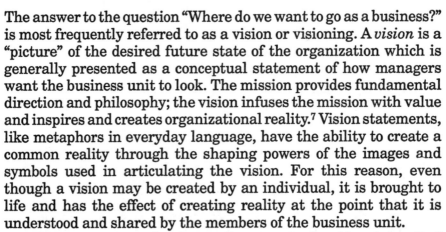

The answer to the question "Where do we want to go as a business?" is most frequently referred to as a vision or visioning. A *vision* is a "picture" of the desired future state of the organization which is generally presented as a conceptual statement of how managers want the business unit to look. The mission provides fundamental direction and philosophy; the vision infuses the mission with value and inspires and creates organizational reality.[7] Vision statements, like metaphors in everyday language, have the ability to create a common reality through the shaping powers of the images and symbols used in articulating the vision. For this reason, even though a vision may be created by an individual, it is brought to life and has the effect of creating reality at the point that it is understood and shared by the members of the business unit.

The importance of vision at the executive level has been cited as the distinguishing characteristic between those companies that were successful in integrating acquisitions and those that were not.[8] The vision for a business unit can be useful for surfacing, recognizing, and reconciling alternative and frequently competing beliefs about a business's future state. Brad, a manager whom we worked with recently, had a vision for his unit that was dramatically different from the vision held by the majority of his direct reports. The disparity between Brad and his direct reports had become apparent over a period of months as Brad took actions that moved the business unit in a very particular direction. After a series of management meetings over a six-month period, Brad was able to articulate the vision and develop momentum for enacting that vision from all but two of his eight direct reports. The result was that substantial new commitments were made by Brad and the team to move in the direction defined by the vision.

An example of a vision statement from one particular business unit reads:

> The Controller's Department vision is to become an integral and pivotal part of (the organization) by successfully executing its mission statement. Our department will help drive the conscience and energies of (the organization) from a marketing only perspective to a fully integrated subsidiary of the (parent company). In order to obtain the greatest added-value of our department we expect to focus on accounting and treasury functions, while providing direction and leadership in the areas of compensation, budget

and planning, marketing research, and systems administration. It is our intention that the barriers of field versus administration be disassembled and that we become the financial resource for the whole organization. The Controller's Department should be part of any solution which has financial impact and involves the compliance of internal control policies.

The process used in the creation of this vision statement was deliberate, thoughtful, and inclusive. It incorporated the ideas of a number of individuals from the business unit. After the development of the statement, the manager and the direct reports indicated significantly greater clarity in their priorities and direction. There had been a long-standing belief that substantial overlap existed between this Controller's Department and another business unit. The articulation of this vision triggered a series of discussions that helped to resolve the dispute.

More problematic in visioning are those situations when a vision is articulated but not embraced by key members of a team. In one situation we witnessed, Pat, a manager, was hired by Jim, an executive, to facilitate the creation and implementation of a new vision for a particular business unit. Although Jim said that he supported the vision, over a period of time, Jim took a number of actions that suggested he did not really support Pat. Pat was able to generate significant momentum from most of the business unit, but two key subordinates realized that Jim was waffling and chose not to support the new vision. The result was that Jim left Pat "hanging," which led to Pat's leaving the firm.

In this instance, the manager group had been in place and working for Jim before Pat joined the organization. Pat was hired to be the interface between Jim and the group because the existing reporting relationship was disruptive to Jim and the organization. Because several key subordinates of the group did not like having an intermediary, and Jim did not support Pat's vision and actions at critical meetings, the new vision was not embraced by the group. When the new vision failed to be embraced by these two key managers, Jim reverted back to the previous working relationship.

For some managers, the process of conceptualizing a future state is easy; their challenge lies in creating acceptance for, and commitment to, the vision once it has been articulated. This can be facilitated by involving multiple layers of the business in the development of the vision, and once it is developed, communicating the vision to the entire business. For others, visioning is difficult. Some managers have asked their subordinates to develop a vision for their respective units or functional areas. These visions are then combined as a way of developing a vision for the business.

The introduction of *perestroika* in the USSR is an example of the former process. Gorbachev has created and articulated a vision. He faces a middle-management rank, in particular some Communist party members vested in the previous system, as well as local politicians within each of the republics, who are resisting the proposed new vision. Resistance from these individuals could become the source of failure for Gorbachev and his vision. In response to this, Gorbachev has chosen to communicate the vision directly to the Soviet people in an effort to create pressure for change from the society at large. What has been unleashed in this process may have gone beyond what Gorbachev expected, as a series of competing visions from a variety of stakeholders has emerged.

The absence of a vision can have profound consequences. Although organizations can survive and even prosper with vague or nondirective missions, the lack of a clear vision of where one wants to be five to ten years from now can be a fatal shortcoming. NASA in the 1980s was an example of an organization that lacked a clear vision. In the early 1960s President Kennedy was able to create a vision for the space agency by proposing that an American land on the moon by the end of the decade. His vision was easily understood and provided both direction and a rallying point for activity. Since the moon landing, there have been several inconsistent visions developed within NASA. First, it was to be a builder of unmanned space vehicles to distant planets, then the developer of the manned space shuttle. Now the space station appears to be the focus of a new emerging vision. In each instance, the vision has been partially accepted by some stakeholders but not fully accepted by enough stakeholders, including the public. This may have occurred because there were numerous visions operating simultaneously within NASA, each competing for the same limited resources, and a charismatic champion to shape the vision did not emerge.

The NASA situation illustrates another concern related to the question of "Where do we want to go?" Is there an appropriate time or planning horizon to use when visioning? The answer depends on both the industry and the level within the organization at which the question is being asked. Aerospace organizations, such as NASA, have a planning horizon of 20 or more years. Yet individuals both within NASA and outside seem to operate within a much shorter time frame. In particular, this may be true for some members of Congress; the U.S. electoral process tends to require a project to demonstrate a payoff of expenditures over four to six years, rather than 20.

In contrast, the merchandising industry operates with a planning horizon of two years. Managers within retail store chains such as Hills Department Stores, Inc., or speciality stores like The Limited tend to operate with a two-to-eight–month planning horizon for their products and services, and a somewhat longer-time horizon for operational and physical needs.

Finally, vision does not equate with a definitive plan. When Mikahil Gorbachev was asked if he had a grand plan as he introduced *perestroika* into the USSR, he noted:

> I had an idea—an idea to change our society on the inside and also to change what is going on outside, around our country, and to do so on the basis of new realities. But when people speak to me of various models and timetables, as though all this had happened according to a train schedule, I can only smile.[9]

The plan, to the extent that there is one, is addressed through the development of objectives, goals, and strategic actions.

WHAT DO WE WANT TO ACCOMPLISH AS A BUSINESS UNIT?—OBJECTIVES AND GOALS

Establishing objectives and goals (and adopting strategic leadership practices generally) is intended to enable a manager to improve efficiency (i.e., do the same amount of work in less time) and to be more effective (i.e., exercise control over what activities are being assigned to and completed by the business unit). This involves both doing things right and doing the right things.

Even though a great many things are important to the continuing operation of a business unit, *objectives* signify those activities that are most important for the unit over the current planning horizon. Objectives can be identified by asking, "For the entire unit, what are the key outcomes that will indicate our success during this planning period?" Sometimes objectives are initiated by the executive level. For example, "reduce expenses" may be established by senior management as an objective to be put into practice by everyone in the organization. At other times, objectives emerge through the collective discussions of those in the business unit. "Improving customer service quality so as to distinguish ourselves as the best in our area" is an example of an internally generated objective for one customer service unit with which we have worked. When a decision has to be made to allocate incremental resources to task A or task B, the business unit's objectives should dictate which task to select. Responsibility for realizing objectives is not necessarily assigned to any one individual or subunit. Rather, objectives tend to be qualitative statements of the things that the business unit is trying to accomplish. Objectives are often a collective responsibility.

Goals are the specific outcomes that objectives are intended to achieve. Goals are generally quantitative statements that succinctly describe what is to be achieved, by whom, and by when. Examples include: "We want the mix of wholesale to retail business to evolve from 35 percent/65 percent to 25 percent/75 percent over the next twelve months," or "We will introduce two new products into 80 percent of our distribution channels by the end of next quarter." The "we" in each of these statements is a specific unit; specific managers are generally held accountable for the accomplishment of these goals.

The motivational and compensation practice of management by objectives (MBO) is a direct outgrowth of translating the objectives of an organization into goals for specific individuals to accomplish in a specified period. Many MBO programs have annual contracts that are signed by both the manager and his or her boss. These contracts provide specific direction on what is to be done and implicitly indicate that there will be things that the manager can postpone or avoid doing because such tasks were not part of a given year's MBO plan.

The benefits of an MBO program include identifying key tasks, holding people accountable for task completion, and empowering the people who have accepted task accountability to work on that task and not on other tasks. Extensive behavioral science research supports the value of goals as motivators of behavior. When goals are clearly understood and accepted by both the boss and subordinate, and when they are quantified and measured, they do direct behavior and lead to greater accomplishment than when goals are unclear, not accepted, not quantified, or not measured. By empowering people to say no to tasks that are not on their MBOs, the organization can maintain greater focus and increase the likelihood of accomplishing its objectives in the current operating period.

One potential weakness of an MBO program is in its inflexibility to changing conditions and agendas. MBO programs can become blueprints that are followed quite closely. When this occurs,

MBO programs can be inconsistent with the strategic leadership ideas proposed when deliberate and emergent events, agendas, and strategies need to be merged in real time due to the increasingly turbulent and changing environment. But this inconsistency need not be the situation for managers or an organization. As suggested earlier, plans can be viewed along a continuum of being a blueprint for maneuvering, a game plan, a periodic milestone, or a common context and language for learning (see Figure 4–2). MBOs can have objectives and goals that also vary along this continuum without giving up much precision in terms of the specific results to be accomplished by whom and when.

HOW WILL WE ACHIEVE OUR OBJECTIVES AND GOALS?—STRATEGIC ACTIONS

Strategic actions address **how** objectives and goals are to be accomplished, and they identify the necessary tactical elements of who, when, where, and with what resources the unit is going to accomplish them. Analytic frameworks to use in developing a strategy have been addressed by many authors, Michael Porter being one of the most well known. Our view of strategic leadership does not focus on the identification of a strategy per se, but on the leadership of a unit with whatever strategy is used to contribute to its mission, vision, and objectives.

Strategic actions are frequently the specific and often creative solutions to the question of how a unit intends to accomplish its mission, vision, and objectives. It is this merging of the ideas of mission, vision, and objectives as one grapples with questions of strategy that has led many managers and executives to consolidate their mission, vision, and objectives into a single statement. We refer to such statements as MVO statements. Some MVO statements also specify the strategy to be followed in accomplishing the business unit's goals. We focus on MVO statements below and will return to questions of strategy in Part Three—Making It Happen.

MVO STATEMENTS

MVO statements reflect the essence of planning and can be a useful tool for developing managers' strategic leadership potential. Are MVO statements better than separate statements focusing specifically on mission, vision, and objectives? Are mission-vision (MV) or mission-objectives (MO) statements of more or less value than separate statements or MVO statements? Is this rhetoric, or does it make a difference—will it affect behaviors?

Packaging a unit's mission, vision, and objectives into an MVO seems to do a number of things. First, it requires much more time and effort to get an MVO statement mutually agreed upon among the organization's key executives and managers. Second, each element is more difficult to change once packaged than it would have been to change in an unbundled state. By connecting these three elements, a change in any one element will often affect the other two. Third, once established, MVO provides a more integrated sense of inspiration and direction than any of the separate elements would have done alone. Priorities are generally clearer in one MVO statement compared to three separate statements.

The decision to develop MVO statements versus separate mission, vision, and objectives statements is a judgment that should balance the time available, the need to potentially change one of the elements while retaining the others unchanged, and the degree of integration and inspiration needed. Can we, given our current business situation, develop an MVO statement? Are we clear on mission, but not on our vision or objectives? Are we clear on short-term objectives, but not on our vision or mission? How much time do we have to devote to clarifying MVO? How fragmented are our activities at present? By answering these types of questions, it is possible to determine the type of statement that is most useful to a business unit at a particular point in time.

The components of MVO are frequently developed separately in those situations that assume stability. Each of the components of the MVO statement can be developed sequentially. Some business units start with objectives, others start with vision or with mission. It is useful to encourage the individuals assigned to develop the mission, vision, and objectives to do so in an iterative manner.

Some mission statements have been nearly reified, leading to ponderous descriptions that are intended to "stand the test of time." The usefulness of such MVO statements seems to be measured by the likelihood of their remaining unchanged. This approach is consistent with a stable environment and traditional views of implementing against the one, right answer. In contrast, it seems appropriate for MVO statements that are to be part of the next decade to be less rigid, more directional, and highly motivational. For some organizations, this means that a general sense of vision and objectives is bundled with the mission statement to provide a complete, succinct definition of and direction for the business unit.

Consider the following two statements written by the managers of the same business unit in 1988 and 1990. The first is a mission statement that was written to provide a general sense of direction over a long time frame. It provides little specific direction; such direction was presumably provided by separate vision and objectives statements.

MISSION STATEMENT, 1988:

1. To contribute to (the parent company's) objective of being the quality retail services organization by providing (the noncaptive) distributors quality support services, and innovative products that appeal to upscale personal and business consumers;
2. To contribute to (parent company's) market share by being the premier distributor in (this) services industry;
3. To provide an attractive rate of return on investment on (parent company's) investment in (the subsidiary);
4. To develop new supplemental distribution systems where justified by growth and profit potential.

The second example is an MVO statement that provides substantially more definition and direction. It may need to be revised periodically—which will be an on-going challenge for the business as changes will need to be agreed upon and communicated to managers and workers.

MVO STATEMENT, 1990:

The mission of (the business unit) is to establish a significant, profitable, high-quality (product line) business which:

a. focuses exclusively on the upscale customer market and achieves a 5 percent market share ($100 million in sales) in this market segment by 1995;
b. distributes through selected relationship-oriented wholesale and retail outlets with 50 percent of sales from each distribution channel by 1995;
c. promotes, maintains and services the wholesale and retail distribution systems through a network of manufacturers' reps and centralized service facilities;

d. provides an average return of 15 percent to (the parent company) over the long term on new investments as well as the intangible benefits from our creativity and our ability to experiment aggressively.

The basis of our competitive advantage today is the strength, stability, and integrity we bring to each transaction as the (distributor) of (our parent's) products. By the end of 1991, the basis of our competitive advantage will be the high level of personalized service which we provide to our wholesalers and retailers.

These two statements were written by the managers of a mid-sized marketing subsidiary of a large financial services organization. Guided by the 1988 mission statement, the efforts of this unit had been dispersed over a broad range of activities; the 1990 MVO statement was developed to define, direct, and empower all the members of the unit. The MVO statement is quite specific in identifying the product lines, target markets, distribution systems, and milestones to be reached over the next five years. It has also begun to identify the strategy that the unit is going to pursue to accomplish its MVO.

Implicit within the development of a business's mission, vision, and objectives, or an MVO statement, is that more specificity and therefore more denial is valued. We have found that businesses that are able to deny themselves involvement in activities outside of their MVO are more profitable and successful than those that deny very little. There is always the risk that denial of some activities will lead to a lost opportunity for the manager and the unit. However, most of the business units with which we have worked generally considered too many activities and business lines. Rarely have they considered too few.

The discussion thus far has focused on a set of ideas that can facilitate more effective thinking and analysis on the part of managers. Implementing a business plan and accomplishing MVO must also reflect the routine as well as the spontaneous behaviors that are the core of a manager's day. These behaviors include decisions made during the planning process that are implemented along with incremental actions taken during strategy implementation in response to changes in the environment.

The next chapter, entitled "Strategic Thinking," focuses on those day-to-day thoughts and behaviors that managers need to experience in order to link the strategic plan and MVO to strategy implementation. The intuitive ability to think strategically is relatively rare. Yet once a framework and heuristic approach for strategic thinking are articulated, it is relatively easy to incorporate into one's leadership style.

ENDNOTES

[1]This chapter is based in part on work presented in "Strategic Leadership in Middle Management: Developing the Baseline" by Thomas P. Mullen and Sidney A. Nachman, a Stern School of Business Working Paper, 1990.

[2]G. Majone, and A. Wildavsky, "Implementation as Evolution." *Policy Studies Review Annual II* 1978, pp. 103–17.

[3]Henry Mintzberg, and Alexandra McHugh, "Strategy Formulation in an Adhocracy." *Administrative Science Quarterly*, 1985, *30*(2), 160–97.

[4]This information is based on discussions with Henry Cherrick, D.D.S., who served as Dean of the School of Dental Medicine at Southern Illinois University (1978–81), the University of Nebraska College of Dentistry (1981–88), and UCLA's School of Dentistry (1988–present).

[5]H. Edward Wrapp, "Good Managers Don't Make Policy Decisions." *Harvard Business Review*, September–October, 1967, pp. 8–21, and James Waters, and Henry Mintzberg, "Of Strategies Deliberate and Emergent." *Strategic Management Journal*, 1985, *6*(3), 257–72.

[6]*Our Mission, Our Values, Actions and Goals*, Union Carbide publication, 1987.

[7]Philip Selznick, *Leadership in Administration.* (New York: Harper & Row, 1957).

[8]"The Decade of the Deal," *Business Week*, January 15, 1990, pp. 52–59.

[9]"Gorbachev Interview," *Time Magazine*, June 4, 1990, pp. 26–29.

PART THREE
MAKING IT HAPPEN

CHAPTER FIVE
Strategic Thinking

CHAPTER SIX
Strategic Management Skills

CHAPTER SEVEN
Personal Preferences

CHAPTER EIGHT
Working the System

CHAPTER FIVE
Strategic Thinking

Understanding the roles of middle managers, the complexities of managing in the middle game, and several concepts of strategic leadership is useful but not sufficient for becoming a more efficient and effective manager. The research we have conducted with several thousand managers over the past decade clearly indicates the need to put these ideas into practice in order for them to have lasting value. However, the leadership challenge in applying these concepts is substantial. In the next four chapters, we focus on how the diagnosis of issues, one's strategic management skills, and one's personal style can and must be integrated with the concepts presented in Part Two in order to provide the critical direction, inspiration, and leadership of a business unit.

We envision the integration of these three elements—strategic thinking, skills, and personal style—as three strands of a rope coming together to make the rope stronger than the sum of the strengths of its individual elements (Figure 5–1).[1] Such synergy is obtainable only after managers develop a capacity to think strategically (Chapter Five), evolve a clear sense of their strategic management skills (Chapter Six), and understand the way their personal style affects their individual and group performances (Chapter Seven). Collectively, it is these elements that managers leverage as they learn to make things happen in their organizations (Chapter Eight).

Strategic
Thinking

Style

BEHAVIOR

Strategic
Leadership
Behaviors

Skills

FIGURE 5–1 The Integration of Strategic Thinking, Skills, and Style

Great strategies, like all great things, are 20% inspiration and 80% perspiration.

Adapted from Thomas Edison

Strategic thinking involves identifying alternative ways to attain chosen objectives and then determining what specific actions are needed to get them into their desired position. It is a process that requires the active diagnosis of issues and events followed by analysis, judgment, and choice. Strategic thinking can focus on the objectives of a company, a business unit, a functional area, various groups or subgroups, and/or individuals. Although there is much to read and many case situations to analyze that address questions of strategy, the amount of strategic thinking that is taking place seems to be less than is needed. Many managers, including alumni of the most prestigious business schools in the country, report the need for a greater capacity to think strategically.[2]

Our research supports this finding, particularly as it relates to the quality of thought that occurs in defining those issues the organization needs to resolve in order to ensure its long-term success.[3] The diagnosis and interpretation of such issues determine subsequent decision activity and choice. Such issues are difficult to diagnose because of their ill-structured nature. They are even more difficult to manage because of the subjectivity involved in their diagnosis. These issues tend to be complex, fluid, and often ambiguous, making their management an ongoing, interpretive process. Understanding how managers diagnose such issues is critical to the influence, control, and attention allocation processes that take place as part of the judgmental decision-making activity and change efforts that are a routine part of managing in the middle game.[4]

THE ISSUE DIAGNOSIS PROCESS

A business situation in which a decision needs to be made, embedded in a context that includes all potential environmental and organizational stimuli, creates cues that managers may, or may not, recognize and identify as important. As suggested in Figure 5–2, it is managers' knowledge and values that filter these cues and form their perceptions of an issue and its context. Managers' cognitive base and values restrict their field of vision by filtering out information that is not initially considered to be relevant to their emerging understanding of an issue.[5]

Managers' fields of vision are further constrained to what is within their respective lines of sight. What is over the horizon is quite difficult to see. The horizon can be changed by moving towards it, by moving to higher ground to alter the perspective, and/or by using technology to forecast or articulate what is over the horizon. Such actions on a manager's part are intended to provide a broader and clearer view of what might lie ahead. The ability to envision situations beyond the horizon, that is, to see and articulate a future state for the business unit, is a skill that is valuable to managers as leaders of their businesses.

The stimuli within one's field of vision, however enhanced by one's ability to envision, are not all attended to. Managers are selective in their perceptions of which elements are important in a decision situation. For example, many observable changes in consumer attitudes towards a product or service may not be immediately perceived as threats or changes in preferences by management. It took many years for managers to interpret what seemed to be clear signals from many constituencies that caffeine might be removed from some

FIGURE 5–2 **The Cognitive Process Involved in Issue Diagnosis**

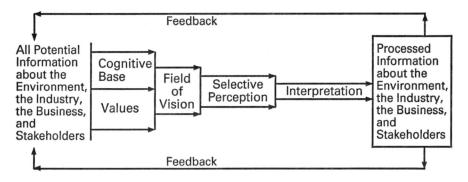

products. It is a manager's unique interpretation and meaning given to the information perceived that becomes each manager's individual diagnosis of an issue.

Different managers' diagnoses of issues are not likely to be random or unmotivated. Issue diagnosis reflects a problem formulation process that can be quite purposive. Some issue assessments may be intended to promote the involvement of select others. For example, we overheard a manager dealing with what was an engineering design issue say to her boss, "We need to get marketing and sales involved in this production issue to be sure that the revised design is something that our customers want." Other issue assessments may be intended to promote specific solutions or outcomes. Many managers have told us of situations in which they knew of solutions that were looking for problems to solve. Finally, issue assessments may be intended to promote self-interests. By knowing the preferences of the people involved in the diagnosis of an issue, one can often predict their likely motivation to support, impede, or sabotage the issue as it becomes defined and acted upon.

"There is no expedient to which a man will not resort to avoid the real labor of thinking."
Sir Joshua Reynolds

By understanding their ability to diagnose issues, managers may be able to improve the effectiveness of their subsequent thinking during the diagnosis, design, and choice activities. Knowing how a decision process tends to proceed permits managers to more precisely assess what additional information may be needed and where their influence attempts are likely to have the desired impact. It can also help to suggest the amount and kind of control needed to achieve that impact. At a minimum, knowing how something proceeds reduces the felt uncertainty and anxiety surrounding the unknown. Think back to the first time you did something that you had never done before (e.g., rode a horse, took a skydiving lesson, gave a public address, opened a new plant, launched a new product). Did the preparation you had for the event affect your skill level or knowledge base? Was the benefit of the preparation greater in terms of an improved skill or reduced anxiety?

A Stockbroker Analogy

Before proceeding with a model of the strategic thinking process, it may be useful to identify an analogy to the complex way managers think as they are investing their efforts and the organization's resources on issues.[6] Consider the following situation: You are a stockbroker for mid-sized institutional clients. Your job is to analyze various financial instruments (e.g., stocks, bonds, options) so as to best serve your clients through recommendations to buy, sell, hold, or ignore specific instruments. You must continuously diagnose and reassess the market in light of environmental factors as well as your clients' intended and emergent goals for risk management and financial success. Since you have many clients and there are many financial instruments, you are often trying to discover possible matches between various instruments and various clients. Since opportunities may not stay in the market for long periods of time, you scan both your client list and possible financial instruments regularly. When you take action, you invest the clients' assets through an expenditure of your personal resources of time, attention, and knowledge. Given the large number of financial products in the marketplace, and the large number of investors, your actions never control the market—but they occasionally have an impact on how others view the financial instruments to which you are actively attending. You may know this, or only suspect it, depending on what information others share with you.

Now make the following substitutions to the first part of the above paragraph. Instead of being a broker, you are a manager responsible for making strategic decisions that affect the long-term viability of your organization. Your clients are various internal and external stakeholders who have resources to invest. The financial marketplace is a market of opportunities and threats within which your organization is immersed. Finally, the financial instruments you buy, sell, hold, or ignore are the strategic issues you support, equivocate about, or suppress.

As a manager, you diagnose issues so as to take actions that invest the organization's assets through the expenditure of your personal time, attention, knowledge, and resources. Your diagnostic process is iterative. You go back and forth with starts and stops depending on which cues are most salient to you throughout the day. Your diagnostic process is nonlinear. You start anywhere; you change your mind without much recourse; and you alter, seek out, or avoid inputs from others as you choose. It would not be easy to program the process you use—nor do you necessarily fully understand the entire process as you live it. Your diagnostic process is heuristic—it aids you in learning and problem-solving. It also aids in the process of discovery. You do not know what insights may be derived from your thoughts and questions. Given the large number of strategic issues in the business at any point in time, and the large number of potentially interested parties in each issue, your actions rarely control the business. However, your actions do have some impact on how others view the issues to which you are actively attending. You may or may not know this depending on what information others share with you.

The broker analogy is a way to explore how issues are diagnosed and how attentional resources are allocated to them. The analogy makes explicit the enormous size of the market for issues and the pressures on managers to match resources to issues in a turbulent, dynamic setting. The matching process involves on-going events that take place with little predetermined order and often involves several iterations of ideas, suggestions, evaluations, more ideas, and so on. The broker analogy makes the distinction between the manager's personal resources and the organization's resources. Managers diagnose and allocate their attention to many different issues in the business, but only a small number of issues are allocated organizational resources. Managers can and do succeed when their choice of attentional investments is imperfect—just as brokers do.

The analogy of brokers to managers raises two general points: (1) Brokers respond to many different cues in diagnosing the risk/return potential of various financial instruments. Many of these cues are known to investors in general. Are there some general cues that managers respond to in their strategic thinking? (2) Brokers use some of these cues to match their recommendations for action with their clients' interests. Which cues do managers use to determine who should be involved in an issue in order to achieve an effective resolution?

OBSERVATIONS OF THE PROCESS

Careful observations and analyses of managerial conversations indicate that managers are rarely linear in the way they present information or act upon it, nor is there any unidirectional cause-effect relationship to behaviors that is sufficiently stable to be predictively useful.[7] By nonlinear, we mean that thoughts and behaviors do not evolve from any accepted and shared step-by-step model. When issues are being diagnosed, the manager's thoughts and behaviors appear to be incremental and iterative. They seem to evolve incrementally from personal motives and perceptions of the then current state of affairs. Different issue attributes may become salient as different managers learn about, and become influential in, resolving a particular issue. Some managers focus only on those issues directly related to their work unit. Other managers focus on issues that represent problems regardless of where these issues reside. These managers are primarily problem-solvers and fire fighters. Even though the critical dimensions of specific decision situations are definable (e.g., our broker can probably tell us after the fact which financial information he or she attended to), how these dimensions are assessed, by whom, and what behaviors will likely follow the assessments are ill-defined.

Seasoned managers have accepted this observation that the process of management, particularly when dealing with the more strategic aspects of management, is not a structured, logical, or programmable process. It is ill-structured, nonlinear (but certainly not illogical), and too variable to be programmed. What was not clear to them or to educators was how important it was for people new to management to know about and respond to this messy process.

As we explored this issue with managers, we found that (1) understanding and accepting the messy process of strategic leadership was critical to their ability to influence the process, exert control over aspects of the process, and feel comfortable with the process, and (2) the use of strategic leadership concepts was primarily a heuristic and diagnostic process. Just as managers had to go through iterations of establishing objectives, examining alternative strategies, reexamining objectives, reconsidering alternative strategies, and so on, they had to use similar nonlinear, iterative processes in many of their activities—particularly those involving important decisions. Having said this, let us try to communicate it a bit more clearly by examining the process most people use when they complete a crossword puzzle.

Reflect for a few minutes on the process you use when you complete a crossword puzzle. Where do you start? Maybe you start with the clue for "1 Across." Maybe not. There is no one correct place to start. You can start anywhere. In practice, people tend to read a few of the clues and then start with the clue that is easiest for them. Do you complete the puzzle in the order that the clues are numbered? Rarely. People tend to focus their efforts on a section of the puzzle, responding to both the across and down clues until they get stuck. Then they move to another section of the puzzle with the intent of coming back to the earlier section when they develop some additional insight. Does practice in doing crossword puzzles improve your ability to do them? Certainly it does in the early stages of learning how to do them. Is completing a crossword puzzle fun? Probably—many people complete them voluntarily each day. Do you have to complete them alone? Not if you choose to involve others (Figure 5–3).

This analogy could go on, but the main points can be made: Strategic leadership is a process much like the process used in completing a crossword puzzle. Both involve aspects of discovery, which can be fun but also frustrating. You can start anywhere in doing a crossword puzzle as well as in strategic leadership. You can

FIGURE 5–3 Strategic Thinking Often Involves a Nonlinear, Iterative, and Messy Process

learn from what you have done before you take additional steps. You can change your mind, and you can alter your approach. Focusing on parts of the whole often makes the task easier. You learn best through practice, and you can get advice and support from others. The process you create is iterative, nonlinear, and not easily programmed. As such, there are times when you feel that things are stalled; wheels may be turning but there is no forward motion. There may also be times when you decide to quit, or to put the puzzle down and come back to it later when you feel refreshed. Your efforts are voluntary and can be attempted as often or as infrequently as you choose.

So why does a process performed by millions of people every day for the fun of it often frustrate and create difficulties for managers? Is it that managers lose sight of their goals once they begin to explore opportunities? Or, is the vision for the enterprise unclear? Could it be that the strategic planning efforts have created the unrealistic expectation that the strategic leadership process will be the systematic execution of the business plan? When this does not occur as expected, one feels pressured, uncomfortable, maybe even no longer in complete control. Based on these questions, our observations, and discussions with managers, we suggest a heuristic model of the issue diagnosis process as we believe it relates to strategic thinking.

TOWARDS A HEURISTIC MODEL FOR STRATEGIC THINKING

We have been able to identify three interrelated sets of ideas that continually need to be discovered, attended to, and acted upon in the process of thinking strategically about one's business unit or functional area: business and individual goals; perceived social, political, and organizational contexts; and business and individual capabilities.

Business and individual goals are frequently alluded to by managers with phrases like: "What we need is a better sense of direction." "What is it that the company really wants, anyway?" "If my boss had given me a bit more guidance, I would have finished this two days ago." "Every year we focus on something different—so why bother trying to keep up, things will change again next year."

The social, political, and organizational context surfaces in discussions of stakeholders. Managers have commented to us: "I need more buy-in on this idea." "I can't seem to get any real support on it." "This project would have really flown if the organization had gotten behind it."

Business and individual capabilities are frequently addressed directly: "We need $2 million to launch this repositioning campaign." "The new building will cost $70 million over the next two years." "We need to hire four more engineers if we are going to make any headway on this project."

These ideas, when reflected in simple language, deal with: **What one wants, what relevant others want, and what one is capable of doing.** By posing these ideas as questions to be answered by managers throughout the middle game, we are able to reflect the diagnostic and discovery aspects of strategic thinking: What do we want? What do they want? What can we do?[8]

Each of these questions is associated with a circle in Figure 5–4. Each circle signifies all of the cognitions and behaviors that are possible answers to one of the questions. Each circle in Figure 5–4 represents the result of the cognitive filtering process (referred to in Figure 5–2) that leads to managerial interpretations with respect to the three "What" questions. Although the circles could

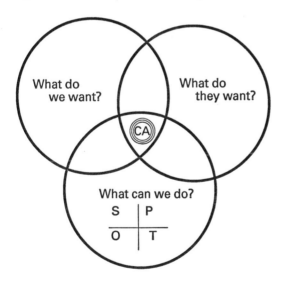

FIGURE 5–4
W-Cubed:
A Heuristic
Model
for Strategic
Thinking

⊚ Target Area   CA — Competitive Advantage

Source: S. A. Stumpf, "Towards a Heuristic Model of Career Management," *The International Journal of Career Management,* 1989, *1*(1), 19. Used with permission of MCB University Press Limited, Bradford, England.

be positioned anywhere in the figure, there is a meaning to the limited overlapping placement that is shown. This overlap signifies the existence of answers that satisfy all three questions simultaneously. We call this area of overlap W-cubed.

The model has been observed to have its greatest impact on managers' thinking when it was used as a diagnostic heuristic—a series of questions managers frequently asked that were rarely answered to their complete satisfaction until they were asked and re-answered many times. Managers record their answers to each question in that question's circle. Out of these initial answers come new insights as to how they could proceed more effectively. The answers are often idiosyncratic to the situation known to the inquirer, but the process of asking these questions and reflecting on the answers is believed to be valid and useful. The answers guide behaviors much the way a physician's diagnostic questions guide the physician's behaviors. The patient's responses to a physician's questions and actions provide information that may lead to additional questions, or discovery.

We have labeled the model shown in Figure 5–4 as W^3 (W-cubed) to signify the three "What" questions that managers need to ask themselves repeatedly in their strategic leadership efforts. W^3 is shown as three overlapping circles. This overlap among the circles is intended to suggest that the most effective ideas will be simultaneously addressing the three diagnostic questions: What do we want? What do they want? What can we do? Business issues are most likely to receive attention and be effectively resolved when the issues fit the multiple goals of different constituencies within the evolving environments and are within the managers' capabilities to address. The $W \times W \times W$ symbolism is also intended to communicate the importance of simultaneously answering all three diagnostic questions. As with any equation involving only multiplication, if any of the elements is zero, the product is zero. Finding answers to each of the three questions that are consistent and compatible with the answers to the other two questions is critical to strategic thinking.

Each of the three diagnostic questions is a **leading question** —these questions are easily remembered and are used to suggest other, **following questions** germane to the three leading questions. When leading questions cannot be easily answered, following questions tend to emerge. By attending to the following questions, managers frequently generate interesting alternative answers to the leading questions.

What Do We Want?

Organizational and individual goals define the set of valued outcomes that managers intend to seek. The question of whose goals are going to be accomplished by attending to various issues is a critical question. Within the context of the W^3 model, one is asking the question, **Who is we?** It is common and necessary for managers to have more than one point of reference when thinking about issues. Reference points could include the perspectives of the manager of the business unit; someone's subordinate; a peer of other managers; a mentor to one or more of the workers; and possibly a member of a committee, task force, or planning group. Managers are frequently responsible for a business unit or functional area that goes beyond any single individual's wants. What managers want for themselves in their careers may be different from what they want in the positions they occupy. By asking the question "**Who is we?**" managers are able to focus their diagnosis on a single entity at a time. "We" could be "I" personally. "We" could also be the manager in his or her organizational position. "We" could be the entire business unit, or the entire organization. As one may suspect from the large number of "we's," the W^3 model is best applied to one "we" at a time. It can then be reapplied to other "we's" that reflect one's different perspectives on an issue.

The process of identifying what we want may also take the form of eliminating what we do not want—by eliminating some alternatives that are not consistent with the organization's mission and vision. It is easier for some managers to identify the things that their business does **not want** because this can be accomplished by reflecting on policy statements and past actions to identify the not-so-successful situations and events. To determine what is wanted in the future requires knowing or envisioning possibilities—many of which are not part of a manager's experiences or cognitive base.

Asking such questions as **Who is we?** and **What don't we want?** are examples of how W^3 is used as a heuristic.

What Do They Want?

The second set of variables involves the social, political, and organizational contexts of the issues being addressed. These contexts house various stakeholders—those individuals, groups, and institutions that have a stake in the actions managers take. The number and divergent interests of the various stakeholders make their assessment problematic. Yet, by asking **"What do they want?"** and **"Who are they?"** managers are able to simplify their environmental analysis without losing much rigor. Stakeholder research has examined these questions and supports the importance of articulating the multiple "theys" and their wants. It is the stakeholders who create and define the environments managers subsequently perceive. By determining who the relevant "theys" are and what they want, possible barriers or constraints are identified. Stakeholder information can be collected by asking the various parties questions about their wants, not just once, but periodically throughout each year. Obtaining such information does not seem to obligate the managers to satisfy the wants of these stakeholders; rather, it identifies areas where there could be mutual benefits and areas that might be best avoided.

The overlapping circles shown in Figure 5–4 suggest that managers have indicated to us in our research that the easiest ideas to implement were those ideas that were able to satisfy their wants and the wants of critical stakeholders. The greater the overlap (i.e., the greater the consistency of the goals of affected parties), the greater was their success in implementing their ideas. To the extent that some of their goals were not consistent with the goals or constraints imposed by relevant others (i.e., the two circles were not concentric), their efforts to attain those "inconsistent" goals were often stalled, compromised, or made ineffective by people in those environments who had a stake in the issues being addressed.

What Can We Do?

Developing an understanding of the business unit's strengths and capabilities is an idea that is central to the strategic planning process. It is similarly essential to strategic thinking. Organizations and individuals perform more effectively when they are predominantly using established capabilities. This does not imply that new strengths should not be developed; rather, the development of new capabilities should consume a relatively small amount of energy so as not to distract managers from leveraging existing strengths. This is particularly critical in the middle game because the organization has already moved away from a focus on entrepreneurism to a focus on productivity. The costs of developing new strengths is high relative to the cost of using a developed strength to achieve growth and profitability objectives.

One widely used tool for accomplishing a **What can we do?** analysis is SPOT (or SWOT); SPOT involves examining the business's strengths (S), problems (P) [or weaknesses (W)], opportunities (O), and threats (T). This is shown inside the **What can we do?** circle in Figure 5–4 and again as a separate model in Figure 5–5.

The SPOT model encourages managers to assess their business's capabilities as part of a detailed analysis of their business situation. SPOT does not replace other assessment tools such as MIS reports, accounting information, market research, and the like. Rather, the insights gained through such assessments can be recorded on a SPOT chart as a way of visually presenting the analysis. SPOT can be used in the same heuristic, nonlinear manner as W^3. It is a diagnostic and discovery model whose four elements can collectively provide meaningful insights into those business actions that are likely to be more viable.

FIGURE 5–5 SPOT Analysis Model for "What Can We Do?"

Strengths: What do we do well now?	Problems: What is wrong now?
Opportunities: What possibilities exist?	Threats: What can go wrong?

Source: Adapted from S. A. Stumpf, "Towards a Heuristic Model of Career Management," *The International Journal of Career Management*, 1989, 1(1), 17. Used with permission of MCB University Press Limited, Bradford, England.

The word **strengths** in the SPOT model is a label for those particular capabilities that the business has now. Each strength a manager lists on the SPOT chart needs to be linked to the context in which it is a strength. For example, Levi Strauss is one of the world's largest sellers of bluejeans. This may be a strength for the company in terms of name awareness in the jeans market. But it is probably not a strength for Levi in the market for designer dresses. For a manager to state that Levi name awareness is a strength is not sufficiently precise to be useful; it may even be misleading.

The value of examining **problems** is to identify those aspects of the business where there are known gaps between where the business is now and where it was forecast to be. A problem is something that managers might choose to deal with by expending time and energy to solve or overcome it, or it may be something that managers choose to ignore. Identifying problems can lead to a reexamination of the business's goals and strengths. It is through confronting the things that are not working out as intended that managers are led to use the W^3 model iteratively. Solving problems can be fun to do, but it can be frustrating as well. Not all problems need to be solved. The art of sidestepping some problems is a skill that many managers learn.

Opportunities are the possibilities that exist in the future. There may be opportunities for opening new distribution channels, running a special sales promotion, or improving the product's quality through a new manufacturing process. Some opportunities can be created by managers when they have a strong sense of what they want and then find ways to achieve it. Other opportunities are identified by a boss, peer, or mentor or are suggested by other departments. Opportunities may also just present themselves to whoever is at the right place at the right time. As a manager identifies opportunities, they must be sorted. The task is one of choosing from among the opportunities those that draw on the business's strengths and are more likely to help the business accomplish its goals.

Threats are the things that can go wrong in the future. If things have already gone wrong, they are best viewed as problems. The value of distinguishing threats from problems is that problems are current issues that seem to demand attention, while threats are risks that may or may not materialize. Managers can protect against threats by developing contingency plans, by taking preventive steps to reduce the risk associated with the threat, or by avoiding high-risk opportunities. It is often possible to assess the level of a threat that one may encounter by asking for more information about the opportunities being considered.

Through conducting a SPOT analysis, managers develop an understanding of their business's capabilities for pursuing various opportunities, overcoming problems, and avoiding or minimizing threats. When they apply a capabilities analysis to a specific business situation of their own, they are assessing the feasibility of whether they and their business can handle a particular possibility effectively.

Target Markets and Competitive Advantage

If the three W^3 circles were concentric, there would be less need to target or focus one's energies on accomplishing some goals, while denying action on others. All of one's wants would be compatible with others' wants and one's capabilities. Over time, everything could be accomplished. As this is rarely the situation, it is important to be able to identify the area of probable overlap. This area is often described as a target market—the market of stakeholders, including customers, that is most likely to want what we want and can offer it. The phrase "The essence of strategy is denial" suggests that strategic thinking requires that many things be denied. The issues that do make a manager's agenda are a small number of those that could have made the agenda. Our research found that managers who were able to keep issues moving, often by diagnosing when the suggested solutions did not satisfy all three W^3 questions and then finding solutions that did satisfy all three questions, were viewed as more influential and powerful by their peers.

"The essence of strategy is denial."

Peter Drucker

Although the W^3 model stimulates thinking around many different wants, constituencies, and capabilities, there will always be a limited set of ideas that simultaneously satisfies the three diagnostic questions. Many of these ideas will not be immediately apparent. This is graphically suggested in Figure 5–6 by the three circles having no one area in common. Creativity is often required, particularly in the ways in which managers define and interpret issues, to shift the analysis of the situation in ways that lead to some useful "overlaps." This might be done by expanding our wants (making the "What do we want?" circle bigger); or it might be done by expanding our capacity or capabilities (making the "What can we do?" circle bigger); or, it might involve identifying some additional customer wants that were not previously considered (making the "What do they want?" circle bigger). Finally, it may involve redefining the situation such that the various stakeholders view the situation differently, thereby finding some areas of overlap or agreement. This would be like moving the circles closer together.

Focusing on a target market that satisfies the three diagnostic questions is not enough to ensure success. Being able to satisfy the wants of relevant others does not necessarily mean that you will be given the opportunity to do so. They may get those wants satisfied elsewhere. The concept of competitive advantage is relevant here because one is in a mutual choice situation. If they must select you as well as you must select them, then a competitive advantage is going to be necessary. What is a competitive advantage? It is the capabilities your business has or the benefits that your business can provide that people in the target market cannot get elsewhere more easily. It is the manager's answer to the question, "Why should they want it from us?" There is a competitive marketplace for most things: ideas, individuals, products, and services. Developing, knowing, and communicating your business's competitive advantage is critical.

FIGURE 5–6 Incompatible Wants within the W-Cubed Heuristic

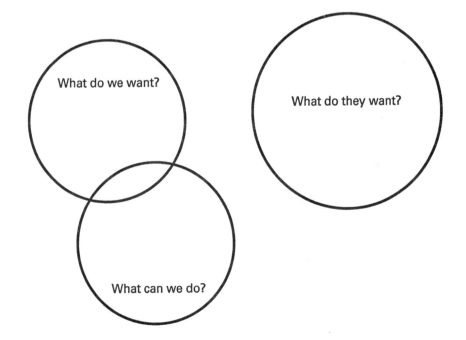

We began with the observation that the diagnosis of issues often involves a nonlinear, iterative process. W^3 is consistent with this observation. Managers often start with different initial questions when contemplating business issues—some start with goals, others with current environmental factors or constraints, and still others with current or planned capabilities. It generally does not matter where they start, what they address next, or how many times they return to a previously addressed question to readdress it in light of subsequent thinking as long as their thinking moves towards simultaneously addressing the three "What" questions. Individuals seem to start where it is easiest or wherever their first awareness of a potential issue surfaces.

APPLYING W^3

In 1986, we began to use W^3 as a strategic thinking tool while continuing to explore its use through our research efforts. We have developed a number of insights into applying W^3 that reinforce our belief that it is this personal discovery mechanism that can improve managers' capacity to think strategically. We share these observations below.

Managers start out using W^3 as an analytic tool—they ask the three questions and generate answers based on some moderate amount of exploration and reflection. They categorize the various ideas that emerge through their analyses on the W^3 and SPOT charts (e.g., Figures 5–4 and 5–5). SPOT is most often used to develop greater understanding of "What can we do?" If there is substantial convergence among the W^3 questions, managers can make fairly clear choices among their business opportunities. As you might guess, a high degree of convergence among the W^3 questions is less common for middle- and senior-level managers dealing with issues in the middle game. What does occur is the identification of many wants that we have, many significant "theys," "theys" with different and often incompatible or unknown wants, and a limited set of "can do's." Now what?

The iterations start. Managers begin to set priorities—which of their goals are most important to them? Which are less important? Which "theys" are most important to them? Which "theys" are most likely to affect goal accomplishment? Are the wants that the "theys" have really important wants? Are the strengths the business has really germane to what the business now wants? Are the areas that one wants to develop important now or at some future time? The questioning continues with incremental answers to many of these questions. When information is lacking, an agenda is often created for further exploration, including discussions with some of the "theys."

If the exploration subsequently done does not lead to clear options, a process of bargaining begins: "That may be what we want, but what can we get?" or "This may be what they want, but what will they accept?" This process increases the amount of overlap among some of the answers to the three questions. Managers begin to focus their energies on some of the business's goals, on key "theys," and on their most important "can do's."

Even after exploration and bargaining, some people are unable to identify opportunities or a clear choice. What we have observed at this stage is a subtle redefining of the business's goals, and its relationship with some of its "theys" and/or the redefining of the managers' roles within the business. This redefining requires a fair amount of energy and openness to alternative ways of thinking about situations. In the most productive instances, managers use this impasse as an opportunity to reflect broadly on their businesses—leading to some exciting business developments at this juncture. Some managers (only a few in our research) get stuck "in neutral." They limit their exploring, they accept their current situation as if it is permanent, they disengage. They have stopped trying to find the overlap among the three questions in W^3. Their strategic thinking has stalled. As we will discuss in Chapters Nine and Ten, comfort with and the ability to persist in strategic thinking processes can be developed. But it takes knowledge of the weakness and motivation to improve it to lead to meaningful development.

ENDNOTES

[1]The metaphor of the rope was first suggested to us by staff at the Center for Creative Leadership in Greensboro, North Carolina.

[2]Lyman Porter and Lawrence McKibbin, *Management Education and Development: Drift or Thrust into the 21st Century.* (New York: McGraw-Hill, 1988).

[3]Over the past eight years, we have observed several thousand managers perform. We have had three-to-five days of contact with each manager, one day of which involved observing the person participate uninterrupted as one of 12 to 20 managers in a simulated company. Another day involved meeting with the managers individually to discuss their management efforts on-the-job. These discussions typically started with the individuals' describing their work situation, discussing their key relationships with others, and then identifying the critical issues that they perceived as most salient at the time.

These managers were volunteers in various executive development programs offered by their companies or educational institutions that focused on developing senior management skills. The typical manager was 41 years old, had been with his or her company for seven or more years, and had five or more direct reports. All had four or more years of work experience. Most were viewed by their bosses as having advancement potential to executive positions within five years. They were employed by a wide variety of organizations and represented many different industries, including banking, chemical manufacturing, utilities, electronics, communications, government, oil, investment banking, and pharmaceuticals.

[4]For a general discussion of strategic decision processes, see H. Mintzberg, D. Raisinghini, and A. Theoret, "The Structure of Unstructured Decision Processes." *Administrative Science Quarterly,* 1978, *21,* 246–75; and M. McCall and R. Kaplan, *Whatever It Takes: Decision Makers at Work.* (Englewood Cliffs, NJ: Prentice-Hall, 1985).

[5]For more information on the cognitive processes and likely filtering biases that may exist in strategic issue diagnosis, see D. Hambrick and P. Mason, "Upper Echelons: The Organization as a Reflection of Its Top Managers." *Academy of Management Review,* 1984, *9,* 193–206.

[6]The stockbroker analogy was developed through discussions with Jane Dutton.

[7]We have conducted extensive observational studies of managers to develop a better understanding of their thought processes. We report the findings in T. Mullen and S. A. Stumpf, "The Effect of Management Styles on Strategic Planning." *Journal of Business Strategy,* 1987, *7*(3), 60–75 and U. Haley and S. A. Stumpf, "Cognitive Trails in Strategic Decision Making: Linking Theories of Personalities and Cognitions." *Journal of Management Studies,* 1989, *26*(5), 477–97.

[8]In an earlier paper we discussed the ideas around a heuristic model of issue diagnosis with respect to people's careers. See S. A. Stumpf, "Towards a Heuristic Model of Career Management." *The International Journal of Career Management,* 1989, *1*(1), 11–20.

CHAPTER SIX
Strategic Management Skills

The distinct nature of skills occurred to us one day on a walk through the SOHO area of New York City. Having glanced into the cellar of a factory, we saw a person building a small table. As we moved on, we discussed our abilities to do what we saw being done. We had most of the same tools and could acquire critical table parts. We knew what steps had to be taken. We knew what the finished product looked like. So why did we feel that we could not do as good a job as the person we just watched?

It was not until we connected our experience in observing the carpenter with our experiences in consulting and educating business people that a preliminary answer to this question emerged. What we lacked was the skill—that learned power of doing a thing competently with efficiency and effectiveness. The field of strategic leadership has emphasized the tools of management (accounting, finance, management roles, statistical analyses, competitive analyses), the knowledge currently amassed (theories, concepts, and models), and examples of good and poor strategic leadership (cases, lessons learned, comparisons of high and low performers). What is missing is an emphasis on the day-to-day skills required to use the tools and turn the knowledge into results in a timely manner. Then a BFO hit (Blinding Flash of the Obvious). The business profession has few (if any) practice sessions, internships, or apprentice programs to develop strategic management skills. Other than on-the-job experiences, it is rare for managers to be asked to perform in the presence of experts so as to receive feedback and develop their skills. This does *not* compare favorably with other professions in which skill training is integrated into the educational process because skills are viewed as critical to effective performance (e.g., medicine, dentistry, the performing arts, the trades).[1]

We began to link our observations of managers to various immediate and longer-term performance indices. By observing the language and concepts used by managers as well as analyzing the behaviors they exhibited, two sets of skills were identified: (1) core competencies and (2) strategic management skills. The core managerial competencies included the ability to motivate others, use influence skills, share and collect information, develop and use communications skills, delegate responsibilities, exert control, use organizational skills, and plan ahead. In our research, these variables *did not* distinguish the managers who were rated by their bosses and peers as being effective managers from those who were rated as needing development in strategic management. A second and distinct set of qualities did differentiate between those managers seen as effective in their strategic leadership efforts and those rated as needing development in strategic management. These strategic management skills involve a manager's ability to: (1) know the business and markets, (2) manage subunit rivalry, (3) find and overcome threats, (4) stay on strategy, (5) be an entrepreneurial force, and (6) accommodate adversity.[2]

Effective managers in the middle game have developed their ability for complex thinking. They are adept at interpreting, analyzing, and applying information. They truly **know their business and markets;** they know how the business makes money, which trends could affect the business adversely or favorably, and what consumer behaviors are needed for the business to be successful. They can ask the thought-provoking questions that stimulate others to expand their thinking. They are able to arrange the same information in more than one way, thereby generating more alternative courses of action for their business to consider and greater insight into various decision situations. Such insights help them to develop a conceptual understanding of the business's past actions that can be shared to inform and motivate others.

The second strategic management skill—**managing subunit rivalry**—focuses on the manager's ability to obtain the most benefit for the organization from subunits that have competing or incompatible goals. The production system wants efficiency, constant rates of production, and the homogeneous manufacture of a stable product line. Marketing and sales want flexible product features and delivery schedules that meet customer demands. Someone must manage the rivalry created by pressures of respective subunits to reach incompatible goals. The effective manager is able to handle both the business side and the human side of situations so that one subordinate's business does not inappropriately benefit at the expense of another's.

The third skill—**finding and overcoming threats**—needs to precede problem-solving. Managers continually diagnose threats to their intended actions. They are able to view issues from many perspectives, consider many alternatives, and remain open to new ideas. Strategic managers monitor and diagnose key information much in the way a doctor practices medicine—by combining and recombining bits of information into theories of what can go wrong. Then they act to protect against or overcome the threat before it becomes a serious problem. Because their first thoughts may sometimes be in error, more detailed information helps redefine events that have occurred in light of their latest diagnosis.

Strategic leadership involves **staying on strategy** once a business plan with the preferred strategy is articulated. This skill is comprised of: (1) recognizing and capitalizing on the organization's current strengths, (2) continually enhancing its competitive advantage, and (3) focusing on specific target markets as well as knowing which markets to avoid. The skill of staying on strategy requires that each significant business action be assessed against the strategy: Is the action appropriate? Does it draw on our strengths, reinforce our competitive advantage, and focus on our target markets?

Effective managers act as an **entrepreneurial force** for their unit. They are sensitive to the relationships between their organization and its environments because they recognize that strategy formulation and implementation are often concurrent activities. They are able to envision a desired future position for their companies in clear, concise detail. They can articulate this vision in sufficient detail to convince others of its realistic possibilities. They are able and willing to champion innovative ideas, even when faced with doubt, skepticism, and resistance.

Finally, effective strategic leadership involves being able to **accommodate adversity.** Taking risks as an entrepreneurial force leads to some failures. Managers bounce back from their mistakes just the way a champion does in any occupation. They are resilient and flexible. They try new approaches if the old ones are not working. They function effectively in ill-structured situations because they tolerate and cope well with ambiguity.

This set of strategic management skills differentiates the apprentice manager from the craftsperson manager. Although exhibiting core competencies will help one to reach a management position, being effective in managing the middle game demands more skills—skills that most managers have not had a chance to develop because their organizations are not clear on the need for such skills, and the demands and hectic pace of their middle-game jobs leave little time for them to acquire these skills along the way.

We turn now to discuss the research that led to the identification of the strategic management skills and our observations of how the skills actually make a difference for managers in the middle game.

IDENTIFYING STRATEGIC MANAGEMENT SKILLS

Our research involved meeting with each manager individually prior to his or her participation in an executive development program. These meetings permitted the program staff to learn about the managers' jobs, current business concerns, and self-assessed managerial skills. In several hundred cases, we were able to obtain assessments of the participants' skills from their real-job bosses, peers, and subordinates. These co-worker appraisals were generally summarized and individually shared with participants early in the program. The availability of these appraisals allowed us to compare the boss's assessment of each manager's skills to staff observations during the executive development program. We knew before actually observing the managers what their bosses thought of their skills. Since these assessments were not available to the program peers, it was possible to empirically examine the extent to which real-world bosses and peers in an executive development program agreed on the skills that each manager exhibited.

The Research Measures

Based on the management literature and our earlier work, separate instruments were used to assess managerial core competencies and strategic management skills. The core competencies questionnaire consisted of 50 items that reliably and validly measure nine managerial skills—setting objectives and priorities, organizing one's work, sharing information, delegating responsibility, relying on structure, involving others, motivating others, communicating effectively, and thinking strategically. The strategic management skills (SMS) questionnaire consisted of 20 items derived from the literature, from conversations with managers dealing with middle-game challenges, and from observations of managers' performances. After preliminary use of these items with over 600 managers, the SMS questionnaire was analyzed to better understand the factor structure of the items and to estimate the reliability and validity of the questionnaire for measuring strategic management skills.[3]

One of the first questions to address was the extent to which the two skill areas—core competencies and SMS—are separate and distinct from each other. Are there unique strategic management skills, or are they simply skills that have been overlooked or labeled something else? We addressed this question in two ways. First, if the skill sets are separate, then factor analyses employing the nine core competencies and six SMS should result in two separate factors. This analysis was done and supported the hypothesis that the skill sets are distinct. Correlational analysis of the two sets of skills also indicated weak and nonsignificant relationships between core competencies and SMS. Possessing skills in one area has little to do with having skills in the other area.

A second way to examine the unique character of the two skill sets was through examining whether the program participants' real-job boss, peers, and subordinates felt that each skill was needed on-the-job. Both sets of skills were consistently viewed as needed for participants whose real-job was in middle or senior management; only the core managerial competencies were consistently viewed as needed for supervisors or lower-level managers. This finding supported our observations that SMS were critical to the middle level of organizations.

Further support came from examining which real-job co-workers felt development was needed in each skill area for people in middle manager and executive positions. There were not meaningful differences in co-workers' views of development needed in the core competencies. However, there were significant differences in co-workers' perceptions of development needed for the SMS:

1. Bosses (compared to subordinates or peers) were up to twice as likely to say development was needed in knowing the business and mar-

kets, finding and overcoming problems, and staying on strategy. When managers view their subordinates, they perceive a need for those subordinates to develop a better understanding of the entire business and market forces, diagnose issues earlier, and manage their units consistently with the broader organization's strategy.

2. Subordinates were 1½ times more likely than bosses to say that development was needed in managing subunit rivalry.

3. Managers' self-reports indicated a greater need to accommodate adversity (by 150%) than did assessments by co-workers. Managers perceive a need to develop their flexibility and resilience more often than do their bosses, peers, or subordinates.

4. The skill most in need of development from all points of view was that of being an entrepreneurial force. People want their co-workers and themselves to have energy, to be willing to champion ideas, and to excite people to take desired actions.

The Research Setting

Studying managerial and strategic management skills required a setting in which we would have knowledge of the domain of possible strategic actions and in which the managers would be involved in a realistic situation that provided the opportunity to identify issues and take actions. An experimental setting was rejected as being too artificial to generate meaningful results. Field interviews were rejected since the information collected would be at best a manager's recollection.

The invention of large-scale behavioral simulations that were not computer games was a viable alternative.[4] Use of behavioral simulations as part of an executive development program permitted research to be conducted without the managers' becoming unduly sensitized to the research questions. Because the researchers were also the training staff, their observations could be shared with participants after the simulation as part of an entire day of personal and interpersonal feedback.

During the authors' initial observations of a program using a behavioral simulation, the 20 participants, each in a different corporate role, became extremely involved in the six-hour exercise; they seemed fully immersed in the simulated company and appeared to ignore the staff observers entirely. Postsimulation interviews with participants unanimously confirmed these observations.

As participants, the managers reported feeling engrossed in the simulation, claimed that their behaviors were representative of their work behaviors on their actual jobs, and said that they did not notice the presence of the observers after the first hour. The simulation was sufficiently complex to provide ample opportunity for strategic management. The observation period (six hours) was long enough for detailed researcher notes and program peer observations of each other's performances.

This latter point was important since the staff observers typically had access to the managers' real-job boss's assessments of their skills, but other program peers did not. The primary assessments to be used in the research were peer assessments. These assessments were made by managers of comparable experience who had not worked with each other prior to this research nor would they necessarily work with each other in the future. Yet, they would go through a common experience that paralleled their real-job context.

The Participants

The participants in this phase of our research were all volunteers in executive development programs offered either within their companies or publicly to develop their overall management skills. They were not attending for remedial training purposes. These managers were certainly not the victims of ineffective corporate bureaucracies—most had partial responsibility for implementing their companies' strategic plans, and all were identified as having advancement potential. A typical manager was 41 years old, had been with his or her company for seven or more years, and had direct responsibility for five or more subordinates.

The corporations involved are frequently cited in *Fortune, Business Week,* and *The Wall Street Journal* as models of excellence in terms of management, the products or services offered, and the value of their stock. Industries represented included chemical manufacturing, publishing, securities brokerage, banking, oil, health and beauty products, insurance, telecommunications, steel, and pharmaceuticals. In total, managers from 64 companies were involved. Five companies generated nearly half of the observations made: Dow Jones, Citicorp, Data General, the New York Stock Exchange, and Metropolitan Life.

EXAMINING STRATEGIC MANAGEMENT SKILLS

The six strategic management skills identified in our research seemed to be the skills that the more effective managers used to link their conceptual models of strategic planning to their managerial actions. Each of these skills is discussed below along with examples of the effect these skills have been observed to have on managerial effectiveness.

Knowing the Business and Market

For nearly 100 years, beginning with the development of the principles of management, managerial emphasis has been on division of labor—breaking complex tasks into distinct, knowable, and trainable parts that can be subsequently integrated into a meaningful whole. This has led to formalized policies and procedures, work standards, and an operations management approach to running organizations. However, what this has unwittingly done is to implant the idea in much of the managerial workforce that has come up through the ranks that the whole is always equal to the sum of its parts.

The whole probably is equal to the sum of its parts when the system is deterministic. But much of strategic management does not involve deterministic events. The unpredictability of competitors, customers, regulators, employees, and interest groups, as well as the rapid rate of change in technology, social norms, and the economy—have left the sum of the parts equal to something that is outdated or not wanted by the time it reaches the market. The skill that is needed to alter this way of thinking is to know the entire business and its markets, not just a part of the business or one functional area, such as marketing, finance, or production. This involves understanding the whole business, how the parts come together to make money or accomplish the goals of the business, and what products and services customers want—today and over the next several years. It also involves **updating and using** this knowledge continuously—not just during the strategic planning process each year.

Knowing the business and markets sounds obvious—but frequently it is the absence of this skill that has cost businesses millions of dollars. Take the conventional bankcard as an example. Just how does one make money as an issuer of a bankcard like Visa or Mastercard? They are *not* like many consumer goods—when you sell a box of Cheerios at 30 percent above your costs, you make money. You make nothing when a consumer accepts your bankcard—in fact, you incur about $35 of account maintenance costs annually with no guaranteed revenue ever—unless you charge an annual fee. The question of how money is made through bankcard use is often answered "on the interest payments." But revolving credit is not like an installment loan. People must first use the bankcard, then they must *not* pay it off entirely each month, then they must make payments against the revolving line of credit. Notice all the consumer behaviors the bankcard issuer must influence. It was not until consumer bankers got more strategic in their thinking about the bankcard business that the projected profits began to materialize (e.g., what behaviors do we need to encourage to generate revenues?—frequent use of the bankcard on high-priced items by credit worthy people). Unfortunately, the skill of knowing the business and markets had to be learned the hard way for many—with more than $1 billion in operating and credit losses between 1976–1978 alone.

Managers who are most effective know their businesses and the marketplace well. They have taken the time to learn it, piece by piece. Because of this, they cannot be transferred into different organizations and industries without some loss of effectiveness.[5] They need to be able to identify and interpret trends that could affect the business, a skill that is developed through active diagnosis of the environment and experience in a business. The trends might be social—such as the effect of the growing number of two-career couples on the demand for convenience products and services—economic, political, technological, or demographic. They are also able to articulate a conceptual understanding of the business's past actions—and do so to anchor employees in a meaningful history and culture. They continuously ask thought-provoking questions that relate to the business's future actions of the people around them—whether those people are peers, subordinates, or others within the executive's network. These abilities—to explore consumers' wants, identify trends, share one's conceptual understanding of past actions, and ask thought-provoking questions—lead to the generation of more viable alternatives that can be analyzed for likely contributions to organizational effectiveness.

Figure 6–1 presents the results of our research on the skill cluster, Knowing the Business and Markets. The horizontal axis indicates whether a manager's boss assessed him or her as either: (1) needing development with respect to a specific skill or (2) exhibiting that skill effectively. The vertical axis is a peer assessment of the contributions made by each participant during his or her management of the simulated organization. The bar graphs indicate the amount of contribution a manager's peers in the study perceived him or her as making for those managers

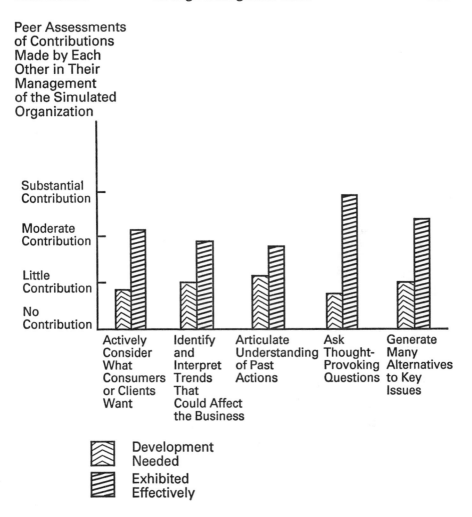

Boss Assessment of Skills Exhibited Based on On-the-Job Behaviors

FIGURE 6–1 **Knowing the Business and Markets**

whose bosses saw them as needing development and for those managers whose bosses saw them as exhibiting the skill effectively. Since the boss ratings were not available to the peers in the simulation, there was no possibility of these assessments being contaminated by the views of the other party.

Figure 6–1 suggests that the most important aspect of knowing the business and markets is being able to ask thought-provoking questions. It was not only what managers knew personally (e.g., being able to actively consider what customers want and generating many alternatives to key issues), but also what managers were able to share and learn through asking questions that stimulated the thinking of their peers.

What we consistently found (as shown in Figure 6–1 and Figures 6–2 through 6–6 to follow) is that managers who were observed to exhibit strategic management skills by their bosses were viewed by their peers in the education program as making more contributions to the running of the simulated organization than those individuals viewed by their bosses as needing skill development.

Through our observations of these managers' running the simulated company and post-simulation interviews, we were able to identify specific behaviors that we believed led the participants to assess the contributions of each other differently. By discussing our observations with these managers after they completed their ratings (typically the following day), we were able to establish which of our observations were consistent with their views. We summarize and share these observations for each strategic management skill cluster as a way of providing detail around what these skills look and sound like in practice. Specifically, how does one exhibit the skill of knowing the business and markets? The observations we share are the observations participants stated led them to believe that a particular skill was being used either in the simulation or on-the-job, and that resulted in their assessment that someone was making greater contributions to the management of the simulated company.

Observation 1: People demonstrated an understanding of the revenue-generating and cost components of the business by being able to explain the meaning of and reasoning behind key entries on MIS reports, financial statements, and budgets. By creating and using ratios, such as the inventory turnover rate or net customer revenue per full-time employee, they were able to examine aspects of the business that others tended to overlook. When such ratios were out of line with expectations or changing in unexplainable ways, it was easy to direct managerial efforts to the areas of concern.

Observation 2: Individuals who asked many questions about their customers were able to communicate to others a solid sense of the market. Examples of the questions asked were: Why do customers buy our products? How do they use the products? Where do they live? What are their shopping habits? What don't they like about our products or services? What do they like the best? The product and marketing ideas suggested by the managers who asked and got answers to such questions tended to receive sufficient internal support to be considered as viable alternatives.

Observation 3: People who were able to share relevant, graphic experiences about the products offered or the services received captured the attention of others. This tended to require a knowledge of the product from both the employee's and customer's perspectives—which sometimes involved shopping the firm's products and services as well as those of competitors. One conversation that we overheard is a good example of an experience that communicated knowledge of the business and markets: A customer service representative had called a customer to inquire about unusually high activity on her credit card. The discussion that followed helped others understand what the customer wanted (i.e., not to have her card used in an unauthorized manner and to have a higher credit limit when her card use was going to be greater in the months ahead) as well as what the bankcard issuer wanted (to encourage active use of the card, but only by qualified customers).

Managing Subunit Rivalry

The challenge for single-product firms with one or two product lines has generally been to coordinate sales and production so as to enhance manufacturing efficiency. The rivalry that exists is between the salesforce's desire to sell whatever the customer wants and the manufacturing system's desire to produce it in a timely and cost-effective manner. As the number and types of products increase, and as entire firms merge with other firms in different businesses, the task of managing subunit rivalry grows disproportionately. The discipline of portfolio management has emerged to help managers deal with the complexity of this challenge. To manage subunit rivalry effectively, senior executives need both analytical tools to examine alternative portfolio possibilities and people skills to manage the conflict that is generated when resources are spent on one part of a portfolio and not on others. Managing subunit rivalry involves allowing conflicts and tension to exist within certain boundaries in such a way that it is productive.

As suggested by Figure 6–2, this requires the active management of interdepartmental communications and relationships. It puts a premium on developing clear, agreed upon, and measurable business unit or functional area objectives, and then managing the portfolio of businesses and people to attain those objectives. This indicates a somewhat obvious linkage between the skill of managing rivalry and the ability to apply the concepts of the "mission-vision-objectives-strategy."

There is a critical need to manage subunit rivalry in firms like General Motors or Ford. The Pontiac and Chevrolet divisions

FIGURE 6–2 **Managing Subunit Rivalry**

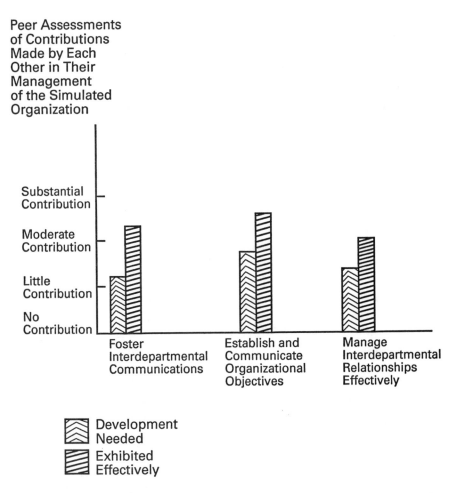

Boss Assessment of Skills Exhibited Based on On-the-Job Behaviors

within General Motors compete for internal resources as well as customers; the managers in these divisions may also compete for rewards, promotions, publicity, and the like. Although the divisions share enormous amounts of technology, have many auto parts in common, and serve many of the same external stakeholders, the managers may not share at all. It is a strategic management skill to be able to attend to these issues in such a way as to make the human rivalry productive. This has not been learned easily by the major auto manufacturers. The time and energy wasted getting "common" parts approved *and* used without modifications has been in the hundreds of person-years. Why? Because each engineer and his or her manager tend to believe that their product design is best for their product-market segment. Once they have invested in it, why should they share it, or give it up to use some other auto part developed by someone not quite as capable as they are? The result: more expensive cars and lower corporate profits.

Another form of subunit rivalry occurs in firms that do extensive product-market segmentation. For example, consumer package-goods firms such as Proctor and Gamble, Unilever, and General Foods are typically organized by product line whereby product managers of similar products within the firm are near-competitors. The stated goal is to have similar products effectively positioned and sold to different market segments (e.g., users of skin-care soaps versus users of deodorant soaps). In practice, the market segments overlap, with some cannibalization of each other's sales. The rivalry intensifies when managers are evaluated and rewarded based on their product's sales, particularly when the product features are not perceived as meaningfully different by consumers. Effective strategic management involves the diagnosis of rivalrous conditions and managing the interpersonal conflict inherent in such situations. For consumer-goods firms, it may mean promoting competing products based upon their primary, differentiated consumer benefits—and not mentioning all of the product's other benefits.

Observation 4: *People who focused a major portion of their attention on the people and issues at the interfaces between specific functions, among similar products targeted to different market segments, and on areas competing for limited resources or rewards were able to identify potentially rivalrous situations. By identifying the potential rivalry, they were frequently able to redirect others' attention to the area of concern before conflicts became dysfunctional.*

Observation 5: Once rivalry was identified, people who devoted their energy to involving the affected parties in the decisions of how to proceed had the greatest positive impact on the situation. Creating new and productive ways of dealing with the rivalry were common once it was openly acknowledged that the rivalry was inherent in the objectives of the different units, and such objectives were accepted as legitimate. For example, one group decided to alter the compensation system from an individual incentive program to an incentive system that reflected the combined sales of rivalrous products relative to the sales of their top three competitors.

Finding and Overcoming Threats

Much of management is solving problems—handling equipment breakdowns, improving sluggish sales, replacing key personnel who have left for other positions, and so on. Chances are that today's problems were threats that could have been diagnosed a few days (or weeks or months) before. Yet, so much of a manager's day involves working on problems that the phrase "management by exception" is popular. Managers attend to the "gaps"—those discrepancies between where they are now and where they thought they should be. They manage in an incremental way, taking small steps to solve problems or attain goals. Actions or decisions that depart a great deal from the current state of affairs are often viewed as too risky—even if they may solve a problem or move one closer to accomplishing a goal.

An alternative to management by exception is management by objectives (MBO). Many MBO efforts encourage managers to look to the future, set goals, and then seek those goals. Exceptions or problems are dealt with to the extent that they affect goal accomplishment. An MBO approach typically directs one's attention to future accomplishments—issues or events that are not built into one's MBOs often get ignored or given low priority.

The strategic management skill of finding and overcoming threats is an antecedent to both the incremental and MBO managerial approaches. Figure 6–3 indicates that it involves the diagnosis of issues before they become problems, coupled with the ability to address the implications of an issue should it become a problem. To accomplish this, managers must be able to diagnose threats, as well as frequently redefine issues and problem symptoms so as to understand them and their implications before they

Peer Assessments
of Contributions
Made by Each
Other in Their
Management
of the Simulated
Organization

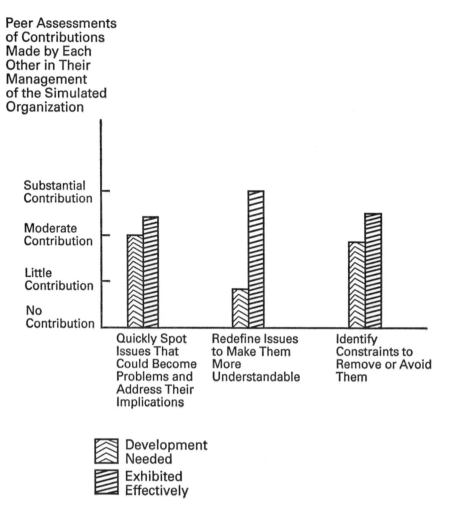

Boss Assessment of Skills Exhibited Based on On-the-Job Behaviors

FIGURE 6–3 Finding and Overcoming Threats

become known to others. They must be able to identify the constraints inherent in the systems around them in order to remove or avoid such constraints.

The aspect of finding and overcoming threats that was most strongly related to peer assessments of contributions made by others was the skill of redefining issues to make them more understandable. Not only was this skill important, but the lack of it was viewed as a sizable weakness. When we asked managers what they meant by the need for someone to redefine issues to make them more understandable, they frequently elaborated on "communication problems." Since this was not what we thought that we had observed, we asked for clarification. The understanding that emerged in our discussions was that for issues to be heard, they needed to be presented as questions or possibilities, **not** solutions. The communications problem that was frequently identified was really a problem of managers' accepting a solution to an issue before the issue was accepted as something with which to contend. Once issues were raised as issues (not solutions to problems or opportunities to take), then they were more easily understood.

Finding and overcoming threats is a skill much like the skill of a good sailor who can interpret the wind, tide, and weather conditions so as to identify possibilities and avoid being caught in a storm. Managers need to be able to continually diagnose and interpret customer and other stakeholder wants, their unit's objectives, their personal goals, and the capabilities of the organization in order to find and overcome threats before the threat has become an "exception" demanding resolution. They need to be cautious about reaching conclusions and recommendations too early—particularly if others have not yet diagnosed an issue or placed an issue on their agenda.

Managers we have studied who possess this skill are both proactive and interactive with their environments.[6] By proactive we mean that they are thinking about what is next as well as what is after that. They focus as much on the future as the present. They are frequently asking of themselves and others: What can go wrong? By interactive, we mean that they are questioning and learning from the people and systems around them. It is through interaction with others that they frequently develop their new ideas—their redefinitions of previous ways of thinking. The interactions also help to identify the constraints—those obstacles or barriers that they will have to overcome if they are to be successful.

Observation 6: Managers who regularly identified threats before their peers were active readers, listeners, and explorers for more information. They probed their peers for information on whatever issues were being discussed. They frequently asked the generic question, "What can go wrong?" in many different ways (e.g., What if the projected level of demand does not materialize? How much capacity do we have to store this inventory? What if the economy does not come out of the recession by May? What if a competitor offers a similar product this year? What if the government asks us to stop offering the product until more testing is done?). Yet, these people were not skeptics. They asked questions to define the level of threat, determine the likelihood of threat, and identify possible ways to reduce or minimize the risk of the threat materializing.

***Observation 7:** When threats were identified, but could not be reduced, contingency plans and back-up systems were suggested. One contingency plan for the risk of a supplier not being able to provide the volume of a raw material desired was to preselect and prequalify a second supplier. One back-up system involved providing a second computer system in the event that the main system failed.*

Staying on Strategy

For the last two decades, most Fortune 500 companies have developed annual and five-year business plans based on elaborate strategic planning processes. Many corporations use Porter's book, *Competitive Strategy,* as a guide; others employ Ackoff's interactive planning model; still others develop their own internal process based on an array of published ideas and/or the assistance of consultants.[7] In each instance, the objective is to develop a business strategy that will increase the likelihood of the organization's reaching its goals for profitability, growth, market share, customer service, employee welfare, and the like.

Given the extensive consumer, competitor, and employee research data typically collected, and the sophisticated analyses and expert judgments made, it is fair to assume that many of the business plans proposed are logically sound and viable. Yet the success of firms employing elaborate strategic planning models and processes is not substantially greater than that of firms not using them. Apparently strategic planning alone is not enough. Somehow the main elements of the plan must become part of the thinking of employees throughout management.

The strategic management skills we observed that address this issue are shown in Figure 6–4. We refer to them as staying on strategy because it was generally the business plan and strategy proposed therein that systematically identified the organization's strengths, proposed a competitive advantage, and identified the target markets. Staying on strategy is more than taking actions consistent with the business unit's mission, and it should not imply

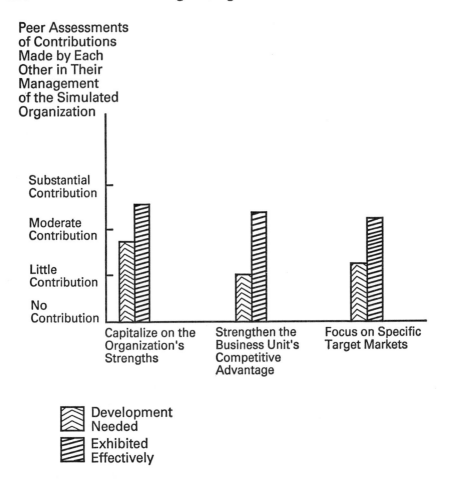

Boss Assessment of Skills Exhibited Based on On-the-Job Behaviors

FIGURE 6-4 Staying on Strategy

that strategies are cast in stone and should be followed blindly. Strategies need to be defined and agreed to by key decision-makers; this is the purpose of the strategic planning process. Once this is accomplished, people need to manage consistent with the strategy and not deviate substantially unless a thorough analysis is again conducted. This means an on-going examination of possible actions to determine: (1) how the action will lead to mission accomplishment by capitalizing on the organization's strengths, (2) how the action is supported by a competitive advantage that can be sustained and enhanced, and (3) how the action targets specific markets. All too often managers chase opportunities that they see—or their subordinates see—that are not related to the business unit's mission or strategies for attaining that mission. Such opportunities rarely capitalize on the organization's strengths and seldom contribute to the organization's competitive advantage for the target markets selected. The result is a diversion of management's attention and organizational resources to alternatives that are unlikely to have the desired payoff even if successfully implemented.

The skill that the more effective managers exhibited in our study was that of continually evaluating ideas, opportunities, and alternatives against the mission and strategy of the business unit they were managing. If opportunities drew or capitalized on the organization's strengths, enhanced its competitive advantage, and were consistent with the chosen target markets, they received additional analyses and consideration. If such a fit was not apparent, the ideas were tabled for future consideration when the business situation changed.

In contrast, either not staying on strategy or frequently changing strategies seems to be linked with poor business performance. Examples where a particular strategy has led to substantial success, and changing that strategy has not sustained that performance, are common. For example, Seven-Up's strategy of being the alternative to cola beverages ("the uncola") was very successful in distinguishing its product from other noncola beverages. Through this positioning, it gained market share. Seven-Up has not done as well with its subsequent strategies to position Seven-Up as the "no caffeine" beverage, or as the "fruit or natural" beverage.

Observation 8: Managers who used the information and ideas contained in the business plan were able to make more convincing arguments than those who seemed to ignore the plan. Those who did use the results of the strategic planning process to guide day-to-day decisions were more likely to capitalize on the organization's strengths, enhance the businesses' competitive advantages, and focus on select markets or target groups.

Observation 9: It was particularly difficult for the managers to deny courses of action that looked promising, even when such actions were not likely to support the existing mission and strategy. As Peter Drucker aptly put it, "The essence of strategy is denial." If one does not deny the business those alternatives that are "off-strategy," then the strategy has little value. Yet the tendency we observed most often was to treat each alternative or option as if it were independent of the mission and strategy of the firm.

Being an Entrepreneurial Force

The need for entrepreneurism and intrapreneurism in organizations today is as strong as ever—and the challenges facing such product or business championing are far greater than just a few decades ago. The dollars required to support a new idea and the potential costs of failure make it difficult to develop and maintain an entrepreneurial spirit. Quinn's research suggests that companies that wish to stay innovative and in tune with their markets need to create internal corporate venture units that act like small entrepreneurial ventures.[8] The managers of these units must have an entrepreneur's spirit, energy, vision, and commitment to making a new venture become a success.

We have observed a similar entrepreneurial spirit in the more successful managers in our research. As suggested by Figure 6–5, the greatest contributions were believed to be made by those managers who were able to create a vision of what a company can be and to articulate that vision so that others are able to understand it, share in it, and become excited about it. But creating the vision was only part of it. They were an entrepreneurial force—they championed innovative ideas, even when faced with skepticism, risk, and resistance. They were able to influence and excite others to take desired actions.

Even though many of the managers we observed attempted to create a vision and champion their ideas, it took tremendous energy and enthusiasm to be a strong enough force to get the organization to move in the desired direction. Such energy is frequently written about in the press—and not just for new ventures. Hewlett-Packard, 3M, Federal Express, Apple Computer, and Citicorp have been kindling an entrepreneurial spirit in their managers for years. Effective strategic management requires that this force be directed towards accomplishing the organization's goals through its strategy. This should not imply that every individual in a firm necessarily agrees with a particular goal or strategy, but that the goals and strategy do need to be accepted so as to channel energy towards the desired actions.

Observation 10: Managers who created a vision of what the organization could be and let others know about it inspired people to attain that vision. The benefits they obtained from publicly sharing the vision outweighed any benefits that might have accrued by keeping the vision a secret.

Observation 11: Individuals who became a product or service champion—even when faced with skepticism and re-

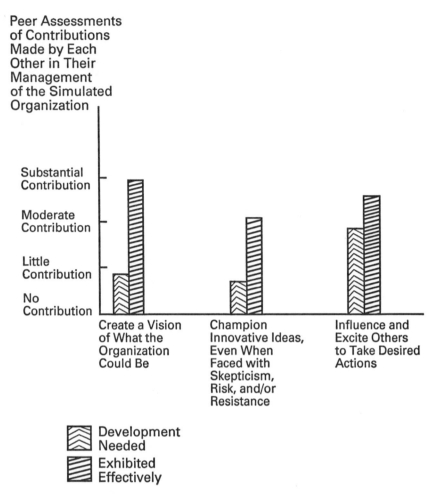

Peer Assessments
of Contributions
Made by Each
Other in Their
Management
of the Simulated
Organization

Substantial
Contribution

Moderate
Contribution

Little
Contribution

No
Contribution

Create a Vision
of What the
Organization
Could Be

Champion
Innovative Ideas,
Even When
Faced with
Skepticism,
Risk, and/or
Resistance

Influence and
Excite Others
to Take Desired
Actions

Development
Needed

Exhibited
Effectively

Boss Assessment of Skills Exhibited Based on On-the-Job Behaviors

FIGURE 6–5 **Being an Entrepreneurial Force**

sistance—were viewed as the strongest contributors to the organization by their peers. The most important challenge for the product or service champion was to show that what was being advocated was consistent with the business unit's mission and strategy.

Accommodating Adversity

Although the public likes to read about a business success, it seems to buy even more papers when the headlines cry failure. And failures are commonplace when changes are being sought, when new products are introduced, or when the business environment shifts quickly in ways that are difficult to predict. Research by MacMillan, Block, and Narasimha suggests that a manager's experience with failures increases the likelihood of his or her future successes.[9] Our research supports their findings with respect to corporate venturing as a strategic management skill.

We labeled the strategic management skill observed when managers were dealing with failures as accommodating adversity (see Figure 6–6). The more effective managers were able to accommodate difficulties—ignoring, denying, or making futile attempts to avoid adversity wasted time, diverted energy, and reduced the

FIGURE 6–6 Accommodating Adversity

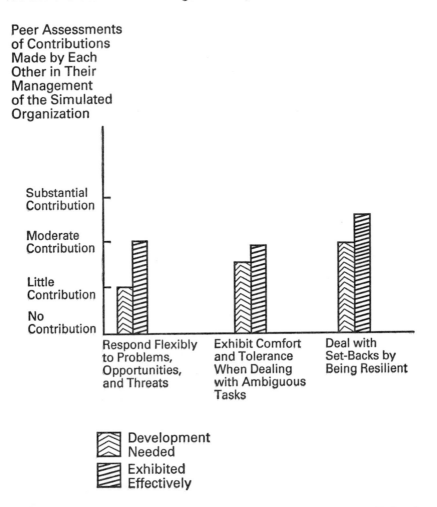

Boss Assessment of Skills Exhibited Based on On-the-Job Behaviors

managers' power and influence over others. Individuals were most successful if they could accommodate adversity by being flexible, altering their approaches, or redefining their situation. This required that they be comfortable and tolerant when dealing with ambiguous situations. Not pressing for an answer or closure prematurely was the best solution to some issues. When set-backs materialized, the most effective managers were highly resilient. They would take the set-back in stride and move on. Signs of mourning, guilt, and self-deprecation were absent. Their energy was quickly directed to the future—What do we want now? What can we learn from this to excel tomorrow?

Examples of accommodating adversity abound and complement the skill of being an entrepreneurial force. Entrepreneurism involves risk-taking, and many risks taken do not yield the benefits intended. The bankcard business provides an example of an unsuccessful large risk taken and a resilient comeback. Citicorp acquired hundreds of thousands of new cardholders in the late 1970s—and the red ink poured in over the following three years. How did Citibank bounce back to have one of the largest and most profitable bankcard portfolios by 1984? By being resilient—it learned enough from its mistakes in accepting bad credit risks to create an excellent credit scoring system for the acquisition of new cardholders. Did the people who designed or approved the 1977–1979 mail solicitations that led to the hundreds of millions of dollars in losses get asked to leave, or leave due to their feelings of failure? No, and many are still at Citicorp more than a decade later, several levels above their positions back in 1977.

Observation 12: Those who took calculated risks seemed to accept the possibility of failure by responding flexibly to problems, opportunities, and threats. They were able to minimize losses and learn from what went differently from the plan.

Observation 13: Managers were able to deal with set-backs by being resilient. Having failed, they appeared to be more sensitive to the forces that conspired against them and were able to use this knowledge as a strength in their next initiatives.

Using Strategic Management Skills

In addition to the above observations and findings regarding each strategic management skill, our work with the managers in this research led to several additional observations.

Observation 14: People were perceived to make the greatest contributions when they were able to apply the strategic management skills collectively. This meant finding and overcoming problems in rivalrous situations, staying on strategy while attempting to champion a new idea by being an entrepreneurial force, and using their knowledge of the business and markets to overcome the adversity in their personal situation. The strategic management skills seemed to depend on each other for maximum managerial effectiveness.

Observation 15: The strategic management skills could complement an effective strategic planning process and plan; they could not substitute for them. If the business had not gone through the strategic planning process, there was a clear gap in the knowledge of the business and markets, in understanding where rivalry was likely, in sensitizing people to potential problems, and in being able to articulate the business proposition.

Observation 16: Managers who accepted the uncomfortable reality that strategic management is an on-going process were able to influence the process to fit their personal style. They involved others who had abilities that complemented theirs, and they forced themselves to attend to aspects of the business regularly that had been easy for them to ignore in the past. If strategic management is a journey, not a destination, then it becomes important to select your travel partners and to frequently consider and reconsider the itinerary—that is, develop a strategic management team and frequently consider and reconsider the business proposition.

Observation 17: Once managers became aware of these skills, there was a fair amount of interest in them. These skills were not beyond the reach of the managers in our research; having seen a skill in action, they wanted an opportunity to personally develop more of it.

THE IMPACT OF STRATEGIC SKILLS ON PERFORMANCE

Even though the staff observations and peer assessments of managers' skills reported above are interesting and support the value of strategic management skills, we wanted to know whether or not these skills had any effect on other indices of individual and organizational performance. In our research, over 2000 manager-participants had become members of the top management team of one of three different fictitious companies—Metrobank (a $1.5 billion in assets commercial bank), Investcorp (a mid-sized securities-brokerage firm), or Looking Glass, Inc. (a mid-size glass manufacturing firm). What could we learn from their collective performances? Before sharing our answer to this question, we need to better describe the use of behavioral simulations in our research. Several common characteristics of behavioral simulations are shown in Figure 6–7. The manager-participants actually manage a company for a day—they have personal offices, hold meetings with peers and subordinates, write memos, discuss issues, set priorities—they do whatever they think will be effective in moving towards accomplishing any goals they have set for the company. They are in complete control, and there are no demands to do anything or to make any decisions. As a result, and because the company is a simulated organization, it is possible to determine whether or not exercising skills has an effect on organizational performance.

FIGURE 6–7 Characteristics of Leadership Simulations

⇨ Each involves an intensive, interactive experience that recreates a day in the life of top management.

⇨ Each generates managerial behaviors observed by a trained staff and reviewed by participants as part of the feedback process

⇨ Each contains multiple problems and opportunities ranging from tactical to strategic. The situations cover several areas including sales, marketing, personnel, research and development, finance, and operations.

⇨ Each has many distinct roles that contain extensive information on past business decisions, current issues, problem symptoms, and decision situations.

⇨ None requires past knowledge or experience in the specific industries or companies simulated.

⇨ Each allows participants to control the simulation outcomes. Depending on the goals, skills, and styles of participants, different issues may become important, or different solutions may be found for the same problem.

⇨ At the end of each simulation, participants fill out questionnaires that uncover information on manager's mission, vision, objectives, and strategy; decision-making; the use of power; work-group climate; and how each participant viewed the other participants with whom he or she worked. Combined with the observations of professional staff, this information forms the basis for diagnostic and developmental feedback on individual performance.

The results of this research supported many of the earlier findings: Individuals and groups who exhibited greater proficiency in the areas measured by the strategic management skills performed at higher levels on many performance indices than those who had not exhibited the same levels of proficiency. Three different, independent measures of performance and three measures of strategic management skills were used. The measures of performance were: (1) the quality of actions taken and decisions made by participants throughout their management of the simulated company, (2) their boss's (within the simulated company) assessment of their overall managerial effectiveness in the simulated company, and (3) their self-assessment of their overall managerial effectiveness in the simulated company. The three measures of SMS, each employing a 20-item SMS questionnaire, were their real-job boss's appraisal of the six SMS, an average of three to five real-job peer appraisals, and a self-appraisal.

Support was found for each of the SMS: knowing the business and markets, managing subunit rivalry, finding and overcoming problems, staying on strategy, being an entrepreneurial force, and accommodating adversity. Individuals whose real-job boss and/or real-job peers appraised their knowing the business markets as being exhibited effectively made higher quality decisions and obtained higher overall management effectiveness assessments by their simulated company bosses.

Individuals whose own appraisals as well as those of their real-job bosses indicated a need to develop skills to manage subunit rivalry and find and overcome problems were observed to be relatively ineffective in managing the simulated company strategically. Their simulated company bosses assessed their managerial effectiveness as low—which was often consistent with their own self-assessments.

Staying on strategy, being an entrepreneurial force, and accommodating adversity, as appraised by real-job bosses, were each positively related to the quality of actions taken and decisions made in the simulated company. In addition, managers' self-appraisals of effectively accommodating adversity related positively with their self-assessment of their managerial effectiveness within the simulated company.

These research findings become more vivid when the performances of two simulated companies are compared: one in which the simulated company was managed by a group of people exhibiting strategic management skills; the second by a group that needed substantial development of its strategic management skills. In the comparison of Metrobank A and C below, both groups were composed of managers from the same consumer banking organization who were given identical preparatory materials and instructions. Participants were randomly assigned to teams of 10 in one of 12 simulated Metrobank companies and had only a few days of contact with each other before their participation in Metrobank. The two Metrobank company performances described below reflect the degree of goal specificity, kinds of actions taken, and climate created by managers exhibiting SMS versus those not exhibiting SMS.

Metrobank A: Creating Excellence

The managers in Metrobank A collectively exhibited effective strategic management skills based on self-reports of SMS and staff observations. The group knew the consumer banking business well; they knew about their markets in terms of consumer wants and current trends. They managed the inherent rivalry among competing business units within Metrobank in such a way that no one perceived his or her unit to be shortchanged. They found and overcame many different and ambiguous issues. They established clear goals, designed strategies to accomplish their goals, and stayed with the strategies. Several of the managers championed innovative ideas and excited others to take actions in support of their ideas. Top management created a vision for Metrobank's future and communicated it well and often. When adversity was confronted, people remained flexible and tolerant.

How did these behaviors affect Metrobank's performance? Metrobank A increased after-tax profits by $3.7 million—a 23 percent increase year-to-year. They increased total earning assets by 13 percent; total liabilities by 20 percent. They decided to purchase a failing savings and loan association for a fair price, enhancing their presence in a rapidly growing community and appeasing anxious regulators.

Metrobank A established five goals for itself and was able to take a large number of actions that contributed to the accomplishment of these goals. Their goals were to continue to grow regionally, to diversify their product lines within the financial service area, to integrate their activities with a recently acquired consumer finance company, to focus on customer service as a point of differentiation in support of their competitive advantage, and to develop their internal human resources to meet the challenges ahead.

Some of the over 35 strategic actions taken were to expand operations and data-processing capacity over the next three years (an \$11 million capital project), purchase more card-processing equipment to support their growing credit card business, hire more computer programmers, cross-sell branch banking products to credit card customers, pilot several new product ideas, target market specific corporations for a major selling effort, recruit and promote more women and minorities into managerial positions, increase their branch presence in key markets, and emphasize customer service in all aspects of the business.

The climate created by the managers of Metrobank A was goal-oriented, with thorough analysis and information sharing followed by actions whenever feasible. Issues raised that did not relate to expressed goals were given lower priority. The energy level of the managers was high; teamwork and cooperation were frequently observed. People tended to be supportive of each other and reported a desire to continue working for Metrobank at the end of the simulation day.

Metrobank C: Struggle for Survival

The managers in Metrobank C exhibited few SMS. They established two goals (a customer service focus and the development of Metrobank human resources), but they took few actions to support these goals. They spent much of their day floundering—their focus was more on symptoms of problems than on diagnosing strategic issues. They seemed not to know the consumer banking business particularly well—even though they were consumer bankers. Unproductive rivalry was common and tended to result in lengthy, ill-structured discussions. No strategy was articulated, nor were innovative ideas championed or adverse situations accommodated effectively.

The financial performance of Metrobank C was poor. It had a 54 percent decrease in after-tax profits totaling a \$4.7 million decline year-to-year. Total earning assets increased only 3 percent; total liabilities increased by 14 percent. No merger or acquisition activity was considered. The large number of issues that were left unattended resulted in a 20 percent increase in annual operating costs.

Metrobank C managers collectively took 20 actions that could have some strategic impact on the organization. Fifteen of these actions addressed current operations and marketing problems; none involved a capital investment or a solution that would be long term. Several of the actions were realized to be ineffective by the managers after the simulation in light of the data available.

The climate created by the managers in Metrobank C involved much ambivalence. People attempted to solve problems individually rather than as a team or company. Information was reluctantly shared; power and influence were often used to get what one wanted—independent of whether or not the customer was being served well. For example, a decision was made to phase out savings passbooks because they were no longer easily supported by new technologies—yet a large percentage of Metrobank's customers were long-time, elderly users of passbook savings accounts. People rarely supported each other's ideas and reported that they would prefer not to continue working at Metrobank another day.

DEVELOPING STRATEGIC MANAGEMENT SKILLS

The above results suggest that a challenge facing organizations is to develop managers with the strategic management skills needed in order for them to be effective in the middle game. Within the broader context of strategic leadership, managers must have the competencies to both create and implement their plans in order to bring their businesses from a current state to a desired future state. They must have the cognitive and emotional flexibility necessary to develop and implement strategies in what is often a complex and competitive marketplace. Strategic leadership is not just a set of concepts and models. It is a way of thinking and acting. Methods are needed to assess managerial abilities in the areas associated with effective strategic leadership and integrate the use of these skills into the business unit. We will discuss these ideas in the chapters that follow.

ENDNOTES

[1]These insights led to some interesting questions about the nature of the skills required of middle managers involved in the middle game. We began to more rigorously assess strategic leadership skills and boss/peer perceptions of these skills in our research.

[2]The strategic management skills were first reported in S. A. Stumpf, "Leadership and Beyond: The Need for Strategic Management Skills." *Advances in Strategic Management*, 1989, *5*, 245–61. See also S. A. Stumpf, "Using the Next Generation of Assessment Centre Technology for Skill Diagnosis," *The International Journal of Career Management*, 1990, *2*(2), 3–14.

[3]The factor analysis of the 20-item questionnaire yielded six distinct, non-overlapping factors which were given the six strategic management skill labels.

Each scale exhibited good internal consistency reliability (the median reliability estimate was 0.76) and modest validity as indexed by the correlation between a manager's real-boss assessment of his or her strategic management skills and the manager's performance in the executive development program simulation. Follow-up research in one organization indicates that individuals who exhibited greater strategic management skills as indexed by the confidential feedback received in the executive development program have advanced to the next level of management sooner than those who received less favorable feedback. Since the organization was not made aware of the feedback received by any of these managers, the predictive value of the strategic management skills and executive development efforts is encouraging.

[4]The management situations used are multiple, interlocking in-basket exercises that collectively create a fictitious company; they are not computer simulations. As such, they employ no algorithms to connect choices to outcomes. For information on this type of management development tool, see S. A. Stumpf and J. Dutton, "The Dynamics of Learning Through Management Simulations: Let's Dance." *Journal of Management Development,* 1990, *9*(2), 7–15, and R. Dunbar and S. A. Stumpf, "Trainings That Demystify Strategic Decision-Making Processes." *Journal of Management Development,* 1989, *8,* 36–42; and P. Petre, "Games That Teach You to Manage." *Fortune,* Oct. 29, 1984, pp. 65–72. For more information on how language and cognitions are observed and coded in our research, see T. Mullen and S. A. Stumpf, "The Effect of Management Styles on Strategic Planning." *Journal of Business Strategy,* Winter 1987, pp. 60–75.

[5]J. Kotter, *The General Managers.* (New York: The Free Press, 1982).

[6]R. L. Ackoff, *Creating the Corporate Future.* (New York: John Wiley & Sons, 1981). See also R. L. Ackoff, "The Circular Organization: An Update." *Academy of Management Executive,* 1989, *3,* 11–16.

[7]The number of textbooks and journals devoted to issues of strategic management has expanded severalfold in the past decade. Representative texts include A. A. Thompson, Jr. and A. J. Strickland III, *Strategy Formulation and Implementation,* 3rd ed. (Plano, TX: Business Publications, Inc., 1986); G. A. Steiner, J. B. Miner, and E. R. Gray, *Management Policy and Strategy,* 3rd. ed. (New York: Macmillan, 1986); and H. I. Ansoff, *Implanting Strategic Management* (Englewood Cliffs, NJ: Prentice-Hall, 1984). Michael E. Porter has written extensively on competitive analysis; see his books on *Competitive Strategy* (New York: The Free Press, 1980); and *Competitive Advantage* (New York: The Free Press, 1985). See also his "Corporate Strategy: The State of Strategic Thinking." *The Economist,* May 23, 1987, pp. 17–22. For a practical viewpoint, see K. Ohmae's, *Mind of a Strategist.* (New York: Penguin Books, 1982); D. K. Hurst, "Why Strategic Management Is Bankrupt." *Organizational Dynamics,* 1986, pp. 5–27; and D. K. Hurst, "Creating Competitive Advantage: Welding Imagination to Experience." *Academy of Management Executive,* 1989, *3,* 29–36.

[8]J. B. Quinn, "Managing Innovation: Controlled Chaos." *Harvard Business Review,* May–June, 1985, pp. 73–84.

[9]I. C. MacMillan, Z. Block, and P. N. Suba Narasimha, "Corporate Venturing: Alternatives, Obstacles Encountered, and Experience Effects." *Journal of Business Venturing,* 1986, pp. 177–91.

CHAPTER SEVEN
Personal Preferences

The personal style that managers bring to the middle game is partially based on their personality and natural preferences. We view personal style as distinct from skills for several reasons. First, we assume a Jungian view of personal style that proposes that there are different personality types based on the different cognitive patterns individuals use to perceive information and make judgments.[1] Hence, style is a natural personal preference.

Second, one person's style is not necessarily better than another person's style. Styles are different in predictable ways, each with its own relative benefits and weaknesses. This is generally not the case with skills. Having more skill is implicitly better than having less skill. It may be that one's skills are not always needed, but their existence is generally viewed as a strength.

Third, one does not develop style through practice and feedback in the same manner as one might develop skills through practice and feedback. There is no learning curve for one to climb in developing a style. This is not meant to imply that one cannot develop a better understanding of his or her style or alter a personal style in a specific situation to be able to identify and evaluate things in a different way. Certainly one can and may well benefit by doing so on some occasions. But one's personal style—one's personality type preference—remains dominant.

Before suggesting the possible effect of personal style on management and strategic leadership efforts in the middle game, a short discussion of different personality type preferences is needed. Carl Jung proposed that people develop preferences for the ways in which they identify and evaluate information at an early age. **Identifying** is the process of becoming aware of people, things, ideas, or events. **Evaluating** is the process of coming to conclusions about what one has identified. Preferences for different forms of identifying and evaluating lead to differences in how people understand themselves, their associates, and their life and work situations.

The two dominant forms of **identifying information** are defined as **sensing** and **intuition.** Sensing-dominant people prefer to focus on facts and details with a strong practical, present orientation. Intuition-dominant people prefer to focus on patterns with a strong innovative, future orientation.

The two dominant forms of **evaluating information** in order to reach decisions and take action are defined as **thinking** and **feeling.** Thinking-dominant people prefer to make judgments objectively, impersonally, by considering the causes of events and by analyzing where different choices may lead. Feeling-dominant people prefer to make judgments more personally, weighing the values of choices and how the choices will affect others.

In addition to preferences for the forms of identifying and evaluating information, people also have preferences for either **judging** or **perceiving.** Judgment-dominant people prefer to live in a decisive, planned, and orderly way, aiming to regulate and control events. Perception-dominant people prefer to live in a spontaneous, flexible way, aiming to understand life and adapt to it.

Finally, Jung proposed that people have preferences for where they look for information to begin with. One's preferences may flow from interest in the outer world of actions, objects, and people—referred to as **extraversion**—or, preferences may flow from interest in the inner world of concepts and ideas—called **introversion.**

Figure 7–1 summarizes the four dimensions defined above in the order in which they are usually introduced when one learns about personality type preferences. A letter is associated with each of the anchors of each dimension as a short-hand notation. It is the combination of preferences on each of the four dimensions that leads to one of 16 types of personal style. For example, an **ESTJ** manager is one who has preferences for Extraversion (looks to the outer world for information), **S**ensing (focuses on facts and details), **T**hinking (prefers to make judgments objectively and imperson-

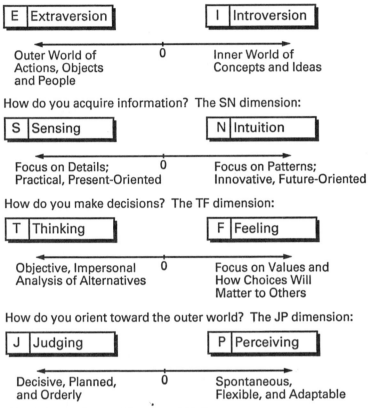

Where do you prefer to focus your attention? The EI dimension:

| E | Extraversion | | I | Introversion |

Outer World of   0   Inner World of
Actions, Objects   Concepts and Ideas
and People

How do you acquire information? The SN dimension:

| S | Sensing | | N | Intuition |

Focus on Details;   0   Focus on Patterns;
Practical, Present-Oriented   Innovative, Future-Oriented

How do you make decisions? The TF dimension:

| T | Thinking | | F | Feeling |

Objective, Impersonal   0   Focus on Values and
Analysis of Alternatives   How Choices Will
                                  Matter to Others

How do you orient toward the outer world? The JP dimension:

| J | Judging | | P | Perceiving |

Decisive, Planned,   0   Spontaneous,
and Orderly   Flexible, and Adaptable

FIGURE 7-1 **Dimensions of Personal Style**

ally), and **Judging** (prefers to live in a decisive, planned, and orderly way). An **INFP** manager would have preferences at the opposite end of each continuum (note that the letter **N** is used to signify intuition). The remaining 14 types would have preferences that reflect different combinations of these four dimensions.

THE EFFECT OF STYLE ON MANAGEMENT
IN THE MIDDLE GAME

Each of the four dimensions pictured in Figure 7-1 can have a significant impact on the way managers approach strategic issues, deal with others regarding work, and cope with the challenges of managing in the middle game. It is important to note that Jungian theory and one popular measure of it, the Myers-Briggs Type Indicator (MBTI®), describe preferences, not skills or abilities.[2] The MBTI helps us to identify our preferred way of thinking and doing, other things being equal. The profiles developed from this instrument are intended to help managers identify what they prefer to do, not what is more effective or less effective behavior in a particular situation. The MBTI describes rather than prescribes. Finally, all preferences are likely to be equally important over the course of one's workday. Types are not good or bad, but different types have different strengths and weaknesses.

As the continuum below indicates, each of the four dimensions can be thought of as a scale with a zero at the midpoint. The MBTI profile does not suggest that people are either completely one way or the other on any of these four dimensions. Some managers have qualities on both sides of one or more of the four preference continua. Others have a decided preference for one side or the other. The stronger an individual preference for either side of the dimension, the greater the probability that the strengths associated with that side will be accessible as true strengths, with the strategic leadership strengths associated with the opposite end of the continuum being potential weaknesses. For example, if an individual has a very strong thinking preference, then that person is less likely to identify and incorporate the impact that decisions will have on others into the decision-making process. Yet in strategic leadership, incorporating the human dimension early, particularly as it relates to subordinates in the strategy development process, can have significant impact on ultimate success during implementation. Similarly, if a manager has a strong perceiving preference, that person may be able to incorporate many changes into an evolving situation but may have difficulty bringing activities to closure. A manager with a strong intuitive preference may be good at conceptualizing the big picture but may not have the details to support a position.

Where do you prefer to focus your attention?

Extraversion   Introversion

E <--------------------------- 0 ---------------------------> I

The difference between an extravert and an introvert is that an extravert "talks to think," while an introvert "thinks to talk." Extraverts look outside themselves for energy and ideas. In their work environment, extraverts prefer varied and action-oriented situations where they can be around and with others. Introverts, on the other hand, look inward for their energy and ideas. They have a preference for work environments that are quiet and concentrated where they can work and be alone. When in doubt, extraverts interact, while introverts reflect.

Imagine what it would be like to be in a work group of extraverts. There would be lots of discussion and sharing of information and ideas. People tend to build trust through sharing information. This trust could create a strong positive extraversion-oriented work environment. For many groups, the talking would represent a sharing and bonding of like behaviors. Now, add an introvert to that group. The introvert would probably be asking himself or herself why people do not collect their thoughts before sharing their ideas. The extraverts would be wondering why the introvert is not sharing information at the same level as everyone else. At best, the extraverts may think that the introvert is different; at worst the extraverts may think that the introvert is thinking things that the introvert does not want to share.

In contrast, imagine a work group of only introverts. Meetings would probably reflect somewhat more thoughtful discussions. Each individual would tend to reflect on the conversation and consider his or her comments before sharing them. Now add an extravert to that group of introverts. The extravert could easily be frustrated by the pace of discussion.

Strategic leadership strengths of extraverts would include gathering information from others, and based on their skills in interacting with others, extraverts may also be effective at persuading others to embrace new ideas once they have been articulated. Strategic leadership strengths for an introvert would include activities in strategy formulation, including thinking through issues and managing the planning process.

Seventy-five percent of the general population has a preference for extraversion and 25 percent of the population has a preference for introversion. In a group of 14,000+ individuals attending a management education program, the breakout was 52 percent extravert and 48 percent introvert.[3]

How do you acquire information?

Sensing   Intuitive

S <---------------------- 0 ----------------------> N

The sensing-preference person needs to work through a problem to see the result. In their work environment, sensing-preference managers like to use learned skills and apply standard solutions to problems. Generally, sensing-preference managers are considered patient with details and tend to make few factual errors.

The intuitive-preference person frequently sees the results or solution to a problem at the beginning. In their work environment, intuitive-preference managers like to add new skills and identify new solutions to problems. Intuitive-preference managers look for patterns and the big picture and are patient with complexity.

In a work group of sensing-preference managers, there would be significant discussion about the details of a situation and the accuracy of the available information. There would also be considerable skepticism regarding ideas that could not be supported by the available information. Now add an intuitive manager to the group. The intuitive manager may wonder why there is such a great concern for the details when the more important thing is to understand the "big picture." The sensing-preference managers would wonder about the legitimacy of any statement about the "big picture" when there is insufficient detail to support the conclusion.

A group of intuitive-preference managers on the other hand may show considerably less concern about the accuracy of any particular piece of information. The focus of this group would tend to be on the patterns that emerge from the information. The intuitive-preference managers would focus on what those patterns show that is new or suggests a new possibility. A sensing manager added to the group may wonder when the group will get its discussion back to the available facts and where the factual support is for the ideas suggested by the group.

Strategic leadership strengths of sensing-preference managers are based on their ability to work with and master information. In both developing and implementing plans, the sensing-preference managers bring a practical and efficient approach to the task of strategic leadership. The intuitive managers have a significantly different set of skills. These individuals will be more comfortable looking for innovative approaches; they prefer attending to possibilities rather than realities. They have a strong preference for conceptualizing and visioning future activities and future achievements. The intuitive-preference managers may be more effective at identifying the appropriate stakeholder map, and the sensing-preference managers may be more effective at gathering the information about the stakeholders. Combined with a preference for extraversion, an E-S manager may also be effective at gathering information from stakeholders.

Seventy-five percent of the general population has a preference for sensing and 25 percent of the population has a preference for intuition. In the management population described earlier, the breakout was 52 percent sensing and 48 percent intuition.

How do you make decisions?

Thinking   Feeling

T <---------------------- 0 ----------------------> F

The third dimension provides insight into how individuals make decisions. Thinking-preference individuals will tend to be more objective and impersonal when reaching conclusions. Their decision-making is based on logic and their focus is on correctness and accuracy. In their work environment, thinking-preference managers are brief and businesslike. Others tend to see thinking-preference managers as treating people fairly.

Feeling-preference individuals tend to be more subjective and personal when reaching conclusions. Their decision-making is frequently based on a set of values and on how decisions will affect others. In their work environment, feeling-preference managers are characterized as naturally friendly and tend to treat others as those individuals want to be treated. Both thinking and feeling are equally rational approaches to decision-making. The thinking-preference managers' process is based on logic, and the feeling-preference managers' process is based on values.

In a work group of thinking-preference managers, discussions would center on making decisions that are fair and logical. The framework for conversation would be based on truth and balanced intellectual criticism. Now add a feeling-preference manager to the group. The thinking-preference managers would wonder why the feeling-preference manager is introducing values into what should be an impersonal discussion and decision. At best, an intolerant group of thinking-preference managers would consider the feeling-preference manager less rigorous; at worst, the thinking-preference managers would consider the feeling-preference manager illogical and more of a social worker than a business person.

A group of feeling-preference managers presents a different situation. Their discussions would center around their core values, values that could influence the decision-making process and its outcomes. There may be a significant focus on how particular decisions will affect others. There is likely to be a greater sense of loyalty to each other and the organization in this group and a greater value placed on tact and harmony when dealing with others. When a thinking-preference manager is introduced into the group, he or she may wonder why there is a seeming lack of logic operating in the group. The thinking-preference manager would search for the underlying logic of the situation in order to make a decision.

Strategic leadership strengths of thinking-preference managers are rooted in their ability and willingness to apply logic to a wide range of decisions. These are individuals willing to make tough decisions which may cause people discomfort and pain. The feeling-preference managers understand the importance of people's feelings and the impact that those feelings can have on the organization. Some managers may say that the thinking-preference managers should make the decisions and the feeling-preference managers should figure out how to implement them in the workplace. A more productive approach may be to include the feeling-preference managers throughout the strategy process, in order to incorporate organizational values and human issues more fully into the strategy crafting process.

The general population is evenly divided (50/50) on the preference for thinking versus feeling. This is the only dimension of the four that shows a gender bias. The thinking preference is dominant for six out of 10 men, while the feeling preference is dominant for six out of 10 women. Among the 14,000+ participants in the management education program mentioned earlier, 75 percent expressed a thinking preference and 25 percent expressed a feeling preference.

How do you orient towards the outer world?

Judging   Perceiving

J <---------------------- 0 ----------------------> P

The fourth and final dimension on the MBTI looks at the preference for collecting information versus making decisions about that information. Judging-preference managers like to get things settled and make decisions. In the work environment, judging-preference managers focus on identifying only the essential information necessary to complete a task.

Perceiving-preference managers like to gather information, initiate tasks, and leave things open. In the work environment, perceiving-preference managers focus on getting things started, postponing decisions until they must be made, and identifying all there is to know about a job, rather than just the essentials. In short, judging-preference managers run their lives, while perceiving-preference managers live their lives.

A work group of judging-preference managers would be characterized as decisive, purposeful, and exacting. They would work best with a plan and would not like loose ends in their activities. A perceiving-preference manager joining the group may feel that some things were being brought to closure prematurely—that simply wanting closure may not be a good enough reason to conclude an activity. The judging-preference managers may view the perceiving-preference manager as not focused and working on too many things without getting closure on outstanding activities.

A work group of perceiving-preference managers would probably be characterized as curious, adaptable, flexible, spontaneous, and tolerant. They would work best in situations where there is no schedule or set of rigid procedures. A judging-preference manager joining the group may feel that nothing is getting done and that the group has no discipline. The perceiving-preference managers may view the judging-preference manager as impatient and narrowly focused.

Strategic leadership strengths of judging-preference managers revolve mainly around their willingness and ability to control resources, deny activities, and take immediate action. Their decisive approach to tasks enables them to create structure, order, and predictability. Perceiving-preference managers have different strengths. Their preference enables them to have greater adaptability and flexibility, which can be critical in businesses experiencing high rates of environmental and technological change. Perceiving-preference managers are generally willing to consider more alternatives and remain open to and consider new information as it emerges.

Fifty percent of the general population has a judging preference, and 50 percent has a perceiving preference. In the management population described earlier, 75 percent prefer judging, and 25 percent prefer perceiving.

As noted earlier, these four dimensions do not act in isolation, each person has an MBTI type preference—one of 16 different combinations of E-I, S-N, T-F, P-J. Figure 7–2 displays the 16 profiles that can result from these four dimensions. In each box are the four letters associated with that particular profile and some suggested strengths that that personality-type preference manager would have in strategic leadership settings. Included in each cell is the percentage of 14,000+ individuals attending management education programs at the Center for Creative Leadership who have this particular profile. (The Center for Creative Leadership is a research and management training and development organization in Greensboro, North Carolina.)

ISTJ – 17%	ISFJ – 4%	INFJ – 2%	INTJ – 10%
I Thinking through issues	I Thinking through issues	I Thinking through issues	I Thinking through issues
S Mastering the facts	S Mastering the facts	N Developing the vision	N Developing the vision
T Logic and analysis	F Articulating values	F Articulating values	T Logic and analysis
J Being decisive	J Being decisive	J Being decisive	J Being decisive
ISTP – 3%	**ISFP – 1%**	**INFP – 3%**	**INTP – 7%**
I Thinking through issues	I Thinking through issues	I Thinking through issues	I Thinking through issues
S Mastering the facts	S Mastering the facts	N Developing the vision	N Developing the vision
T Logic and analysis	F Articulating values	F Articulating values	T Logic and analysis
P Being adaptable	P Being adaptable	P Being adaptable	P Being adaptable
ESTP – 3%	**ESFP – 1%**	**ENFP – 5%**	**ENTP – 8%**
E Talking through issues	E Talking through issues	E Talking through issues	E Talking through issues
S Mastering the facts	S Mastering the facts	N Developing the vision	N Developing the vision
T Logic and analysis	F Articulating values	F Articulating values	T Logic and analysis
P Being adaptable	P Being adaptable	P Being adaptable	P Being adaptable
ESTJ – 16%	**ESFJ – 4%**	**ENFJ – 3%**	**ENTJ – 13%**
E Talking through issues	E Talking through issues	E Talking through issues	E Talking through issues
S Mastering the facts	S Mastering the facts	N Developing the vision	N Developing the vision
T Logic and analysis	F Articulating values	F Articulating values	T Logic and analysis
J Being decisive	J Being decisive	J Being decisive	J Being decisive

FIGURE 7-2 The 16 Types of the Myers-Briggs Type Indicator®: **Contribution Made by Each Preference to Strategic Leadership in the Middle**

Note: Myers-Briggs Type Indicator (MBTI) is a registered trademark of Consulting Psychologists Press, Inc., Palo Alto, CA.

"If there is time, I want it done perfectly. If there isn't enough time, I just want it done."

ISTJ Manager

THE IMPORTANCE OF PERSONAL STYLE

Sharing an example can serve to highlight the importance of personal style in strategic leadership. One manager we worked with was rather dogmatic in his approach to tasks. Although he was somewhat open to future-oriented ideas from his peers and subordinates, he only wanted to pursue ideas that were grounded in facts backed up with detail. This style had served him well for many years and was part of what he believed had led to his success. In his words, "I eliminate a lot of the bull around here by sticking with the facts and good analysis; completed staff work, that is what I expect and get from my people."

In the context of an executive development program, the manager completed an instrument that helped him to diagnose his personality type preferences based on his view of himself. He had scores that reflected strong **Sensing** and **Thinking** preferences and more in-between scores on the other two dimensions. It was not until he was dealing with a manager in the same executive development program who had scores that reflected strong **Intuition** and **Feeling** preferences that a "communications problem" was detected. The latter manager would raise ideas based on perceived patterns of information, without necessarily being able to provide supporting information at the time. These ideas were quickly dismissed in conversations with the sensing-thinking manager. The intuition-feeling manager would also suggest that certain courses of action being proposed would negatively affect some individuals and thereby lead to some resistance if the ideas were to be implemented. This was also dismissed by the sensing-thinking manager. As you might guess, there were times during the educational program when the intuition-feeling manager's ideas were insightful and concerns well justified. More importantly, the sensing-thinking manager could not see this as information he wanted to surface due to his resistance to the other manager's orientation.

An individual conference with the sensing-thinking manager later in the program resulted in an interesting personal disclosure: "I've missed a few really good opportunities and lost several good people through my intolerance of other's wishy-washy ideas, or their concerns about how someone will feel if we take a particular action. By better understanding my style, I think I can use it to my advantage more effectively and also learn to draw on the advantages of other styles when the situation warrants."

It was this last point that reinforced our emerging view that it is critical to have all strands of the rope equally strong. Strategic leadership demands that one be able to tap into the elements of concepts, skills, and personal style at any time. Different business situations, particularly those involving the diagnosis of issues and decision-making, place heavy but unequal demands on a manager's ability to apply concepts and strategic management skills and to leverage the strengths of one's personal style, or adapt to its limitations.

PERSONALITY TYPE PREFERENCES: CREATIVITY, BIASES, AND ACTIONS

Managers with different personality types are predisposed to deal with information in particular ways. Such predispositions can lead to cognitive trails—patterns of thinking that pervade managerial actions. One stream of research has identified a relationship between certain personal style preferences and creativity. Other researchers have identified some of the cognitive biases that managers exhibit based on their preferences. It is proposed that systematic biases exist in the ways that managers with different personality type preferences diagnose and analyze issues, make choices, and take actions. Still others have extended these ideas to incorporate cognitive biases within groups. We explore each of these topics below.

Personal Style Preferences and Creativity

Peter Drucker has argued that given the nature of industrial organizations, companies have fostered adaptive behavior, "to do things better," rather than innovative behavior, "to do things differently."[4] Managers who demonstrate **adaptive** behavior generally accept the definition or paradigm used to address a particular business issue and seek to resolve the issue within the accepted frame. Managers who demonstrate **innovative** behavior are more likely to question the definition and existing paradigms used to address the issue in favor of alternative definitions and different paradigms.

Recent studies have provided significant evidence that managers who have a sensing preference on the Sensing-Intuitive dimension and a judging preference on the Judging-Perceiving dimension have a preference for adaptation over innovation. Similarly, managers who have intuition and perceiving preferences have a preference for innovative over adaptive behavior. To the extent that these relationships exist, S-J managers are more likely to demonstrate adaptive creativity, while N-P managers are more likely to demonstrate innovative creativity.

Change initiated through adaptive behaviors tends to be incremental and acceptable to a larger portion of stakeholders. It does not, however, involve much reconceptualization of the issue. Change initiated through innovative behaviors tends to be radical relative to existing practices and is often less acceptable to a significant portion of stakeholders.

Companies in the personal computer market provide us with examples of firms that have responded to these two archetypes of change behaviors. The innovative response in this marketplace came from Apple Computer. Primarily through its introduction of the Macintosh operating system, Apple was able to create and market a different type of personal computer to both existing and emerging market segments. In contrast, the adaptive response to this environment was embraced in such organizations as IBM, AT&T, and Zenith. Their decisions to adopt (or continue) the Microsoft DOS operating system led them to present a different product line to the marketplace.

Which of these organizations' approaches was more effective is not a question with an easy answer. It was in the nature of an organization such as Apple to stimulate innovative change. Innovation was part of the essence of the Apple organization at that point in time. IBM, AT&T, and Zenith reflect values that are rooted in adaptation. Their philosophy in the personal computer market has been to wait for others to innovate and then to pursue a technological innovation with market muscle after it has exhibited technological success.

One can argue that when measured within the context of their respective values and beliefs, these organizations are equally effective. More recently, IBM has made the decision to adopt a GEM operating system, which replicates on an IBM machine what is already available on a Macintosh. But even this response can be positioned as part of IBM's posture of adaptation rather than innovation. Apple led the way in shifting the frame or dominant paradigm in this industry during the 1980s, and IBM adapted within this paradigm once the paradigm became generally accepted.

For some managers, adaptive change is appropriate because that style fits the nature of their organization or business unit. This may be the case for the sensing-judging managers in organizations such as IBM. In other organizations, innovation may be the norm; managers with intuitive-perceiving preferences can use their ability to consider innovative change more freely. The challenge for managers is greatest when their personal style strengths for creativity are counter to what the organization or their business unit wants. The stress is most apparent for the intuitive-perceiving manager in a unit that restricts its creativity to adaptation, not innovation.

Adaptive managers and innovative managers are equally capable of developing creative ideas or solutions. The difference lies in the nature of their contribution. Building on the comments of Peter Drucker, other writers have suggested that at the extremes, the adaptive-innovative continuum represents two types of creativity: "Adaptive behavior generates a high quantity of ideas which recognize environmental constraints and are aimed at doing things *better.* Innovative behavior does not focus on generating quantity, but rather on testing the definition of the problem; stretching environmental constraints aimed at doing things *differently.*"[5]

Personal Style Cognitive Biases and Preferences for Strategic Action

The two middle dimensions of the MBTI define preferences for acquiring information (sensing versus intuition) and for making decisions (thinking versus feeling).[6] Based on these two dimensions, particular types of action-taking are suggested. Four types of managers and their preferences for action are described: Sensing-Thinking (S-T), Intuition-Thinking (N-T), Sensing-Feeling (S-F), Intuition-Feeling (N-F).

Sensing-Thinking Type Managers. Sensing-thinking managers (S-Ts) appear to perform best when they can impose models on a decision situation in such a way as to specify the relevant data needed and then provide formats or rules for logical analysis. S-Ts have preferences for quantitative, aggregate data and often have a distaste for qualitative data. This can lead to an oversimplification of decision situations to give order and meaning to data and lead to selective perception biases by failing to incorporate new data that do not fit initial cues. Such new data, if incorporated into the analysis, may suggest that one make changes to the actions proposed. The failure to incorporate such data reduces the likelihood that the solutions generated will involve much change, thereby implicitly supporting actions that involve only incremental adjustments in the current state to get to the desired future state.

Selective perception tends to reflect excessive reliance on certain types of information and problem-solving methods. S-T managers often use standard operating procedures to solve problems; these procedures identify the unusual aspects of the more innovative alternatives. S-T managers may reject novel or entrepreneurial solutions because prevailing systems fail to support them. For example, managers may deal with nonpreferential alternatives through inferences that the nonpreferred alternatives are impossible or too radical for the organization to adopt. Selective perception can also result in the rejection of the more feasible alternatives due to premature acceptance of courses of action that do not require the generation of new knowledge.

This profile suggest that S-Ts take actions that reflect selective perception biases more often than the other personality types. Such actions rarely involve radical change. S-Ts' actions tend to be quick-fix solutions to problems, involve low levels of risk, and reflect standard operating procedures.

Intuition-Thinking Type Managers. Intuition-thinking managers (N-Ts) tend to see patterns in structured data and ignore cases that negate their beliefs. N-T managers often persevere in their beliefs in spite of contradictory evidence. NT managers' preferences for holistic information, and their problem constructions that ignore disconfirming information, would seem to encourage positivity biases. Although positivity biases are similar to selective perception biases in that both involve selective use of information, positivity biases specifically involve the selective recall of positive, confirming information rather than negative, disconfirming information with respect to given alternatives. Positivity biases are most easily accepted as being fair arguments in decision situations involving longer-term opportunities where little specific data exist. In such situations, negative or disconfirming information can be discounted as conjecture; managers introducing such information may be viewed as blocking progress or not being fully committed to the management group. N-T managers favor these open-ended situations; they enjoy moving from abstract needs and opportunities to creative responses. By testing their ideas on hypothetical possibilities, they may deny the importance of gaps between goals and outcomes and cling to their preferences.

Given this profile, N-Ts are likely to take actions that reflect positivity biases more often than the other personality types. Such actions often involve a substantial amount of radical change. N-Ts' actions tend to seek opportunities, focus on the positive aspects of the opportunity, and ignore the risks or threats involved in implementing the action.

Sensing-Feeling Type Managers. Sensing-feeling managers (S-Fs) often place substantial importance on people-oriented information. They are inclined to suggest consultative, group-process approaches to issues because such approaches provide for a way to reconcile facts that give rise to conflicting sentiments. A potential weakness of this style is that S-F managers may appear to be more interested in promoting discussions about premises than in exploring the premises in detail.

Because S-F managers place importance on interpersonal relations and social approval, they become more susceptible to social-desirability biases. Managers exhibit social-desirability biases in their actions when they do what they sense that other people would want them to do. It is probably S-F managers' acute need for acceptance by others that prompts them to seek and often promote others' ideas. Promoting others' ideas may well lead to moderate degrees of change for the decision-maker if the ideas are accepted. However, such changes are likely to be of low risk and use the existing knowledge base since they reflect ideas already familiar to the system. S-F managers, in their zeal to achieve consensus and acceptance, often restate their viewpoints to reflect the arguments used by others.

Given this preference, S-Fs are likely to take actions that reflect social-desirability biases more often than the other personality types. Such actions would typically involve a moderate amount of change within the organization. S-Fs' actions tend to conform to socially accepted norms and values, yield social approval, and satisfy the wants of significant others.

Intuition-Feeling Type Managers. Intuitive-feeling managers (N-Fs) often rely on relevant anecdotes, catchy symbols, and vivid imagery to make their points. They often ignore traditional methods and standardized procedures in favor of novel ideas. N-Fs like ingenious and entrepreneurial solutions to the issues they confront. They often excel at poorly structured decision tasks: N-Fs attempt several dissimilar approaches on issues to see where each leads; such false starts, if followed by incubation periods, can lead to insights. This suggests that N-F managers may be inclined to seek changes that are more radical for the organization, particularly when the changes reflect their values.

It has been suggested that N-Fs use a simplifying process to help them formulate new ideas: They develop analogies in order to draw inferences from simple, vivid situations to more complex ones. This process, referred to as reasoning-by-analogy, is often dominated by the use of images and metaphor. Reasoning by analogy helps to describe environmental uncertainties and can lead to creative solutions to problems that involve the organization-environment interface. When one perceives environmental uncertainty as moderate or low, he or she is likely to consider more radical actions since the outcomes of the actions are believed to be more predictable. However, this process can also lead to simplistic views of complex situations. N-F managers may mistakenly think their problems are more simple and familiar than they really are.

N-Fs are likely to take actions that reflect reasoning-by-analogy biases more often than other personality types. Such actions frequently involve substantial, more radical changes that affect the organization-environment interface. N-Fs' actions tend to be novel and are often based on analogies between the present situation and purportedly similar situations.

Research Support. Research in this area generally supports the proposed relationships between personality type preferences and the pattern of choices made in strategic decision situations.[7] The pattern of choices made by individuals reflected their predispositions and the biases contained in those predispositions. These biases may stem from the cognitive trails etched in the minds of individuals based upon years of thinking that has been affected by one's personality type preferences.[8] Specifically, sensing-thinking preference managers were observed to take more and a greater percentage of actions suggestive of selective perception biases than other managers; intuitive-thinking preference managers were observed to take more and a greater percentage of actions suggestive of positivity biases than other managers; sensing-feeling preference managers were observed to take more and a greater percentage of actions suggestive of social desirability biases than other managers; and intuitive-feeling preference managers were observed to take more and a greater percentage of actions suggestive of reasoning-by-analogy biases than other managers.

The actions examined varied on dimensions that were linked to different cognitive biases. Actions suggestive of selective perception biases rarely involved radical change, had greater short-term financial benefits, and generally involved fewer people in the discussion or approval of the actions. Actions suggestive of positivity biases generally involved more radical change, had greater variation and risk associated with the financial and quality aspects of the actions, and involved more people in the discussion and approval of the actions. Actions suggestive of social desirability biases involved a substantial amount of change for the internal structures of the organization (but not the environment), were generally of higher quality in terms of the organization's responsiveness to its stakeholders, and generally involved fewer people in the discussion and approval of the actions. Actions suggestive of reasoning-by-analogy biases were generally the most radical actions and involved attempts to change the organization's environments.

Implications of Personal Style Preferences for Group Composition[9]

Just as one's personal style preferences suggest differences in individual behaviors, the predominant personal style preference in a group can provide some insight into group dynamics and group decisions. A group composed of managers with a preference for extraversion would look, sound, and function quite differently from a group composed of managers with a preference for introversion.

Within a business unit, the manager and those individuals working closely with the manager form a work group. If this group is at the top of the business unit hierarchy, it has substantial formal power and authority to establish the group's direction, norms, and protocols. Strategic leadership for many of these groups reflects an S-T approach: Information is identified and analyzed, and logical decisions are made based on that analysis. The philosophical base for this orientation is rooted in the assumption that reality exists "out there" and if enough resources are put against the effort, what is out there is knowable. Once it is known, the appropriate use of analytic tools can lead to optimal solutions.

As we suggested in Chapter Four, independent of philosophical considerations, the rapid rate of change in the environment should lead one to question seriously the viability of the assumption that what is out there is knowable. The organizational reality that managers experience is the interaction of an objective reality, the reality that is discovered by the work group, and a subjective reality—the reality that is created by the work group or imposed by others.

That is not to say that the analysis and decision-making done by a group with a sensing-thinking preference is not useful. It is perhaps more useful today than in the past, as it can assist a group in analyzing and incorporating environmental changes as they occur. In many instances, the responses from a group with a sensing-thinking preference will represent effective adaptive behavior. The group may well be creating and implementing strategies that do things better but may not necessarily be doing them in innovative ways. Whether or not innovation or adaptation is the appropriate response is a function of the situation and the environment. It is likely to be the managers who can create work groups that embody both sensing-thinking and intuitive-feeling preferences that will prosper.

Figure 7–3 suggests five alternative group compositions, each group's likely time horizon, and the likely strategic focus of the group. Each of the five groups has a different cognitive composition.

FIGURE 7–3 Suggested Relationship between Group Composition, Time Horizon, and Strategic Focus

Group Composite Preference*	Time Horizon	Strategic Focus
Intuition and Feeling	Future	Newness
Thinking and Sensing	Near-Term Future and Past	Improvement
Sensing	Present	Analysis
Feeling and Sensing	Past	Caution
Mix of Intuition, Feeling, Thinking and Sensing	Past <--> Future	Renewal

Source: Figure adapted from D. Hurst, J. Rush, and R. White, "Top Management Teams and Organizational Renewal," *Strategic Management Journal*, 1989, 10, 87–105. Reprinted by permission from John Wiley & Sons, Ltd., Sussex, England.

These differences are identified based on the **strongest prefer-ence (in bold in the figure)** operating within the group. For example, in the first instance, the group's strongest preference is **intuition** with some in the group who have feeling as a strong preference. In this group, the time horizon is the future and the strategic focus is on newness. In the second instance, the strongest preference in the group is thinking with some individuals having a preference for sensing. For this group, the time horizon is near-term future and past, and the strategic focus is on improvement.

The strongest preference for the third group is for sensing, the time horizon is the present, and the strategic focus is analysis. The fourth group's strongest preference is feeling with some preference for intuition. Their time horizon is the past, and in an attempt to preserve the past, their strategic focus is on caution. The last group incorporates a blend of preferences and shifts its time horizon to reflect the preference that is dominant at the moment. In this instance, the strategic focus is renewal, where renewal means preserving the past by building on a business unit's core capabili-ties and allowing the on-going examination and redefinition of that core as a part of building for the future.

As Figure 7–3 suggests, groups are likely to have a cognitive composition that reflects the personal style preferences of its mem-bers. This tends to create a specific time and a strategy perspective bias. The appropriate mix of personal style preferences is largely determined by the needs of the business unit at a point in time and the organizational environment within which the business unit is operating. If the organization has a near-term focus and is rewarding behavior that fosters doing things better, a manager needs to take that into account in determining the appropriate amount of hetero-geneity that should be present in the group. If the strategic focus is renewal, this suggests a very different group composition for the work group having strategic leadership responsibility for the business unit.

OVERALL IMPLICATIONS

Managers are continually taking actions that reflect their under-standing of their business situations. There is a tendency for managers or groups of managers with specific personality type preferences to take actions suggestive of certain cognitive biases. This latter decrement to effective decision-making could be reduced by accurate diagnosis of the decision situation followed by asking people with different personality types to address each issue so as to minimize the risk of any particular bias materializing. Alternatively, individual managers could develop sufficient sensitivity to their predisposed style so as to guard against the bias by exhibiting flexibility in the style they chose to use in a specific situation. They would be able to switch to S-T, N-T, S-F, and N-F styles as the situation required. The most effective managers would be able to diagnose and understand differences in decision situations so as to involve other managers with styles that were the least susceptible to bias and/or to modify their cognitive style to complement the situation. However, these ideal decision-making approaches may not be practical or feasible. Managers may not have clarity on their own styles and/or understand the strengths and limitations of that style. Managers may not know the style of other managers; forming a decision-making group composed of managers with different personality type preferences may not be possible.

Attending to questions of the composition of the group to address strategic decision situations is important, but a more vital area to address may be the on-going, nonlinear, and iterative process that is typical of most such situations. Are the kinds of questions raised throughout the decision-making process encouraging the decision-makers to think through the potential biases suggested by their personality type? For example, to reduce their tendency to exhibit selective perception, managers might frequently ask themselves (or be asked by others): "What other areas might be considered?" and "How might other units view this?" The positivity biases exhibited most frequently by N-Ts might be reduced through thoughtful answers to the questions: "What can go wrong?" and "What is the down side of this action?" Social desirability biases observed most frequently in the actions of S- Fs might be reduced by looking for solutions that simultaneously answer the two questions: "What do we want?" and "What do they want?" Reasoning-by-analogy biases exhibited most frequently by N-Fs might be reduced by simply challenging the analogies: "Is this a complete analogy?" or "What are the limits of the analogy in our present situation?" Similar questions could be equally applicable to intact work groups who have a preference bias.

Regardless of the approach taken, personal preferences can play an important role in understanding the behavior of both individuals and teams in strategic settings. Coupled with strategic thinking and strategic management skills, they can aid managers in diagnosing and improving their strategic leadership.

ENDNOTES

[1]For more information on Jung's theory and personality type preferences, see C. Jung, *Psychological Types* (London: Routledge and Kegan Paul, 1923); I. B. Myers, *The Myers-Briggs Type Indicator* (Palo Alto, CA: Consulting Psychologists Press, 1962); and G. Lawrence, *People Types & Tiger Stripes,* 2nd ed. (Gainesville, FL: Center for Applications of Psychological Type, Inc., 1980).

[2]Myers-Briggs Type Indicator and MBTI are registered trademarks of Consulting Psychologists Press, Palo Alto, CA. For more information on Jung's theory and personality type preferences, see I. B. Myers, *The Myers-Briggs Type Indicator.* (Palo Alto, CA: Consulting Psychologists Press, 1962).

[3]The general population numbers are taken from D. Keirsey and M. Bates, *Please Understand Me: Character and Temperament Types* (Del Mar, CA: Prometheus Nemesis Book Company, 1984). The manager population numbers are from a series of executive education programs offered through the Center for Creative Leadership, Greensboro, North Carolina.

[4]P. F. Drucker, "Management's New Role," *Harvard Business Review,* 1969, 47(6), 49–54.

[5]See S. Gryskiewicz, "Creative Leadership Development and the Kirton Adaption-Innovation Inventory," presented at the 1982 Occupational Psychology Conference of the British Psychological Society. Greensboro, NC: Center for Creative Leadership, 1982.

[6]See S. A. Stumpf and R. Dunbar, "The Effects of Personality Type on Choices Made in Strategic Decision Situations." *Decision Sciences,* 1991 (in press); and U. Haley and S. A. Stumpf, "Cognitive Traits in Strategic Decision Making: Linking Theories of Personalities and Cognitions." *Journal of Management Studies,* 1989, 26(5), 477–97.

[7]Stumpf and Dunbar, "Effects of Personality Type."

[8]Haley and Stumpf, "Cognitive Traits."

[9]Many of the ideas in this section are adapted from D. Hurst, J. Rush, and R. White, "Top Management Teams and Organizational Renewal." *Strategic Management Journal,* 1989, 10, 87–105.

CHAPTER EIGHT
Working the System

What does it mean to "work the system?" To some, it means getting the system to work for them. It means understanding the organizational structures and habits that exist and leveraging them for the benefit of one's unit. For others, it means being political, or playing organizational politics: being manipulative, executing power plays, operating with hidden agendas, fighting turf battles, back stabbing, and looking good without the substance to back it. Still others interpret the phrase to mean figuring out who you need to deal with to get an idea placed on the agenda or a decision approved and working with others to satisfy their concerns while maintaining the integrity of the proposed ideas.

Each of these views has some validity and some advocates. Understanding and leveraging organizational structures and habits can be efficient. Playing organizational politics is viewed as appropriate and necessary by those who do so, and quite questionable by those who do not perceive themselves as doing so. It is the third view noted above that we have observed to be most efficient and effective in organizations. **Working the system involves managing multiple agendas in an ethical manner to simultaneously accomplish individual, organizational, and societal goals.**

In a cognitive sense, this means making decisions that are consistent with the ideas proposed in Chapter Five on strategic thinking—that is, simultaneously attending to what we want, what they want, and what we can do (i.e., decisions that are at the center of W-cubed). In a behavioral sense, it means taking actions that leverage one's skills (Chapter Six) and are consistent with one's personal style (Chapter Seven).

A manager's first step in working the system is a choice to become involved in the strategic processes of the organization and his or her unit. The choice to get involved is more than a decision. It is a commitment to strategic thinking as a business framework coupled with a willingness to act. It means putting the organization's values and mission first, diagnosing who the key players are in each situation, and understanding the preferences of these key players (i.e., Who are they? and What do they want?). We discussed this process as part of a stakeholder analysis in Chapters Three and Four; DeLuca explores this idea as "mapping the territory."[1]

Mapping the territory begins with a designation of the key players—those who are likely to get involved in the issue. The relative power and influence of these players need to be assessed along with their likely support or resistance to the actions proposed. Managers must also estimate the extent to which the potential influence will be exercised, for how long, and with what impact. Given this political map, a strategy needs to be developed to accomplish the chosen objectives, and tactical actions must be developed and implemented. Before we entertain ideas of strategy and tactics for working the system, it is important to establish the strategic leadership values that we believe should underlie any strategy, as well as aspects of the organization's culture that will constrain or enhance the success of the various tactics that are implemented.

STRATEGIC LEADERSHIP VALUES

Our discussion of strategic leadership, we have been implicitly communicating a set of values with respect to people, managerial practices, and business activity. Three values that have been espoused, although not necessarily identified as values, are essential for strategic leadership in the middle game: valuing the past, valuing the vision for the future, and embracing change. Valuing the past permits one to become more efficient. Valuing the vision of the future permits one to become more effective. Embracing change permits one to cope with a turbulent environment, uncertainties, and ambiguity. Without sharing and balancing these values as suggested in Figure 8–1, it is difficult to make things happen in organizations. That is, it is difficult to manage multiple agendas in an ethical manner to simultaneously accomplish individual and organizational goals.

Valuing the Past

Valuing the past allows one to benefit from the organizational and individual efficiencies that have been designed into systems or have evolved as individuals and organizations learn from their repeated actions. Benefiting from known efficiencies means "doing things right" more often. Valuing the past implies a respect for the history of the unit—personal history as well as organizational history. It means valuing the foundations on which an organization was created. It means taking pride in the unit's successes, feeling part of its progress, and collecting the learning that occurs—however haphazardly—to create an accumulated knowledge base.

FIGURE 8–1 **Maintaining a Balance among Three Values**

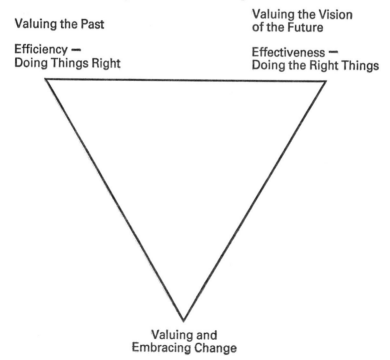

Valuing the past does not necessarily mean that one wants to perpetuate all past actions, as some of those actions were not as efficient as expected. Valuing the past does mean that one is open to learning from it so as to do more things right in the future. When managers answer the question, "What can we do?," they are trying to derive knowledge from past actions, events, and performances. The detailing of an organization's strengths in a SPOT analysis is one way of developing an understanding of the past. If strengths are those things that individuals or organizations can leverage to address a problem or opportunity, knowing the organization's strengths requires the synthesis of the key factors that contributed to successful past performances.

Valuing the Vision of the Future

One of the most common criticisms of the executive ranks by managers is the lack of direction provided to them by their bosses. For some, direction means a specific list of things to do by when. For others, direction means a shared mission and vision for their business unit within which they can exercise discretion. It is this latter sense of direction and vision that is essential for strategic leadership.

Valuing the vision of the future is linked to organizational and individual effectiveness—doing the right things. What is "right" for managers to do should be guided by their understanding of the organization's desired and somewhat idealized vision for the future. For example, if the vision involves "changing the world through making personal computers available to the average person," then "right" would be defined to include a strong emphasis on user-friendly software and price-quality-capability trade-offs that reflect the average person's user requirements.

> ## "In the absence of a vision, personality will prevail."
> ### *Dan Boffey*

Creating a value for and around the organization's or business unit's vision is a critical aspect of inspiring and motivating oneself and others to perform at high levels on those tasks that are believed to lead to the attainment of that vision. Motivating workers is very different from motivating managers. Linking pay to performance can motivate workers to produce more; it is more myth than reality that stock options and bonus plans per se motivate middle-level managers to do things differently. It is the challenge of accomplishing meaningful goals—whether they be financial, growth, distribution, or developmental in nature—that motivates managers. We have known this for decades through the research and writings of McClelland and Maslow; yet we have been slow in applying it to managers. The fear of executives is that managers will become too empowered; they will accomplish things that have yet to be approved at higher echelons. One solution to this conflict between motivation and control is to establish a value for the organization's vision, letting the vision be the control and motivational mechanism. In the absence of a vision and the valuing of the vision that is espoused, managers act more like workers than executives.

Embracing Change

The third value that is essential to "working the system" is embracing change. Embracing change implies an openness and responsiveness to proposed changes—changes that could be internally or externally initiated. Embracing change might mean altering an organization's structure, reward systems, operating systems, or control systems. Because one is managing in the middle game, changes often involve redeploying resources—undoing something as well as doing it differently. Such changes may require unlearning some things before becoming willing to learn a new way of accomplishing goals. In these instances, it is frequently necessary to deconstruct one reality or set of operating conditions before reconstructing a new set of operating conditions.

For many managers today, the necessity to embrace change is a precondition for adapting to the current business environment. The challenge lies in helping the operating core of the business unit to put this idea into practice. In working with others to embrace change, it is important to recognize that people do not resist change per se. What people resist is the uncertainty of change and the threat that they will not be effective and efficient in the business unit as it evolves. Ironically, it is often the perception of the operating core in the business unit that it is the managers who are most resistant to change. To the extent that concerns such as these are addressed, all who are involved in the efforts to embrace change can contribute.

Embracing change can mean trading off the efficiency of the current way of doing something for the potential future effectiveness of an alternative way of doing it. This trade-off is difficult for managers to make since the current operating system tends to prefer the status quo. Although organizational systems are initially designed around both efficiency and effectiveness criteria, the use of the systems often leads to organizational habits that get sustained over time based on their efficiency, not their effectiveness. Individuals are encouraged to keep doing it right; someone else has already determined that what is being done is the right thing to do. Although this may be a reasonable approach for some parts of a business, it needs to be questioned by managers in the middle game. Since many reward systems are designed around efficiency, not effectiveness, embracing change is difficult for many managers to do. Doing things right implies standards for performance that are measurable, particularly in the short run. Doing the right things requires an understanding of the desired future state and is best measured over a substantial time period. The continual adjustment needed between doing things right and doing the right things requires that one value and embrace change.

Challenges Implied by These Values

Simultaneously valuing the past, valuing the vision of the future, and embracing change is particularly difficult for managers in the middle. These values can often suggest inconsistent actions. They may even suggest an unresolvable paradox to some people. The career paths leading to middle management in many organizations have not helped managers to develop an understanding of the possible complementarity of these values. Most career paths to management require one to specialize in a business function (e.g., marketing, finance). Specialization breeds efficiency and a value for the past way of doing things right. By becoming an expert in a specific area, one learns how to do things right in that area, often to the detriment of other areas. For example, production expertise is often focused on the development of timely, standardized outputs of a product or service of some desired quality. Marketing expertise is often focused on identifying product-market segments, product variations, and price-quality trade-offs that meet with consumer interests. Accounting expertise is often focused on the collection and organization of information for regulator-induced reporting requirements. MIS expertise is often focused on the dissemination of information for internal evaluation and decision-making purposes. People in each of these functions are rewarded through pay raises, promotions, and increased responsibilities as they master their respective specializations and are able to make their functional areas more efficient.

As managers move into the middle ranks and middle game, a series of challenges emerges that were not present during the functional specialization phase of their careers. David Kolb identifies and discusses eight of these middle-game challenges as part of the adult development process that is necessary for one to make a successful transition from a specialist or technician to a strategic leader in middle management.[2]

The Challenge of Wholeness. Strategic leadership requires that one approach tasks in a holistic manner, which often involves more synthesis than analysis. Meeting the challenge of wholeness may necessitate initiating more cooperative problem-solving efforts, involving ideas and people from different functions and specialities, and using more group decisional processes. Because of the time demands associated with involving more people and perspectives in the managerial process, effective managers need to become more focused and selective in determining which problems and opportunities are the priorities to be addressed. There needs to be a conscious effort to choose the right issues, not just deal with issues in the right way.

The Challenge of Generativity. Strategic leadership is taking care of the people, the products, and the ideas that one has come to value. It is assuring that the past is not forgotten for the sake of the future or a current change effort. It requires one to be both mentoring and directive with respect to the people, products, and ideas that have become the foundation of the business. It involves a loyalty to the past and a commitment to the vision of the future by simultaneously assuming responsibility for others and exercising direction.

The Challenge of Change and Complexity. Strategic leadership is coping with change and complexity. It is learning from change, and it is learning how to manage in the midst of change. It requires one to be able to formulate scenarios, beliefs, and intentions that anticipate the future through a continual reexamination and debriefing of past experiences.

The Challenge of Time. Strategic leadership is regaining control over how one invests time. It uses visioning so as to always have an intentional action framework to guide one's choice of actions. It requires one to be able to sustain excitement about the possibilities 10 years from now while taking actions to resolve today's priorities.

The Challenge of Moral Leadership. Strategic leadership is value-intensive decision-making. It is being a public person, representing others, serving as a model for others to follow, and creating a culture that supports ideal values even in the most complex of circumstances.

The Challenge of Interdependence. Strategic leadership is a group activity that often involves integrating diverse knowledge specialities into coherent actions. It requires a dynamic team-building process whereby power is given to those on the team whose capabilities best respond to the particular issue at hand.

The Challenge of Ordinary Life. Strategic leadership is a human endeavor. It is a balance between the application of knowledge and the humble recognition that begins with the discovery of the limitations of knowledge. It recognizes that learning is often an experiential process and that having had an experience does not make one better than someone else. It is not elitist.

The Challenge of Facing Challenges. Strategic leadership is the development and maintenance of courage. It is staying positively engaged in the social world, being resilient, and responding with a hardiness to stress. It requires a continual learning process that embraces change.

Although the challenges of strategic leadership are many, there is an intensity and excitement in addressing these challenges, in learning from past experiences in dealing with these challenges, and in envisioning ways to deal with them more effectively in the future. It is this intensity and excitement that keeps pulling managers back into the middle game. It is also this intensity and excitement that stimulates some managers to start new ventures when the organizational environment and culture are not supportive of their efforts to be loyal, to learn, and to progress. There are times in chess matches as well as in business when one departs before the end-game—sometimes the departure leads to the starting of a new game, sometimes it involves entering another game in the middle. In either case, many of these strategic leadership challenges persist because they reflect what is needed in the managers' personal development as well as in the leadership of a business unit.

ORGANIZATIONAL CULTURES

Strategic leadership values reflect an individual's perspective for working the system; the organization's culture is its view of how its systems should work. If observers were to describe the different organizational habits they witnessed—those rather repetitive ways by which the organization's members seem to get things done—they would be describing the organization's culture. Although organizational culture is an abstract concept, its power becomes concrete when a manager violates a cultural norm. Actions that run counter to the organization's culture are like "shooting yourself in the foot." To highlight this point, DeLuca shares what could be foot-shooting actions in different organizations if an underlying cultural norm is being violated. Consider the following alternative cultural norms of different organizations:

- ⊃ "Keep your peers involved from the very beginning or they will shoot it down once the proposal is finalized."
- ⊃ "Don't let your peers know about the idea until you have all your ducks in a row or they move in and take it over."
- ⊃ "Strike back immediately when someone attacks or they write you off as a wimp."
- ⊃ "Never strike back in this department or they think you are petty."
- ⊃ "Skip the motherhood and apple pie and get to the numbers."
- ⊃ "Make sure you wrap the numbers in the company's value statement."
- ⊃ "Once the initiative has been accepted, 'ride herd' on implementation or nothing happens."
- ⊃ "After you've got the idea sold let go of it so someone else gets credit for making it happen."
- ⊃ "Social gatherings are prime time for influencing executives."
- ⊃ "Never bring up business issues at parties etc. because you get labeled as pushy."
- ⊃ "Innovation is highly prized."
- ⊃ "Couch your innovation in very traditional terms so it looks like a small improvement rather than a radical one."[3]*

Each pair of statements represent opposite cultural norms. Knowing what norms apply to a specific setting can mean the

*Note: List adapted from J. M. DeLuca, *Political Savvy*, 1991. Used with

difference between a successful approach and a failed one. In order to influence strategy, managers need to diagnose and attend to the organizational habits and operating norms of the organization and business unit. Since such habits and norms tend to focus on the process for doing things, rather than what specific outcomes should be achieved, it is often necessary to adjust the means used to reflect the organizational culture in order to accomplish the desired ends.

Does this imply that the end justifies the means? We think not. It implies that there are many different ways to reach desired endpoints or accomplish the business's goals. Choosing a way that reflects the culture of the organization can be every bit as ethical and moral as alternatives that do not reflect the organization's culture.

Even though organizational cultures vary along many attributes, there are some distinguishable patterns of organizational habits and norms that suggest discrete cultures. At the risk of oversimplifying the complexity of issues that managers confront in diagnosing and responding to different cultural norms, two cultures are described.

A Profit-Center Culture

Many businesses organize their various product lines into profit centers. Each line of business typically has bottom-line responsibility. The executives in charge, who might be middle managers in a functionally organized company, are CEOs of a subsidiary profit center. They are often masters of their own business. They have the autonomy to organize their business in whatever way they feel will best reflect the skills of their people, their distribution channels, their product offering, their manufacturing system, and the like. The executive ranks expect most profit centers to be self-funding and/or profitable within a few years of being established.

Once organized as a profit center, many businesses begin to develop what we refer to as a profit-center culture. For example, one large financial company developed a profit-center structure for its 20+ consumer businesses in the early 1970s. By the mid-1970s, a profit-center culture dominated how things got done in each business. This culture remained until a major restructuring and change of personnel took place in 1989. Working the system during the 1975–1989 period involved each business unit's manager's:

⊃   operating in an independent, autonomous manner,

⊃   tailoring products and services to local market conditions,

⊃   actively competing with other business units within the corporation that served the same customers,

⊃   developing depth in general management skills,

⊃   encouraging creativity and innovation within his or her market to best serve the consumer and develop a local competitive advantage,

⊃   providing rewards and promotions based on merit using easily measured performance criteria,

⊃   hiring the best talent available from within or from outside the company,

⊃   using expert consultants to develop solutions to problems,

⊃   treating people as if they were only as good as their last accomplishment,

⊃   managing the business to obtain immediate growth and short-term profitability.

If one puts aside personal preferences for working within a profit center, then the above attributes are neither good nor bad. They simply reflect the kind of culture that emerged within most of this financial institution's business units as a function of the mission, vision, and objectives established by the parent organization. The types of people that these business units recruited, hired, and retained tended to reflect this culture. They tended to be independent, aggressive, and self-sufficient. Conflict among managers over issues was openly accepted and often encouraged. Training programs stimulated friendly competition among participants through the way case materials were designed and used. Developing creative solutions to the case situations was encouraged to the point that the next new idea was more highly valued than finding additional applications for the last new idea.

The level of excitement, energy, and intensity at the offices of managers within this firm was high. People came in early and stayed late. They rarely stayed in one position or business for more than a couple of years. If someone was in the same job for four years, he or she risked being labeled "plateaued" or an "empty shirt." These were fast times in the financial services industry, and this organization wanted to be a major player. Work hard, play hard, and win might be a fair description of the culture.

A Shared-Accountabilities Culture

An alternative culture to the one created in the profit centers is a culture that reflects the sharing of accountabilities and resources across functional and business unit lines. Such a culture could reinforce an organization's focus on the customer or customer relationship instead of the specific and discrete products or services that the customer uses or consumes.

The financial company discussed above appears to be shifting its mission and vision for the next decade from that of being a financial services institution to becoming a global financial and information-services provider. The desire to change its vision to one that is more customer-relationship–oriented is one outcome of its change in mission. This has led the executive ranks to reevaluate the firm's past culture and to pursue the development of a shared-accountabilities culture for the future.

Central to managing in a shared-accountabilities culture is for managers to be able to solve problems and take initiatives that are in the best interest of the organization as a whole while: (1) not having sole responsibility and accountability for these actions, and (2) not necessarily perceiving the actions as being in their personal, business, or functional area's short-term best interest. Managers need to accept the efficacy of investing their efforts to accomplish organizational goals at some cost to individual goal accomplishment. This value is particularly important to reinforce because managers may not always get personal acknowledgment for their positive contributions to attaining the organization's goals, but they will likely feel some blame for their lack of contribution to organizational goals that are not accomplished.

Consider the following ways in which managers of this organization are learning to work the system within a shared-accountabilities culture:

⊃   operating in an interdependent, collaborative manner,

⊃   offering a uniform set of products and services to all markets,

⊃   actively collaborating with other business units within the corporation that serve the same customers,

⊃   developing depth in functional and technical skills so that knowledge and successes in one area can be transferred to other areas,

⊃   encouraging consistency and excellence in execution within each market to serve the consumer effectively and to develop a national competitive advantage,

⊃   providing rewards and promotions based on loyalty and merit using subjective and objective performance criteria,

⊃   transferring the best talent available around the organization and using outside resources only as a last resort,

⊃   using process consultants to facilitate discussion among parties in conflict,

⊃   valuing people for their collective contributions and on-going development,

⊃   managing the business to sustain moderate growth and long-term profitability.

Like the profit-center culture, a shared-accountabilities culture is neither good nor bad per se. It is certainly different from the profit-center culture that had emerged and been reinforced over the previous decade. This change in culture has not occurred quickly, nor without extensive executive communications, discussion, and education. Specific concepts and ideas that have been incorporated into the management development curriculum to facilitate the cultural change include:

1. managing change and ways of dealing with ambiguity,
2. understanding the meaning of cooperation, coordination, and collaboration,
3. developing mechanisms for improving coordination, such as liaison and integrator roles, diagonal slice groups, task force activities, collateral organizations, and so on,[4]
4. developing influence skills, particularly as they relate to peer relationships,
5. conducting stakeholder analyses and developing skill in resolving conflicts,
6. understanding the importance of interpersonal trust, and how to develop it,
7. learning to facilitate teamwork, networks, and interpersonal relationships,
8. understanding the effects of personal style and background on one's perspectives and behaviors.

Although not inclusive, these topics are suggestive of the kind of learning that is viewed as needed by one firm to change its organizational habits of getting things done from a profit-center culture to a shared accountabilities culture. The more successful strategic leaders in this organization are being asked to embrace a tremendous amount of change, while maintaining a high level of efficiency and retooling their approaches to be more effective in the future. How do these managers and others like them in other organizations that are initiating a change in mission, undergoing organizational renewal, or experiencing a radical change in their culture maintain a balance between efficiency and effectiveness? This is a question of personal strategy and tactics to which we now turn.

DEVELOPING AN APPROACH AND ACTING UPON IT

Making things happen in the middle game requires managers to draw upon the concepts of strategic leadership to think strategically, to apply their strategic management skills, and to use their

FIGURE 8–2 The Integration of Strategic Thinking, Skills, and Style

knowledge of their personal style as a strength in their interactions with others. By combining these elements with strategic leadership values and a knowledge of the organizational culture, managers are able to develop more useful answers to the question, "How can I best contribute to the business?" As suggested at the beginning of Part Three, we picture this integration of strategic thinking, skill, and style as three cords of string becoming entwined to form a rope (see Figure 8–2). In the process, each piece of string loses some of its distinctiveness while it makes an important contribution to the newly constructed whole.

Applying the Concepts

The objectives of analyzing the business environment, conducting a stakeholder analysis, and identifying organizational habits are to: (1) become familiar with the context in which one is expected to lead (e.g., it is like studying the chess board before making another move), and (2) find inspirational elements in that context that stimulate a sense of mission, vision, and objectives. Having felt that inspiration, managers need to develop a strategic agenda and strategic action plans.

If all that is needed is for each manager to have a strategic agenda, then organizations would run efficiently and effectively once a "good" analysis was completed and shared with others. Since we know that this is not the situation in practice, more must be necessary. Good analysis is a necessary but not sufficient condition for personal and organizational success. In recognizing this reality, managers begin to ask the question, "How can I be more effective in working the system and in making the things that I want happen?" Many answers have been suggested, but DeLuca captures them quite succinctly in *Political Savvy:* Develop a coalition, link agendas, build momentum, and customize your influence attempts.

Develop a Coalition. Coalitions—groups of people who share specific values, interest in issues, and goals—are a natural part of organizations. The influence of a coalition in supporting a change initiative is derived from the collectivity as well as the individual members. The existence of even informal coalitions communicates to the organization that the ideas being pursued have met a minimum test of issue validity and relevance. Several people support the same issue for inclusion on the organization's agenda. The agenda item is not just the beliefs or preference of a single individual. The formation of a coalition around an issue begins to establish the legitimacy of the issue as well as to reduce the ease with which a single advocate could behave in an unethical or selfish manner.

Coalitions are voluntary, somewhat amorphous, temporary entities. They rarely exist because someone said, "Let's form a coalition around this issue to influence management to support our position." They tend to emerge as a by-product of someone explicitly or intuitively working the W-cubed model of strategic thinking (What do we want? What do they want? What can we do?). In the process of diagnosing the business unit's wants and the wants of others, some commonality of goals becomes apparent. The savvy manager uses this newly found commonality of goals to pursue specific issues that are consistent with those goals. To the extent that a common value framework exists among these stakeholders, and to the extent that rapport and trust develop, coalitions begin to precipitate.

For a coalition to develop beyond an informal "sense of the group" viewpoint on an issue into a strategic force within the organization, the issues for which the coalition stands must become the group's issues, not just one or more of the individuals' issues within the group. This requires that the primary advocates permit (and encourage) others to influence how issues are defined and the processes by which issues are advanced for inclusion on the organization's agenda. This sharing of influence among group members must be matched with a sharing of credit for any of the successes that the coalition achieves.

Link Agendas. Most of the people in our research were continually developing and updating their strategic agendas to accomplish their personal and business unit's mission, vision, and objectives. Just how many agendas managers have is not clear, but we suspect that they have at least one agenda for every "we" they consider in response to the questions, "What do we want?" and "Who is we?" "We" can be the individual; "we" can be the business unit; "we" can be the functional area in which one works, and so forth. With so many potentially distinct agendas, it is not surprising that individuals and organizations have difficulty committing to a course of action and executing against it.

One response to the multiple "we's" in organizations is to acknowledge the multiplicity and complexity of agendas, ignoring whether or not these agendas are entirely rational from one's particular perspective, and to look for opportunities to link key issues across agendas. Managers need not buy in to the entire agenda of another manager or business; they may only need to collaborate on some agenda items. Diagnosing and examining the agendas of the significant "theys" in one's organization is a powerful entry point to the process of establishing linkages across multiple agendas. Direct inquiry, the use of information networks, following paper trails of meetings and projects, and careful listening to the language of others are helpful ways to more accurately diagnose the agenda items of others.

Once the potential for linking agenda items is tangible, managers need to seek (or create) win-win-win possibilities. The other party must win, the manager must win, and the organization must win. Even though in most games the idea of winning connotes a short-term success, winning for managers and organizations in the middle is intended to reflect the long run. Winning today through a short-term or tactical response to a long-term or strategic issue can lead to losing tomorrow. Managers and organizations will not really know if they won until the game is over—for individuals and organizations this is the end of their lifetime. As Figure 8–3 suggests, win-win-win possibilities need to reflect the values of people, the organizations they create, and the society in which they function.

Build Momentum. Once coalition members have been identified and some agenda items have been conceptually linked, one needs to build momentum for action. The easiest steps have probably already been taken based on the manager's stakeholder analysis and strategic thinking (W-cubed analysis). Not only is it efficient to take the easiest actions first, it is appropriate to the process of strategic leadership. When confronting nonlinear, iterative, and ill-structured situations, start where it is easiest (remem-

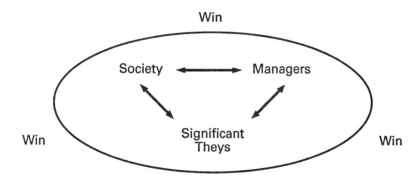

FIGURE 8–3 Customizing Influence Attempts to Win-Win-Win

ber the crossword puzzle analogy to the process of strategic leader-ship). Managers do this fairly well. But then many get stuck or blocked in their approaches or actions. Why? It is quite likely that the initial analysis was useful, but it was not sufficiently compre-hensive or accurate to lead to immediate success.

Because of the often messy and iterative process of strategic agenda building, one needs to generate many possibilities even when an initial alternative looks viable. This can be done through more individual analysis and/or by getting assistance from others. This is what building momentum is about. It involves reviewing and revising one's analysis to reflect an updated view of the situa-tion that captures the diagnostic information collected during the initial development of a coalition and initial linkages of agenda items. Building momentum is particularly difficult work because it often involves readdressing things that managers believe they have already addressed reasonably well. To make this work a bit easier, we suggest that a number of critical questions be answered as part of the momentum-building process:

⊃   Are the emerging mission, vision, and objectives of the coalition (or group that is predisposed to support the issue) consistent with the values and culture of the organization? If not, how can the issue be redefined or altered to be consistent with the values and culture of the organization?

⊃   Have all of the significant stakeholders ("theys") been identified? Are their wants really understood? If we articulate their wants, will they agree with our interpretation of them?

⊃   Have all potential coalition members been identified and ap-proached? How can we identify more potential supporters? How should they be recruited?

⊃   Have any critical agenda items that could alter the positive aspects of the dynamic that is evolving been missed?

⊃   Are there linkages among agenda items, or across the many agendas of the key managers, that could be developed to build a stronger, more cohesive coalition? Are there agenda linkages that could undermine the coalition that is emerging?

⊃   Have we passed the "halfway" point? Is more than half of the influence that is likely to be brought to bear on the issue already in favor of exploring the issue further?

⊃   Is the leadership of the coalition appropriate to the issue as it is now understood? Is the group more likely to achieve a win-win-win situation if the issue is defined more broadly or more narrowly, thereby redefining the role that the primary advocate should play in the process?

⊃   If a group decision is needed, is an interactive group setting the appropriate place to make the decision? Are alternative group structures and processes, such as a nominal or Delphi group, more appropriate for this situation?[5]

⊃   Is the degree of formality associated with exploring and resolving the issue appropriate to the stage of coalition formation, agenda linking, and momentum attained? Are more formal structures now needed (e.g., a task force, committee, policy review board, collateral organization), or should the formal structures that have been created be disbanded?

Customize Your Influence Attempts.   Once some degree of clarity and commitment has emerged around the strategic agenda within a coalition, tactical plans are needed to turn ideas into results. The time spent in planning versus doing is best thought of as another iterative process that managers learn as they lead. In benevolent systems, managers have more freedom to act, as they do in systems that are rich in feedback.[6] In contrast, hostile systems tend to be intolerant of mistakes or activities that are viewed as misusing their resources (including their time). Feedback-poor environments do not provide a timely opportunity to adjust actions in light of emerging events.

Given some degree of planning, managers must then initiate actions within the system to get it to work for them. The greater the degree of change being proposed, the greater the resistance likely to be experienced that will slow or stop action. To overcome this resistance, it is helpful to tailor the influence attempts to the specific individuals involved. For example, time and attention are critical resources of managers and executives. Yet many influence attempts ignore these resources. Once a meeting is scheduled, ideas are presented from the presenter's point of view—including his or her sense of time and issue importance. Jargon is used that does not clearly communicate the idea to the audience. Details in support of the idea are often presented before the idea is even understood. Executives get impatient as they ask themselves, "So what's the issue here?" or "Why is this being presented to me at this point in time?" Tailoring the media, message, and timing to the audience is necessary to get the audience's attention. (Marketers tend to understand this when they pitch their products to consumers.) This is another application of W-cubed: Assess what you want, what they want, and what you can do. Then give them what they want, what you want, what you can do. Without the attentional resources of significant others being committed to the issue, other organizational resources are less likely to be made available.

Leveraging Your Strategic Management Skills

In Chapter Six, we discussed a set of six strategic management skills that are necessary for managers to master in order to be effective strategic leaders: knowing the business and markets, managing subunit rivalry, finding and overcoming threats, staying on strategy, being an entrepreneurial force, and accommodating adversity. Few managers have mastered all of these skills, and even fewer can exhibit them effectively all of the time, but it is important for managers to know the specific skills that they can leverage to work the system. It is equally important for them to know the skills that they lack so as to be able to protect against demands that will require them to exercise skills that they do not possess.

An example may help to highlight these points. Dale, a middle manager in a knowledge-based business, was involved in promoting the launch of a new product that had little known market demand. The new product was a variation of another product that was being offered by another company. The demand for the existing product was minimal, but growing. Conceptually, the new product had strong appeal. Operationally, the new product was difficult to produce and deliver, and it was expensive relative to viable and less complex alternatives.

Dale exhibited strong skills in the areas of finding and overcoming threats, being an entrepreneurial force, and accommodating adversity. Dale's flat side was managing subunit rivalry. A mentor of Dale's was able to recognize this and proceeded to guide some of Dale's activities into developing a coalition that could withstand rivalrous criticism.

During meetings with the organization's executives, relatively little time was spent on the product concept—Dale's entrepreneurism prior to any formal meetings had effectively sold the idea and overcome most problems and threats. The meetings focused on how the product would fit in with the existing organizational structure and other well-established activities—who was to be responsible, how would resources be managed, and the like. It was the presence and advocacy by other members of the coalition that created the necessary momentum to get the idea approved, funded, and introduced into the market. Without question, the idea would not have been supported at the executive level if the rivalry had not been brought under control. The product did not have an overwhelming set of attributes to carry itself.

The scenario above could have easily turned out differently. Most new product ideas in this organization have not progressed past the discussion stage, and many of its middle managers have left after four or five years of service. The organization has no research and development budget to speak of, yet it is one of the more well-known and successful organizations of its kind. It ranks among the top 20 firms in its industry segment, and among the top 50 firms in its industry worldwide.

Working the system in this situation involved leveraging the skills of the product champion and avoiding being blocked due to the champion's weaknesses. It involved developing a coalition and customizing the influence attempts to the executives who were reviewing the proposal. Since the organization's culture involved many characteristics of bureaucracies, it was critical to have the visible and active support of the coalition members. It was not Dale's entrepreneurship and problem-solving skills that were the focus of attention at the key decisional meeting—these skills only gained Dale entrance into the game. They had little to do with the strategy executed during the middle game of this new product approval process.

Leveraging Your Personal Style

Just as managers can leverage their skills, many of the people in our research were able to use their knowledge of their personal style to their benefit as well as the benefit of their units. In Chapter Seven, we discussed 16 Myers-Briggs personality types as a way to understand personal style preferences. Managers have preferences for such things as where they look for information, the types of information to which they attend, and how they make decisions. These preferences affect the types of issues to which managers attend as well as the way they deal with the issues.

A recent situation experienced by Peter, a manager in a large manufacturing firm, exemplifies the importance of knowing one's personal style. Peter was responsible for developing and presenting a major project design to a client. Peter's strong sensing-thinking style was generally a positive aspect of his being assigned to the project. He was well organized, clear in his direction and suggestions, and knowledgeable of the key success factors that needed to be incorporated into the design.

During most of the design meetings, Peter was highly effective in communicating the project design concept, operationalizing important aspects of the design, and the like. However, certain aspects of the design were not being openly accepted by the client. In fact, the client would listen carefully to Peter's points but would provide no clear signal of acceptance or rejection.

One of Peter's colleagues, Susan, had attended most of the meetings. Susan was an intuitive-feeling style manager. She began to notice the passive acceptance of Peter's ideas fairly early in the design process. Although she said nothing about the tentative response she felt that the client was giving, she continued to reflect on it. After the third meeting, Susan approached Peter to discuss the emerging issue—no action was being taken by the client in spite of what appeared to Peter to be excellent meetings and client acceptance of the ideas proposed. Susan suggested that two of the people at each of these meetings didn't seem to be sharing Peter's vision of what the design would look like when it was complete. After some discussion of their style differences, and the possibility that some of the client's managers may have a style that was quite different from Peter's style, Peter agreed to follow Susan's cues at the next couple of meetings. Susan agreed to subtly let Peter know each time one of the clients began to "drift." Peter would then pause in order to direct his attention to that particular manager. Peter sometimes asked an open-ended question, or simply changed his rate of speech or intensity to be more reflective of the audience.

The result was noticeable almost immediately. The client's managers began to engage more often in the discussion of the design, constructive debates often ensued, and approvals began to follow. One of the client's managers commented some days later to

Susan that she was glad that Peter had stopped pushing so hard. Everyone knew that the design was high quality work, but people just didn't feel good about it. Once they got personally involved, their feelings began to change.

This situation is not uncommon—many of the managers in our research would find that their best efforts were not working. They stated to us that they knew their ideas were sound, that their analysis was thorough, and that their interpersonal skills had not hampered them in the past. So why was the system not working? Why was nothing happening? It was not until these managers examined their style, and the style of the people they needed to influence, that ideas were suggested to resolve the situation. Neither the idiosyncratic nature of this scenario, nor the one above involving Dale, should be skipped over lightly. Most strategic leadership initiatives are idiosyncratic. They reflect a different mix of stakeholders as a function of the issues being addressed. They need to reflect the specific skills and personal styles of these stakeholders (who frequently change). They need to reflect the culture of the organization—which can vary substantially from one business unit to another and sometimes within a business unit over time. And, they need to reflect the evolving nature of the business as a function of changes in the wants of its managers and executives, the wants of various stakeholders, and current capabilities. As the strength of and rate of change in market forces increases, the nature and magnitude of change that organizations must embrace will also increase. Embracing change will soon become a way of life—which will make managerial and leadership actions appear all the more idiosyncratic. And in practice, they probably will be.

ENDNOTES

[1]For insightful and provocative ideas on working the human system within organizations, see J. R. DeLuca, *Political Savvy*, unpublished manuscript, 1991.

[2]D. A. Kolb,"The Challenges of Advanced Professional Development," in L. Lamden (ed.), *Gladly Wolde He Lerne, and Gladly Tech: Festschrift for Morris Keeton* (San Francisco: Jossey-Bass, 1991).

[3]DeLuca, "Political Savvy," from Exhibit 29, page 8–2.

[4]A diagonal slice group is an ad hoc group that includes members from different levels of the hierarchy as well as from different functional areas within the organization. The phrase, "diagonal slice group," came to our attention through discussions with Joel DeLuca in 1980. The phrase comes from drawing a diagonal line through a typical organizational chart to identify possible group

members. The benefits of using a diagonal slice group are its heterogeneity in both level and function with respect to the issues the group is asked to address.

A collateral organization is a parallel, co-existing group (or organization) that a manager or executive can use to supplement the existing formal organization. Dale Zand introduced the concept in his article "Collateral Organization: A New Change Strategy," *Journal of Applied Behavioral Science,* in 1974. Zand discusses the concept of a collateral organization as it relates to strategic leadership in D. E. Zand, *Information Organization, and Power: Effective Management in the Knowledge Society,* Chapter 4 (New York: McGraw-Hill, 1981). The primary benefit of using a collateral organization is that it can tailor the standards of behavior, decision-making processes, and procedures to the issues at hand, rather than be constrained by the formal organizational systems.

[5]A nominal group differs from the typical discussion group in that its members are not permitted to openly discuss their ideas throughout the group's meeting time. Discussion is not permitted during the generation of ideas and at the time that ideas are being formally evaluated. Ideas from individuals are often solicited first, without the benefit of discussion. Once all group members have had an opportunity to provide their ideas, discussion is permitted. Similarly, the evaluation of ideas occurs individually, with people reporting out their preferences for action without the benefit of group discussion. Once everyone has had the opportunity to express their judgments, group discussion follows. The primary benefit of a nominal group is in its ability to yield more creative ideas.

Delphi groups involve people who never actually meet with each other as a discussion group. All "group" activities are handled by an administrator via electronic or written correspondence. A questionnaire is often used to solicit the ideas and expert judgments of the group members. These results are tallied by the administrator and fed back to the members. These members would then have an opportunity to respond to a second questionnaire that reflects their collective input from the first questionnaire. This process would continue until there is a reasonable convergence of ideas, or a stable, non-changing disagreement among group members. The primary benefit of a delphi group is in its ability to yield a consensus of expert judgments without interpersonal conflict among the experts.

For more information on the utility and rationale for using different group structures, see S. A. Stumpf, D. E. Zand, and R. Freedman, "Designing Groups for Making Judgmental Decisions," *Academy of Management Review,* 1979, 4(4), 589–600.

[6]Ibid., Chapter 10.

PART FOUR
DEVELOPING THE CAPACITY

CHAPTER NINE
Creativity Counts

CHAPTER TEN
Developing a Capacity for Strategic Leadership

CHAPTER NINE
Creativity Counts

Organizations want greater productivity from their workforces—some refer to this as a need for greater efficiency, and others refer to it as a need for excellence in execution. A central ingredient that is sometimes overlooked for increasing productivity is creativity. For managers, particularly those who are not in a research function, creativity often involves ingenuity and resourcefulness. Creativity involves the ingenuity to figure out how to get the tough tasks done in less time for less money; and it involves the resourcefulness to figure out how to bring the people, finances, and inspiration together to actually make it happen. Both of these aspects of creativity are critical to managers.

Creativity for the managers in our research did not appear to come easily. We have observed it to flow readily from some managers, but having ingenuity, championing an innovative idea, and being entrepreneurial presented a sizable challenge for most. Is it that people who get promoted to managerial positions are not creative people? We think not. The managers we have worked with do have many of the characteristics generally considered to be associated with creative people. Many managers are:

⊃ open to the experience and the ideas of others
⊃ able to see things in unusual ways

⊃ curious
⊃ accepting of apparent opposites
⊃ persuasive, persistent, and thorough
⊃ in need of and assuming autonomy
⊃ independent in judgment, thought, and action
⊃ tolerant of ambiguity and comfortable with change
⊃ flexible, yet clear on direction
⊃ responsive to feelings
⊃ able to think in images
⊃ able to concentrate
⊃ able to generate a large number of ideas
⊃ willing to take risks

If managers have many of these abilities and characteristics, why is it that they rarely see themselves as creative people and their practices of management are not viewed as particularly creative by their peers? One possibility is personal style. Those managers whose personality type preferences were for intuition and perception did exhibit more of the characteristics of creative thinking. Although managers whose personality type preferences were sensing and judging had to work harder at accepting and generating new ideas, doing so was not beyond their capabilities. It was not these personal style differences per se that led to the difficulty in applying ingenuity and resourcefulness to a task. It appears to be the challenges of managing in the middle game that create many of the barriers to creative thinking. The organizational culture and habits then serve to either reinforce these barriers or help managers to overcome them.

The three aspects of the middle game discussed in Chapter One that distinguish it from the opening game or the endgame seem to systematically work against managers' being creative. In the middle game: (1) A great number of resources are already deployed, (2) there are few recurring sequences of activity, and (3) the complexity of the situation is at a peak. Coming up with new ideas has little value to an organization unless they can be implemented. Innovations, by their nature, demand additional resources beyond those that are already deployed. During the middle game, most resources are deployed. Innovations also involve a level of risk that cannot be easily assessed. Only hindsight can show that a creative idea was successful.

The combination of the need for additional resources and the presence of ill-defined risks eliminates many creative ideas from consideration. Those that do survive require managers who are able to go beyond the limits of their formal positions to amass power and resources to support the innovation. This is by no means an easy task. There is often substantial momentum to maintain the status quo, political forces are well entrenched so as to actively resist change, and people with less power try to protect their turf. Because of these internal barriers, creative managers often become intrapreneurs or champions of their ideas to the point of being relocated to an R&D unit or moved to a separate area that is to focus on new ventures (i.e., they are moved to a unit or area that focuses on the opening game).

The second aspect of the middle game that works against managers' being creative is that there are few recurring sequences of action that lead to success. One might initially think that this would foster creative thinking. And it can, if the organization's culture and habits foster taking risks and learning through experience. What frequently does occur, however, is that managers feel helpless due to the lack of established patterns of activity that assure success. The statement "I don't know what to do about..." was a frequent communication conveyed to us in our research. Sometimes it was stated as a question, "What do you think I should do about...?" or "What would you do in this situation?" The grappling for ideas was apparent. Yet, many of these managers were able to answer their own questions once they were prodded to use the strengths of their personal style, their strategic management skills, the concepts they had learned about strategic leadership, and their knowledge of the decision-making process. One personal challenge for managers was to overcome feelings of helplessness derived from not having been in quite the same situation before.

The lack of recurring sequences has a potential second negative effect on managers. Rather than accept the newness of each situation, they attempt to force fit situations into known scenarios. The cognitive trails that managers use that stem from their personality type preferences and other patterns of thinking may not reflect the richness of the information available due to their filtering and selective attention to cues in their environments. The result is a biased diagnosis and analysis of an issue or the use of solutions that fit other problems rather than the particular problem at hand.

The fact that the middle game involves the greatest degree of complexity in situations compounds this problem. It suggests that managers need to develop a greater capacity for complex thinking. They need to be able to: (1) view issues from several different perspectives without biasing their view by a personal perspective, (2) consider a variety of responses to an issue, including redefining it, ignoring it, and addressing it, and (3) be cognitively and emotionally flexible in their responses to deliberate and emergent events that result in the implementation of organizational strategies.[1]

When we observed managers who were dealing with issues that were very complex, we saw attempts to simplify the issues for the managers' personal comfort as well as for their ease in communicating complex issues to others. Managers reported that they looked for what was familiar in an issue, then sought known analyses or solutions to familiar issues to apply to the complex issue. Although this works in situations in which there are frequently recurring sequences of events, the lack of patterns in events greatly reduces the benefits of looking for a familiar pattern.

"What is not there should not be found."
Roger L. M. Dunbar

Even though managing in the middle game would seem to work against creative thought, the role demands and position of middle managers in the organization can stimulate it. Middle managers are exposed to greater functional and hierarchical diversity than many others in the organization, thereby increasing the variety of ideas with which they come into contact.[2] Their day-to-day activities involve coordination and collaboration across functions and hierarchical levels. Managers often have multiple reporting relationships and overlapping responsibilities with peers that can stimulate them to think through their own ideas before having to sell them to others. Managers are also information nodes—they are the focal points of more information than is made available to either executives or workers.

Some of the new roles for managers discussed in Chapter Two can also stimulate creative thought. Of greatest significance is their role as the strategic leader of their unit or functional area. In this role, they have responsibilities for ensuring that the unit's mission is clear, that a vision is shared, and that objectives and strategies are proposed. Crafting strategies demands ingenuity and resourcefulness. Managers must be able to analyze the various forces on their unit, including rivalry in the industry, threats from alternative products, the power of buyers and suppliers, and the impact of new entrants.[3] This analysis becomes the material out of which strategies are created.

WHEN IS CREATIVITY NEEDED IN STRATEGIC LEADERSHIP?

Certainly organizations need to have some creative elements; they need to introduce new production and marketing ideas within the organization as well as new products and services to the marketplace. But do managers who are not in a research and development function need to be creative? Do managers of accountants, financial analysts, human resource specialists, market researchers, lawyers, sales personnel, or technical support personnel need to think creatively? In working with hundreds of such managers, we believe that the answer is clear—yes!

Several of the strategic management skills are enhanced through creative thought. The skill of accommodating adversity reflects some of the attributes that have been associated with creative people: flexibility and tolerance of ambiguity. Even though knowing the business and markets sounds analytical and factual, the ability to ask thought-provoking questions and generate many alternatives to key issues involves putting ideas together in new ways. Similarly, the skill of finding and overcoming threats is dependent on managers' abilities to diagnose issues and events with which they are unfamiliar, to redefine issues to make them more understandable, and to exhibit enough ingenuity to remove or avoid constraints. Being an entrepreneurial force requires managers to create a vision, champion ideas, and excite others to support the vision. Can managers see alternative possibilities and form scenarios of the future without creative thought? Creative thinking is part of a manager's strategic management skills.

Fortunately, not all of the agenda items managers face each day require creative thought. The managers studied in our research indicated that most of the issues they deal with on a daily basis did not require creativity in solution or action. They characterized these agenda items as routine. Routine agenda items had a sense of urgency around them, were defined in simple terms, involved only a few people, and lacked political overtones. They generally received little creative thought but did get quick action.

In contrast to routine agenda items, managers report that some of their agenda items each day are complex and convoluted.[4] These agenda items receive extensive thought—often occupying the majority of a manager's day. Actions are not forthcoming because it is not clear what actions could or should be taken. The actions taken are often to delay consideration of the issue and/or form a committee to get a better understanding of the issue. "Let's organize a committee to discuss this issue," or "Let's meet next week to talk about this in more detail," or "Work on that for a while and get back to me when you have some ideas on what we should do" are the words often spoken by the manager in charge.

The reason managers gave for postponing an issue or sending it to committee was that they were hoping to find new ways of thinking about the issue. Applying known problem-solving methods and management concepts did not quicken or improve the decisions made. Some managers simply reported that they were tired of dealing with an issue: "Let someone else deal with it for a while." Letting time pass and involving others was a way of dealing with this frustration, and it might get some new ideas introduced. Yet, a few managers said something quite different to us: "I knew that this issue was going to be a tough one to resolve. I knew there was a solution somewhere to be created or found. I just had to be clever enough to put the pieces together and find it."

Putting the pieces together—being creative. When we asked managers what they did to stimulate their creativity, they typically said, "I shared the issue with my people" or "We held a brainstorming session." We then might add, but what did you do personally? We were surprised at how few creative problem-solving techniques were practiced by managers themselves in the middle game. Issues requiring creativity were delegated; someone else was given the responsibility to be creative, but they were rarely told that creativity was part of their responsibility. Why would the most capable people, occupying critical positions in the organization, delegate the hardest work on the most critical issues to others?

The three reasons cited to us were: (1) I was not aware that being creative was really part of my job. I did not see it as my personal responsibility. Our organization hires creative types for R&D, marketing, and advertising, not for accounting and finance. (2) I am not a creative person. I don't know how to be creative. It is easier to hire someone or retain a consultant to help out in creative problem-solving, rather than learn this skill personally. (3) I don't have the time. Being creative involves lots of false starts, trial and error, and risk-taking. I prefer to concentrate my energies on running the business and let others take the time to develop and suggest creative ideas. My job is to evaluate those ideas, not to invent them.

We were not swayed by these arguments. If the task itself demands creative thought to reach a solution, then delegation or involving others to do the creative thinking is just one of several ways to handle it. Not being a creative person implies that creativity is a birthright, not something that can be developed or expressed intermittently. Managers do not need to be creative all the time—they need to be able to exercise creative muscles from time to time, and they need to know how to use a few tools to stimulate their creativity when it is needed. And the "not enough time" argument? None of the managers had enough time, whether they did a lot of creative thinking or none at all. It is how managers use the time they have that was important, not how much of it there was to use.

What emerged through interviews and discussions with managers was a lack of understanding of the role of creativity in their jobs, too few tools at their disposal to stimulate their creativity, and a lack of motivation to be creative. In listening to these managers, we began to see how many of the strategic leadership ideas could be enhanced through finding new or different ways of combining ideas, events, and agendas. It was rare that a manager simply applied SPOT or W^3 to a situation to reach a viable course of action. SPOT and W^3 provided managers with a way to go about diagnosing a situation. Rarely did something emerge from the use of either tool without creative thought.

METHODS TO STIMULATE CREATIVE THOUGHT

The methods that people can use to enhance their creative thinking fill books on creative problem-solving, entrepreneurship, and innovation. But managers do not go to their bookshelves to learn about such tools when they are in the midst of a middle game. They either have the tool in hand, or no tool is used.

By observing different managers exhibit various creative problem-solving methods on a rather complex set of issues, we were able to identify the tools most widely used by them to manage their agendas in the middle game. Four of these tools seemed to work well for many managers, independent of the managers' strategic management skills or personal style. These tools are:

1. **Redefinition**—defining a situation in a different way than it was initially diagnosed or presented

2. **Negative thinking**—taking a devil's advocate position on an issue or looking for the good in the opposite of what was being proposed

3. **Identifying and overcoming mental blocks**—those preconceived notions of what is inappropriate or impossible

4. **Analogies and metaphors**—drawing parallels or comparisons between the familiar and what is less familiar.

Each of these tools is discussed below along with examples of how each has been used by managers to improve productivity.

Redefining

Redefining was both the simplest and most widely used tool for creative thinking that we observed. In most cases, it was a subtle reframing of an issue, or a shift in the language used to describe a situation. It frequently occurred when someone was brought into a discussion who had missed earlier discussions on the topic. When the newcomer was informed of a complex situation, the situation was described differently from the way some of the managers remembered. In attempts to clarify the situation, it was redefined. On several occasions, the redefinition greatly simplified the issues. In some situations, the redefinition altered the way the business was viewed to the point of identifying new product or service ideas.

There is a tendency for some managers to begin with a single definition of an issue and then pursue it without considering other definitions. Such vertical or linear thinking can be contrasted to divergent thinking—thinking that alters the way in which an issue is being conceptualized. The creativity tool of redefinition requires that managers start with one definition of the situation, then seek to conceptualize the issue somewhat differently without losing sight of the issue or the interests of others. Common ways in which managers redefine issues are suggested in Figure 9–1.

Redefinition of issues in organizations is quite common. Consider how Seven-Up redefined lemon-lime soda—the Uncola! After years of fighting for market share against the cola beverages, someone thought of the situation in a new way. It was not bad to be a noncola beverage. Many soda companies knew this and sold lots of noncola beverages. What was so powerful about redefining Seven-Up as the Uncola is that it redirected people's attention to Seven-Up over other noncola beverages. Instead of competing with colas, it subtly took on all the noncolas without mentioning them at all.

FIGURE 9–1 **Ways in Which Managers Redefine Issues**

Reframing—altering the context of an issue

Changing Language—referring to an issue with new or different language

Divergent Thinking—using an issue to stimulate other, tangential ideas

Another example of redefinition comes out of the financial services industry. Bounced checks are a costly annoyance to the bank, the customer, and whoever tried to cash the check that bounced. None of the parties involved wants the check to bounce. The banking industry simply defined it as an overdraft—an error on the part of the party writing the check. So the solution was a penalty. Punish the mistake. If the punishment is strict enough, the behavior will stop, or at least the bank will recover its costs of handling the mistake.

The first redefinition of a bounced check was to think of an overdraft as the person taking out a loan by way of a line of credit. If the bank preapproved people for a limited amount of overdraft protection, then many bounced checks would become short-term loans. This subtle redefinition has made the banking industry millions of dollars. The creators of this idea captured a notable competitive advantage on what was basically a commodity business (i.e., checking accounts).

The next redefinition that occurred with bounced checks was even more creative. When consumers were asked why they bounced checks, most responded that they did not know that the check would bounce—they thought they had sufficient funds. When this answer was explored, what was found was that the reason why people thought they had sufficient funds was that their checkbooks indicated a positive balance. The error in their thinking was that it took banks anywhere from one day to a week to clear a check. Just because they wrote down the deposit on the day of the deposit did not mean that their account was credited with the money on that day. "Checks as cash" was born (as well as a regulation on how long it can take before a bank must credit one's account with a deposit). This redefinition involved using the savings account as collateral for a deposited, but uncleared check. Customers who signed up for such a relationship, could write checks on a deposited check immediately. If the check cleared, then there was no fee or loss of interest on the savings account dollars that were used as collateral. If the check bounced, the savings dollars were switched from the savings account to the checking account to cover the overdraft. Simple? Fairly. So why did it take the banking industry 50 years to figure this out? Because prior to the no-bounce checking idea, there was no need to do anything about an overdraft. Up until then, it was the customers' problem—they made the mistake, let them suffer the consequences.

The most significant redefinition of all for the money center banks in the banking industry is currently underway. It involves money center banks redefining themselves as a service to customers, not the holders of deposits and granters of loans. Although taking deposits and making loans is what they do, it does not need to be the definition of what they are. Redefinition—the ability to define something differently from how it is currently understood.

The Power of Negative Thinking

We introduced the idea of negative thinking when we presented the W^3 model in Chapter Five. The leading question was "What do we want?" One of the following questions was "What don't we want?" We can also ask "What do they want?" "What don't they want?" "What can we do?" "What can't we do?", or "What don't we want to do?" The idea of negative thinking is easily extended: What do we want more of? Less of? How can we make the product or service more personal? More impersonal? Simple? Complex? Passive? Active?

Thinking in opposites jars people's thought processes to permit them to consider something that was not previously within their cognitive reach. Several rather involved methods have been developed to force people to consider the negative of what they are currently thinking. Assigning someone or personally assuming the role of devil's advocate is probably the simplest of these techniques. The devil's advocate role involves challenging most major premises that are made by considering the opposite. It has worked well in groups to reduce the likelihood of a rapid consensus on what would otherwise turn out to be a poor course of action.

A second area of negative thinking that has already been introduced involves the SPOT model: Threats—what can go wrong? Managers who continually ask this question of themselves and their peers before taking actions on convoluted issues are able to reduce their risks and backstop many of their less than stellar choices before the undesirable actions reach crisis proportions. Of course, determining "what can go wrong" is much easier to do after the risk has materialized. Remembering to ask the question and probing for meaningful answers are part of what creative thinking in the middle game is about.

Overcoming Mental Blocks

Our discussion of personality type preferences in Chapter Seven foreshadowed this tool of creative thinking. People exhibit different preferences in the way they deal with information. Each of these preferences can lock them into certain patterns of thinking and thereby block their ability to think of things in different ways.

Research on creativity has identified several of the blocks to creative thought.[5] Figure 9–2 identifies 10 blocks that are frequently observed in managers.[6]

There Is a Right Answer. For simple agenda items that arise in structured, known environments, there probably is a right answer. Since most people enjoy being right, finding or proposing the right answer feels good. When confronting more convoluted agenda issues, right answers are much harder to assess—particularly at the time they are proposed. If the "answer" involves imple-

FIGURE 9–2 **Ten Mental Blocks**

1. **There Is a Right Answer.** There are likely to be many right answers and many ways of reaching them. More importantly, the right answer may not be needed at all—just a good answer.
2. **That Idea Is Not Logical.** It may not be. That's OK. Logic is fine for the application of ideas, but in the creative phase of management it tends to restrict one's thoughts.
3. **We Must Follow the Rules.** There are no rules for being creative. Most revolutionary ideas have disrupted existing principles.
4. **Let's Be Practical.** In other words, stifle your imagination—a sure way to kill a creative idea.
5. **We Should Avoid Ambiguity.** That is, let's look at any situation in the way we always have. No creativity here.
6. **To Err Is Wrong.** To err is to err. Not to err is not to experiment. When you fail, you learn what doesn't work and you get an opportunity to try a new approach. If you are not failing now and then, you are not being very imaginative.
7. **Play Is Frivolous.** Maybe. It is also fun. People are much more creative when they are having fun than when they are "only working."
8. **That's Not My Area.** True. And it is because it is not your area that you have the greatest creativity potential. This is not to say that every one of your creative ideas will be practical. Leave execution up to the experts.
9. **Don't Be Foolish.** Why not? If we never tried anything that might make us look ridiculous, we certainly would not have airplanes, telephones, bicycles,...
10. **I'm Not Creative.** Maybe. But one of the worst blocks to our thinking is thinking that we can't be creative.

Source: Reprinted by permission of Warner Books/New York from R. von Oech, "A Whack on the Side of the Head," Warner Books, Inc., New York, NY. Copyright © 1983 Warner Books, Inc., New York, NY.

mentation of an idea in a turbulent environment, then what is right today may not be so by the time it is implemented and experienced by those in the environment. Herbert Simon's concept of *satisficing*—finding solutions that meet the needs of most affected parties to some reasonable degree—was part of a theory of economics that won the Nobel Prize. Why managers persist in finding the right answer has more to do with their styles and egos than it does with there being a demand for a right answer to an issue. When managers let go of their quest for a right answer, and began their quest for a good answer that meets the needs of the various parties involved, creative ideas emerge and creative solutions to convoluted issues are proposed.

"Every act of creation is first an act of destruction."

Picasso

That Idea Is Not Logical. Logic tends to be based on a rational, analytic framework or on a rational, values framework. Managers who have a personal style that reflects a preference for thinking (based on Jung's theory) respond to logic based on an analytic framework. Those who have a personality type preference for feeling respond to logic based on a values framework. What is logical is different for people with different personal styles. To restrict ideas because they are not logical generally involves ignoring either the analytic or values perspective in resolving an issue. Some of the ideas proposed in discussions may not be logical from the perspective of some managers. To discard them on the basis of their not being logical may result in some potentially useful ideas being ignored because one's frame of reference was different from that of the idea initiator.

We Must Follow the Rules. Rules are created to restrict thought and behavior. Following rules may be essential for resolving routine issues and ensuring the smooth running of a unit or organization. Alternatively, rules may exist long after the situation that they were introduced to control has changed. In such situations, rules inhibit behaviors that could be productive for the organization. Observing the residents of New York City walk the streets of Manhattan is a case in point. New York does have a no jaywalking law. On a rare occasion, it is enforced. Many pedestrians in New York deviate from the rule of no jaywalking because the rule no longer fits the environment. The unofficial law is "don't obstruct traffic." The personal, logical framework is "don't get hit by a vehicle." The result appears to be chaos; in practice, more people move from one place to another more quickly in New York than in any other city—with a pedestrian accident rate for midtown Manhattan that is not significantly different from other major cities that do enforce their jaywalking laws.

"Rules are for the obedience of fools and the guidance of wise men."

David Ogilvy

Let's Be Practical. What a tough suggestion to turn down. It is as if the only alternative to being practical is being impractical. One might be theoretical, empirical, or analytical. Each has its place in strategic leadership. Although practicality is often an important attribute of a suggestion, it tends to compare an idea to what is already known and has been tried. Creative ideas generally go beyond what is currently available. Practicality may be a criterion to use in evaluating a series of alternatives; it only hampers the generation of ideas and stifles suggestions for alternative ways of doing things.

We Should Avoid Ambiguity. Avoiding ambiguity is based on the premise that when a discussion becomes garbled, clouded, and vague, it is time to move on to something more solid. If things cannot be presented in a clear, articulate way, they should not be discussed at that time. This is acceptable advice for many routine agenda items. But, if an issue is convoluted by its nature, ambiguity as to what the underlying issue may be and how to resolve the issue is likely. Ignoring murky issues, or assuming such issues are resolved because one has lost sight of them, does not lead to their effective resolution. It is the ambiguous issues that reflect the salient responsibilities for managers to resolve in the middle game. They are likely to be closer to ambiguous issues than the executive ranks, and managers have greater resources to expend in resolving the issues than the worker ranks. Avoiding ambiguity only maintains the status quo; accommodating ambiguity may lead to ideas that help resolve the underlying cause of the ambiguity.

To Err Is Wrong. Avoid mistakes! Ten or more years of schooling have driven this idea into most managers' minds. What could we say to change such a viewpoint on errors after a concerted effort to create this viewpoint by the educational establishment? Fortunately, the human trait of making mistakes, of committing errors, remains in spite of the educational system. In practice, educational attainment seems to do more to allow one to gain access to forums in which to make more costly mistakes than it does to enhance one's ability to reduce the number of mistakes made.

Making mistakes is a function of many things, including the amount of experimentation one does. Active experimentation provides an opportunity for learning from the errors made so as to improve in subsequent situations. To err is to try something and find out that one's expectations as to outcomes were not met. Creativity often occurs when one examines how the mistake occurred.

Play Is Frivolous. Managers go to the office to work, they come home to play. This artificial distinction of where it is appropriate to do certain things makes sense only in the extreme definitions of the terms. We have used the idea of play in our chess and crossword puzzle analogies for the reason that many activities typically thought of as play involve many of the same skills and processes as work activities do. Certainly playing is supposed to be fun, it is supposed to be enjoyable. Does this mean that work should not be fun, it should not be enjoyable?

Play is often intended to be a distraction from other events, a diversion of one's energies from other tasks. Is it inappropriate in work contexts to be distracted or diverted? Much of a manager's job involves one distraction and diversion after another—only a few of the many interruptions that occur each day are likely to be called play by managers. Play is often emotional and involves aspects of competition and combat. Denying these elements of a manager's style can be costly in terms of his or her productivity. It is through the frivolous aspects of play that managers can let go of some of their preconceived ideas of what is going on and how to proceed and begin to make room for other ideas.

That's Not My Area. Often managers hold back their ideas in a discussion of an issue that is outside their area of expertise: "If you don't know what you are talking about, don't talk." This advice may apply to the implementation and execution phases of a project. It is premature during the idea generation and analysis stages. Creativity often involves putting known ideas together in ways that are different from the past. The opportunity to do so is greatly reduced when the ideas from different areas are not shared. The most widely used method for increasing creativity in organizations is to bring together diverse people, functions, and interests in a semistructured setting to share ideas. Open idea generation is encouraged and supported, no matter how unknowledgeable a person's idea may seem when it is first presented.

Don't Be Foolish. What is probably meant here is don't embarrass yourself. Don't be careless, irresponsible, immature. It is hard to argue that managers should be these things. The way an idea is presented should not be foolish, but the idea could be foolish. Foolishness is something that is felt at the time of the event; it is often lost thereafter. By accepting the legitimacy of emotions in the workplace, more creative ideas are possible. This does not mean that one should be foolish in front of hundreds of others; be foolish with a few friends, get their reactions, then pose the somewhat refined idea to the group.

I'm Not Creative. We started this chapter with the observation that most of the managers in our research had many of the attributes of creative people. Yet these same managers rarely characterized themselves as creative. Managers think of artists, musicians, and scientists as being creative people—not accountants, financial analysts, or human resource specialists. Once managers label themselves as "noncreative people," they have given themselves permission not to try. Since the dynamics of the middle game make it difficult for them to exercise their creativity, the solution is often to delegate any need for creativity to others. But the demands of their management jobs require creative thoughts every day. Recognizing this, and overcoming these mental blocks to creativity, are essential for their effective management in the middle game.

Analogy and Metaphor

Creative thinking involves seeing what is there in a different way from before. Rarely are new ideas actually the creation of something from nothing. Analogies are descriptions of events or things that have a likeness, similarity, or resemblance to the agenda item or issue that is of interest at the time. To develop an analogy is to draw comparisons between two events or things. A useful analogy is one that is able to approximate many of the critical aspects of a convoluted agenda item by comparison to something that is more familiar to oneself and others.

Metaphor (and similes) are comparisons between two or more seemingly unrelated events or things. The use of metaphor is a way to explain an issue to others by using ideas that are more familiar or graphic to them. Metaphor can make something that is complex easier to understand.

The power of analogy and metaphor in the creative thought process is that they provide managers with a familiar frame of reference to work from in their thoughts about something that is unfamiliar, complex, and convoluted. If the analogy or metaphor captures the essence of an issue, it is possible to develop new ways of thinking about the issue by exploring the analogy or metaphor. We have introduced several analogies and metaphors in earlier chapters. The rope metaphor symbolizes the importance of the three aspects of strategic leadership—strategic thinking, skills, and style. All three aspects work together in a silent, but integrated way.

A number of other analogies and metaphors were introduced: the "river" model of the merging of deliberate and emerging events to form the perceived reality of the middle game; the W^3 model as a mathematical analogy for the importance of simultaneously addressing the three "What" questions; and the crossword puzzle analogy for the nonlinear, iterative, messy process of management. These analogies and metaphors stimulated our thinking about these topics as we discovered them by observing managers in the middle game. To the extent that they were useful comparisons and developed well, they have helped managers understand the ideas suggested by giving them something familiar to use as a point of comparison.

CREATIVITY AT METROBANK

During the development of the materials for the simulated companies used in our research, we had the opportunity to have lengthy conversations with many managers. Whenever an idea was proposed that was sufficiently different from the ideas we had heard from other firms or managers, we would ask how the idea came about. Of the many examples that we could share that highlight creative thought, one in particular warrants discussion.

The organization, call it Metrobank, is a large metropolitan consumer bank. It has many branches located within a 30-mile radius of the heart of a major city; about 25 of these branches were considered by the executives of Metrobank as exemplary of what a branch bank might be. Metrobank had developed a significant competitive advantage in the late 1970s through its use of electronic banking and automated teller machines. This advantage was sustained until the mid-1980s when the network of cash machines and other electronic banking methods substantially reduced Metrobank's competitive advantage. By the late 1980s, Metrobank was seeking a stronger competitive advantage but was having difficulty in determining what it should be.

The managers involved in running the branch system began to look for an analogy to branch banking that might be useful in stimulating ideas around how to develop a meaningful, unique, and sustainable competitive advantage. This process was not new to Metrobank. In the early 1970s, a similar quest led Metrobank managers to compare their check-processing operations to the operations of manufacturing organizations such as Ford. Several insights were gained through this analogy that subsequently led to redefining, streamlining, and automating (as in a production line) the operations function at Metrobank. In the mid-1970s, Metrobank looked to marketing organizations such as General Foods and Philip Morris for ideas on how to better market Metrobank products and services. Dozens of Metrobank employees were hired with consumer package goods experience as a way of developing an internal cadre of people who could talk marketing (up until this time the primary jargon of Metrobank was credit analysis and personal selling). The result has been a wave of market research, advertising, and promotions to target and stimulate sales. These successes were important for other units within Metrobank, but they did not eliminate the challenge of a fleeting competitive advantage faced by the branch banking unit.

Managers began to ask themselves just what a branch is. Is it a transaction depot, a storage place for valuables, a cash dispensing outlet, a place for people to meet, a point of sale for Metrobank products and services, a point of sale for non-Metrobank products, or something else? Since it was many of these things to some people, and some of these things to different people, was there a single analogy that could be useful in helping Metrobank to define and develop a sustainable competitive advantage?

Without a firm answer in hand, management decided to conduct research on how customers saw Metrobank. What was learned was that customers saw Metrobank as a middle-class, mass seller of financial products and services. Even though this image was not necessarily a negative one, it was far from what the executive and manager levels wanted or expected. Metrobank wanted to be perceived as a premier provider of financial services, not a mass seller of them. Additional research was undertaken to develop an understanding of what makes retailing organizations successful and prestigious in the minds of consumers and employees. Metrobank's research suggested the following:

1. Premier retailers are passionate about their business, their customers, and their employees. They communicate this passion with devotion and commitment.
2. Premier retailers organize their enterprise around fulfilling customers' needs.
3. Premier retailers treat their place of business with pride.
4. Premier retailers recognize that the staff members who have the most contact with their customers make the most difference.
5. Premier retailers know how to "keep it simple." They recognize that execution is critical to success.
6. Premier retailers recognize the value of a deep and on-going relationship with customers.
7. Premier retailers look for ways to save money in areas that don't affect the customer. They work to become more efficient and effective in areas that do.
8. Premier retailers look for new and better ways to do things, relying on customers and staff for ideas.
9. Premier retailers promote heavily from within.
10. Premier retailers know how to merchandise their products and services.
11. Most importantly, premier retailers believe that customer satisfaction is the most powerful way to distinguish themselves from competitors—and that customer satisfaction is difficult to achieve and imitate.

Had Metrobank managers stopped their analogy at this point, they would have learned much, but gained little. What was done next to turn these insights into actions involved redefining retailing as they had observed it in premier retailers into branch banking. This process involved both managers and their staffs finding ways to translate each of the 11 points above into specific agenda items for the different levels and functions within the organization. Today these agenda items have been translated into customer service behaviors, branch merchandising efforts, incentive compensation programs, technological additions to branches to measure and shorten wait time, customer and employee satisfaction surveys, an awards program, and more. The vision of being a premier retailer that Metrobank managers created for the branch system has both guided most actions and motivated several thousand branch employees to reach the vision. While the analogy, redefinition, and vision that emerged have led to substantial success for Metrobank, it would not have occurred without a supportive climate and structure.

ORGANIZATIONAL CONDITIONS SUPPORTIVE OF CREATIVE THINKING

Managers cannot be expected to put in the extra effort needed to think creatively while managing the middle game if the broader organization does not reward their actions, or actually hampers their efforts. Several researchers have explored this issue at the organizational level with respect to organizational climates, structures, and support systems. Organizational climates, according to Peters, must support the champions of ideas and encourage "creative swiping."[7] Supporting idea champions involves a climate that encourages champions to come forth and accepts some disruption to its operating systems because of the championing effort. Creative swiping requires a climate that encourages ideas to be borrowed from other areas—such as in the premier retailing ideas above. Every idea need not be invented by the organization—it only needs to be new and useful to the organization, not the world, to be rewarded as "creative."

Fluid and organic organizational structures that are selectively decentralized have also been identified as supportive of creative thinking.[8] Coordination among functions and units needs to occur through mechanisms that go beyond the formal hierarchy, including the use of liaison personnel, integrating managers, and matrix structures.

Rosabeth Moss Kanter identified several organizational structures and processes that provide support for creativity and encourage managers to tackle convoluted issues.[9] The kinds of opportunities that supported managers' going beyond their formal jobs to combine organizational resources in new ways were:

1. multiple reporting relationships and overlapping market responsibilities,
2. an open flow of information to the point of forcing managers to rethink what they really need to know out of the information overload,

3. alternative centers of power, each with budgetary flexibility to encourage managers to champion their ideas,

4. opportunities for managers to obtain positions that had ambiguous responsibilities that they then had to define and defend,

5. frequent and congenial cross-functional contact with an emphasis on lateral, collegial working relationships rather than hierarchical, formal relationships,

6. a reward structure and climate that focused on future accomplishments rather than past services.

Were these conditions present in the Metrobank example noted above? Some of them were. Metrobank's climate does support champions and its use of analogies suggests that everything need not be invented at Metrobank to be useful. Metrobank's structure is highly fluid, organic, and decentralized—to the point that there are few formal organizational charts because the organizational structure is viewed as not stable and constantly changing. Work gets done because of relationships among individuals. The Metrobank branch system has been described as consisting of "organic work units with elastic jobs."

The Metrobank branch system is a separate operating unit with its own mission, vision, objectives, and strategies. This should not imply that Metrobank executives do not oversee the unit's MVO; as any manager within Metrobank will quickly inform you, they do. But, the responsibility for the strategic leadership of the branch system is with the managers of the branches, not corporate executives.

Are Kanter's opportunities for organizations to support creativity present at Metrobank? Our experience with Metrobank for over a decade now suggests that many support structures and processes do exist. Many managers do have multiple reporting relationships. There is a fairly open flow of information. There are multiple centers of power with budgetary flexibility. Some positions do involve substantial ambiguity around responsibilities which the managers must then resolve. Cross-functional contact is frequent and relatively smooth. Problems arising from infrequent cross-functional contact in the 1970s and early 1980s have resulted in strong pressures from the executive level for managers to work together by sharing information, resources, and support staff. Finally, do reward systems focus on investments in people and projects rather than past accomplishments? Without a doubt. To quote the senior human resources manager at a conference of 71 high-potential new managers, "What you did yesterday is interesting, but...what you're going to do tomorrow is critical. Effort and activity are not the same as Results!"

COUNTING ON CREATIVE THOUGHT

Organizations rely on their people to provide stability and certainty as well as to embrace change and manage in ambiguous, turbulent environments. Creative thinking can be used to improve the ways in which stability and certainty are managed as well as facilitate the embracing of change under conditions of uncertainty. Creative thought often leads to a viable way to serve the organization's many stakeholders better. It is creativity that results in a manager's finding a useful action that gets at the center of W-cubed: simultaneously satisfying some of the organization's wants, some of the salient wants of key constituencies, and leveraging the organization's current or emerging capabilities. Organizations need creative thought from their managers many times each day. Without such thoughts, the organization will either persist in old ways of doing things or leave unresolved some of the key issues facing it that would have altered its future.

In this chapter, we have focused on several tools for stimulating creative thought. The thoughts that emerge from the application of these tools are not likely to be uniformly useful. But some of the thoughts will be directly applicable to the issue being addressed or will stimulate other thoughts that are applicable. Learning to stimulate creative thoughts, then selectively capturing and applying those that get at the heart of W-cubed, are essential to strategic leadership in the middle.

ENDNOTES

[1]Jean M. Bartunek and Meryl Reis Louis, "The Design of Work Environments to Stretch Managers' Capacities for Complex Thinking." *Human Resource Planning,* 1988, *11*(1), 13–22.

[2]Rosabeth Moss Kanter discusses the potential for middle managers to be innovators in her article, "The Middle Manager As Innovator." *Harvard Business Review,* July–August, 1982, pp. 95–105.

[3]For further discussion of these points, see Porter's Five Forces Model: Michael Porter, *Competitive Strategy* (New York: The Free Press, 1980).

[4]Many of our observations of managers were guided by the insightful observations reported in Morgan W. McCall, Jr. and Robert Kaplan, *Whatever It Takes: Decision Makers At Work* (Englewood Cliffs, NJ: Prentice Hall, 1985); and Jane E. Dutton, L. Fahey, and V. Narayanan, "Toward Understanding Strategic Issue Diagnosis." *Strategic Management Journal*, 1983, *4*, 307–23.

[5]For a good overview of creative problem-solving, see David A. Whetten and Kim S. Cameron, *Developing Managerial Skills* (Glenview, IL: Scott, Foresman and Company, 1984), pp. 151–64.

[6]Roger Von Oech, *A Whack on the Side of the Head* (New York: Warner Books, 1983).

[7]Tom Peters, *Thriving on Chaos* (New York: Harper & Row, 1987), pp. 278–304.

[8]Henry Mintzberg, *Mintzberg on Management* (New York: The Free Press, 1989), pp. 196–220.

[9]Kanter, "The Middle Manager as Innovator," pp. 104–5.

CHAPTER TEN

Developing a Capacity for Strategic Leadership

Developing a capacity for strategic leadership in the middle game involves discovery and learning. It requires managers to continually diagnose, plan, act, and reflect. Based on the reflective thoughts that managers have, they need to make sense out of what occurred in order to adjust to it, incorporate it into their understanding of the situation, or consciously ignore it. The cycle of diagnosing issues and events, planning agendas, taking actions, and reflecting on the results of these actions is of greatest value when it is short in time frame and frequent in occurrence. Assuming that this is good advice, now what? How is this advice any different from that given to managers before?

Throughout *Taking Charge,* we have shared our research findings and ideas in an attempt to provide useful insights, BFOs, and aah-haas to others. To the extent that we have been successful, we can make a number of suggestions for how managers may be able to develop and increase their capacity for strategic leadership. For many managers, the suggestions that follow will have their roots in personal insights. These will be the most useful suggestions. We present these suggestions here for easy reference; they are a collection of insightful questions and recommendations that managers have shared with us as well as observations that we have made through working with managers in the middle game.[1]*

EXAMINE YOUR TOOLS—ARE THEY IN GOOD WORKING ORDER?

Concepts, skills, and style—these are the different sets of tools needed for strategic leadership. It is certainly easier to construct something when all the needed tools are available and in good working order. When the tools are not available, or when they do not work properly, a two-hour task stretches to a day's work, or maybe several days' work. Sometimes the task gets put off for weeks. Strategic leadership should not be put off.

Concepts: Which Ones Are You Going to Use?

We have offered several concepts to assist managers in their strategic leadership efforts. Choosing the most useful ones for a situation may not be easy, but practice in using the concepts in different situations helps one to make future choices as to which concepts work best for which situations.

One set of concepts plays a particularly important role: Mission, Vision, and Objectives (MVO). After these concepts have been effectively applied, they seem to receive less attention. Managers need clarity on their organization's MVO, their unit's MVO, their subunit's MVO, and any additional MVO ideas upstream of them that need to be nested within the organization's MVO. The most critical of these is the organization's MVO, for without an understanding of it, managers tend to wait for direction rather than provide it. If the executive ranks are not forthcoming with the organization's MVO, then managers need to ask for it. If it is still not forthcoming, it is time to create an MVO for their unit and push it upstream. The critical elements are to seek as much consistency and nesting of MVOs across organizational levels as is feasible and to eliminate the psychological barrier experienced by managers due to the lack of MVOs upstream.

Note: Portions of this chapter are based on the following works: Stephen A. Stumpf, "Towards a Heuristic Model of Career Management." *The International Journal of Career Management, 1989, 1*(1), 11–20; and Stephen A. Stumpf, "Work Experiences That Stretch Managers' Capacities for Strategic Thinking." *Journal of Management Development,* 1989, 8(5), 31–39. Used with permission of MCB University Press Limited, Bradford, England.

Suggestion 1: Develop the mission, vision, and objectives for your unit, share them, and modify them as is necessary to fit the views and values of your workers and the organization. Seek clarity, acceptance, and excitement around your unit's MVO.

Two tools help managers diagnose their situations and craft their strategies and tactics to fit their MVO: W^3 and SPOT. The leading questions in W^3 (What do we want? What do they want? What can we do?) reinforce the importance of being clear about the unit's goals, stakeholders, stakeholder wants, and capabilities. W^3 also focuses managers' attention on seeking answers to the diagnostic questions that simultaneously satisfy the W^3 questions. Since these questions are only the leading questions, they permit managers to develop and ask additional following questions that seem appropriate to their situation in a heuristic manner. That is, managers identify issues and the salient aspects of issues through a personal discovery process that is started by asking the W^3 leading questions. This continues via a process of seeking answers to these and the following questions that can help to identify various target markets and a meaningful competitive advantage for their unit's products and services.

A SPOT analysis (examining the unit's strengths, problems, opportunities, and threats) helps managers advance their understanding of their business situation. The power of the SPOT tool is in helping managers to look at these four elements simultaneously. Managers want to identify those opportunities that can minimize or resolve problems, take important and distinctive advantage of the unit's strengths, and avoid or protect against threats. Such opportunities may not be common or identified. The challenge in such situations is to shift from analysis to creative thinking. Opportunities may be identifiable once clarity is gained on where managers might look. For example, asking the questions, "How can we leverage this strength?" or "What can we do to reduce this risk?" can stimulate creative thought.

Suggestion 2: Use W^3 and SPOT as tools for diagnosis, analysis, and creative thinking. They are critical to the issue identification and the discovery processes.

Concepts: Have You Taken a Personal Perspective?

Although the above suggestions often assist managers in their leadership efforts, managers may not adequately take into account the effects that their personal values, goals, and aspirations can have on their leadership efforts. When personal preferences are ignored or viewed as irrelevant, the potentially useful diagnoses and analyses may not get transformed into the intended strategies or deliberate events that others expect. This suggests that managers and their organizations could benefit from the integration of individual and organizational goals.

The human resource management literature is rich with ideas and models on how individuals and organizations can plan for and guide managerial careers.[2] Such models often suggest that one conduct an objective and systematic assessment of oneself and the work environment. For example, individual development efforts generally involve a self- or counselor-guided assessment of a manager's interests, values, skills, personality, past work accomplishments, and so forth. This information can be used to develop a set of personal themes or identity statements that capture the key factors that managers might consider in making career choices. Managers are also encouraged to establish career goals and objectives. This knowledge of one's self and goals can be used to direct the manager's search for information on different job or position possibilities. Through exploration, managers generate alternative job possibilities and choose positions that have some degree of fit with their themes, goals, and aspirations.

While managers are doing their self-assessment and career exploration, organizations are following a similar process: defining tasks and jobs that need to be accomplished, identifying the skills needed to do the task, recruiting and assessing people for their ability to perform the tasks effectively, and making employment decisions. Often the individual and organizational management development processes pay little attention to what the other system is doing—each is separately trying to attain its goals and maximize the returns on its investments. As a result of this, managers often report being confused about what to do or how to go about doing it. Many report feelings of helplessness, hopelessness, and frustration. Could it be that career planning efforts have created the false expectation that the management development process will be the systematic execution of a career plan in much the same way that the business planning effort has sometimes led to the expectation that strategic leadership is the systematic execution of the business plan? We believe that the answer is yes.

It took us many months to develop and accept this view of management development because it was not what we expected to find. Why was the process not more orderly and predictable for seasoned employees as it seemed to be for individuals entering the workforce out of high school or college? Managers were telling us that the existance of clear outcomes, such as getting their first job, were not as clear for them in mid-career. What we discovered was that the management development process was messy, ill-structured, and nonlinear in much the same way as the strategic leadership process. This led us to the observation that the MVO, W³, and SPOT concepts used in their work situations could also be used to diagnose and guide managers in their personal situations as well.

Suggestion 3: Use MVO, W³, and SPOT for you personally. Use the results of the diagnosis and analysis to guide your management development efforts.

Doing this means that the managers must know their mission—their reason for being. They need to develop a vision of where they what to be in five years and then develop objectives to guide their actions. Applying W³ to oneself means taking actions that are consistent with the answers to three questions: What do I want? What do they want? What can I do? Applying SPOT to oneself means that managers need to identify their skills and capabilities for the goals that they seek: What do I do well now? What problems am I confronting? What opportunities have I identified? What threats could materialize to hamper my career?

LOOK FOR BAD ORGANIZATIONAL HABITS—GET THEM UNDER CONTROL

Organizations have many habits—those attitudes, procedures, policies, and systems that guide managers in their thinking and influence how they interact and lead others. Organizational habits are entrenched in the organization's past. Many organizational habits may reflect well-learned efficiencies, but some of them can reinforce or unintentionally block actions directed towards the MVO of a unit. In many cases, organizational habits are invisible constraints to the thoughts and behaviors of managers. Like brushing your teeth before you take a shower, or eating the salad before the main course, organizational habits are frequently semiconscious acts. Yet embedded within these actions are ways of conducting business that may or may not be consistent with MVO. Below are several examples of "bad" habits, habits that can impede strategic leadership. As with personal bad habits, they need to be diagnosed, accepted as counterproductive, then systematically worked on to be overcome.

Bad Habit 1: Reifying Organizational Structures Rather than Treating Them as a Management Tool

Many managers treat their organizational structure as something that is permanent. This is what "structure" means in many professions. It seems that organizational structures, once codified on organizational charts, are intended to remain fixed. This may occur for several reasons. First, there is a belief in many businesses that structure is or should be stable. One organization recently had the choice of increasing its salesforce to support the infrastructure of the organization or altering the infrastructure. It made the decision to increase the size of the salesforce in spite of industry data that suggested there was an oversupply of sellers. The existing structure was retained out of habit.

Second, changing structure requires resources and necessitates behavioral change. This is especially true in businesses that do not have a norm of examining and refining the structure as part of the management process. The initial upheaval of "that first change in structure" can have significant short-term impact on the performance of the business despite the long-term benefits of the change. Once this inertia is overcome, subsequent revisions in structure tend to be less disruptive.

Third, a given organization structure links individual managers to the hierarchy, to their roles with their businesses, and to a status system. If you change organizational structure, you are implicitly making statements about the quality of the work of some members of management. The linkage of organizational structure to managers frequently means that management does not view structure as a tool or that some members of management (the ones feeling criticized) resist structural changes. The key is to unlink the two ideas in the minds of the entire business unit and position changes in organizational structure as necessary adjustments to changes in the environment. Structural changes are not necessarily criticisms of the existing management practices or individuals.

For managers in organizations such as Citibank, organizational structure represents the vehicle through which activities are conducted. There is a fundamental value within Citibank that supports a flexible attitude towards structure and the rate at which structural change takes place. This attitude is pervasive throughout numerous businesses within Citibank at many levels. The focus of management activity is directed outward towards its critical stakeholders; internal structures are designed and redesigned to meet the changing and emerging needs of these stakeholders.

Bad Habit 2: Looking for the One Right Organizational Structure

This is a corollary to habit 1. A useful example is the discussion surrounding centralization versus decentralization. Organizations often shift between being more centralized to being more decentralized, and back again. One is not necessarily better than the other. Both have benefits. Frequently organizations shift their structures to a decentralized approach because they have captured the bulk of the benefits of being centralized and are now trying to capture the benefits of being decentralized. The same is true in reverse. Organizations seek to centralize because they have captured the benefits of being decentralized and now seek the benefits from being centralized. In many instances, an organization's decision to choose one structure is based largely on its success in the other. Neither approach delivers the one right structure.

In the early stages of a company's development, organizations tend to be more centralized. This is done to facilitate the efficient execution of the organization's mission. As the organization grows, centralized control becomes more difficult, the needs of different product-market segments or lines of business become more complex and varied, and much of the internal structure in the organization becomes insulated and distanced from the customer.

As the benefits of control and uniformity of a centralized structure diminish, organizations begin to decentralize. They may establish separate profit or cost centers for units in the organization in an effort to: (1) bring managers closer to the marketplace, (2) improve operational efficiency, and/or (3) shorten their response time to changes initiated by competitors or emanating from market forces in their environments. Managers in charge of decentralized units often operate autonomous businesses. Decentralization is generally based on particular products, geographic regions, market segments, or distribution systems. Each business unit reports performance to the executive level via business reviews. Through decentralization the organization trades off some efficiency for greater effectiveness—doing more of the right things in response to a demanding marketplace.

The interaction between decentralized business units, the organization, and the environment ultimately brings to the surface new pressures that decentralization cannot accommodate. Pressure to develop strategic alliances within the organizations increases. This in turn can lead to the centralization of selected functions or activities.

Recentralization is done for several reasons, including cost savings through economies of scale, the development of competitive advantages through emerging synergies among businesses, and the need for the organization to present a coherent face to its customers and other stakeholders. The recentralized portion of the organization often includes technical and staff functions. Activities in this core include marketing, manufacturing, operations, quality control, research and development, information systems, finance, product development, human resources, and public affairs. The remaining decentralized portions of the organization are those parts that interface with the marketplace or key stakeholders that have significantly different wants. Understanding the benefits and costs of alternative structures enables a manager to use structure as a management tool.

Bad Habit 3: Letting Policies and Procedures Develop a Life of Their Own

Operating policies and procedures can be a critical stumbling block in developing and implementing a direction for the business. These activities represent the embedded, historic practices of the business. It is exactly these behaviors that can lead a business unit in one direction despite the best efforts of its managers to lead the business in another direction.

Information management is an especially critical procedure that should be examined. The type and amount of information collected and made available to the managers of a business can play a critical role in the business's ability to adapt to change. Most existing systems are not up to the task. Existing systems are often based on regulatory reporting requirements that were established to satisfy the needs of two stakeholders—government and stockholders. The information needed to address other stakeholders and their concerns is often not collected, or if collected, not shared with managers. Examples of such information would include the wants and concerns of customers, employees, suppliers, buyers, and internal units being served by or servicing a part of the business.

Those procedures that use the best sources of information for monitoring stakeholders and processing this information so that it is accessible to relevant managers should be examined. Careful management of this process can directly impact the extent to which managers at all levels can respond to changes in marketplace dynamics.

Bad Habit 4: Seeking Conformity and Stability, Rather than Balancing These Attributes with Diversity and Change

This speaks to a pivotal aspect of strategic leadership—embracing change. By embracing change we mean those behaviors that allow managers to look for information today that they did not know yesterday and to **embrace an attitude of responsiveness** to that information. Acting responsively to new information is a process of turning information into useful knowledge and using that knowledge to enhance one's strategic leadership. The use of strategic leadership practices can help managers organize and clarify beliefs and understandings about the environment so that when information emerges, they have a framework within which to receive and interpret it.

Organizational hiring systems are frequent perpetuators of habits. Many companies that have traditionally maintained an operational focus have implicitly used their hiring practices in support of this orientation. Businesses have selected individuals who have a natural inclination to execute routine tasks within a stable environment. In some organizations, this practice has been followed at many levels for an extended period of time. As a result, the clerical, supervisory, and management ranks are populated with individuals who have achieved success by practicing operationally driven behaviors. As these organizations expand their focus to include a more market-driven orientation, tensions are created for these individuals. They experience significantly more change and must adopt new behaviors in order to manage within this new environment. In some of these organizations, as they extend their focus to be more market-driven, it has become necessary to find a new type of employee. In other instances, it has meant significant training and development activities in order to build the required new skills and ways of thinking within the existing personnel base.

In some businesses, being responsive means downsizing the structure, decentralizing or recentralizing power and authority, redeploying resources, and streamlining the decision-making process to include the minimum number of individuals. In other businesses, it requires more risk-taking and the acceptance of failure as a potential by-product of risk-taking. By identifying procedures to define risks and the acceptable boundaries for prudent risk-taking, managers may be able to control risk while capturing some of its benefits.

Bad Habit 5: Not Linking the Reward System to Mission, Vision, and Objective Statements

The reward system is at the heart of encouraging a strategic perspective in every individual in the business. Yet few businesses do an adequate job of linking performance to rewards. Every organization has unique reward system practices. Managers need to examine these practices and determine if they are structured in a way that will motivate individuals towards the desired goals. As one manager noted, "If you don't aim compensation policies in the right direction, they frequently are aimed in the wrong direction. Misguided or unsupervised compensation policies are like loose cannons on a rolling ship. If you don't have them under control, they could end up sinking the ship."

Businesses should also use reward systems to encourage a balanced perspective between short-term and long-term thinking. Most managers treat their employees as if the employee were going to leave the organization tomorrow. People are certainly more likely to work for a greater number of companies today than 30 years ago, but managers should not encourage the short-term thinking that may accompany this level of mobility. One manager, who holds the position of legal counsel for his organization was recently overheard to say, "By the time they figure out the impact of my legal decisions, I'll be long gone. So who cares?" Using "golden handcuffs" to extend payment of annual bonuses over several years is one example of using compensation to build commitment and direct activity. The employee who accepts this is making a greater commitment than would otherwise exist. The employer is saying "we value you enough that we want to encourage you to stay."

Suggestion 4: Identify the organizational habits that have become counterproductive to accomplishing your MVO. Develop a plan to overcome these habits, solicit support for the plan, and then execute, execute, execute.

PROCESS: WHAT ARE YOUR DAYS REALLY LIKE?

We have characterized the process of creating agendas as an iterative, nonlinear one that is akin to the process used in completing a crossword puzzle. Managers can start their diagnosis or analysis of issues anywhere, they can start where things are easiest for them, they can change their minds as they go, and they can learn from earlier experiences to make subsequent activity easier or more effective. Collectively, this is what managers do across a wide variety of situations and organizational settings. But not all managers choose to follow such a process, nor are all situations and organizational settings conducive to such a process.

What is needed is a way for managers to diagnose the process that they typically use, or the different processes they use in different situations. Once managers understand their enacted processes, they can examine the benefits of those processes for the kinds of work that they do. If the work changes, then they are in a position to reevaluate their preferred process for its relevance to the new tasks. The most common way for managers to diagnose the process they use to create agendas is to keep a diary of what they do, how long it takes, whom it is done with (if anyone), and how it is done (by phone, meeting, delegation). The "what they do" needs elaboration to be of much help in diagnosing the agenda creation process. Under "what they do," managers might add: What issues were discussed? How well-developed is the current understanding of each issue? Which issues are outgrowths or redefinitions of previous issues? and Which issues are nearing resolution or closure? Maintaining a diary for as little as two days can provide managers with enough information to identify patterns in their process that are unique to them and their situations. The benefit of understanding the process is to gain control over it if that is needed and to determine when it is necessary to create more suitable agendas.

Suggestion 5: Personalize your understanding of the processes by which agendas get created by you and your unit. Use this knowledge to control or influence the process to create the desired agendas.

SKILLS: ARE YOU CLEAR ON WHAT YOU DO WELL AND ON WHAT YOU DO POORLY?

Strategic management skills are the third set of tools needed for strategic leadership. Our research suggests that most managers, though not all, had developed skill in the core competencies of delegating, motivating, controlling, and so forth. Gaps in management skills were more apparent with respect to six skill areas we subsequently defined as strategic management skills: knowing the business and markets, managing subunit rivalry, finding and overcoming threats, staying on strategy, being an entrepreneurial force, and accommodating adversity. How does one know if he or she possesses sufficient skill in these six areas to be effective in the middle game?

We have used the items discussed in Chapter Six as a multirater instrument with many organizations and managers. The objective in using a multirater instrument is to obtain assessments of these skills from several different perspectives: a self-view as well as those of peers, bosses, subordinates, and possibly other observers. The assessments from the different viewpoints need to be examined separately whenever possible to identify which skills are exhibited in different settings. For example, one may manage subunit rivalry to the satisfaction of the boss, but not to the satisfaction of those involved in the rivalry. Ideally, both constituencies would perceive equally effective skills.

The managers in our research generally knew about their relative skill levels for the core competencies (often through previous management development efforts on the part of their organizations), but they were generally unaware of their effectiveness level on any of the strategic management skills. They, and their organizations, had not previously identified the strategic management skills in performance appraisals or job descriptions. It was not that these skills were necessarily lacking, rather that they were not identified as being important to the tasks being done. Once the skills were defined, managers were quick to accept their importance and value in the middle game.

Suggestion 6: Diagnose your strategic management skills. Solicit input on these skills from your bosses, peers, and

subordinates in an open but confidential manner. Use the information acquired in your personal SPOT and W³ analyses to more precisely answer the question, "What can I do?"

STYLE: HOW DOES YOUR STYLE AFFECT YOUR COGNITIONS AND ACTIONS?

Style means different things to different people; we have focused on style as defined by Jung in his personality theory and subsequently measured by the Myers-Briggs Type Indicator.[3] There are many other dimensions of style that can affect managerial performance, such as being personable, charismatic, emotionally even-tempered, ambitious, and liking power.[4] These factors, much like the managerial core competencies noted above as skills, seem to be generally understood by managers. In many ways, they are a base line from which managers must develop. Sizable gaps in one's managerial style along such dimensions as being personable and charismatic, liking power, and so on tend to eliminate one from the game.

In contrast, the four dimensions proposed by Jung are not believed to identify any ideal styles that would generalize across a variety of situations. Managers can have preferences for extraversion or introversion, sensing or intuition, thinking or feeling, and judging or perceiving without their preferences enhancing or inhibiting their performances. The importance of style is not to develop the "right" style but to understand the effect that managers' styles have on their preferences for focusing their attention, acquiring information, making decisions, and orienting themselves to their world. The ability of managers to access and exhibit styles that are not their preferences when formulating strategic issues has been suggested as important to the development of executive-level talent.[5] Since the attributes of each of the 16 styles developed based on Jung's theory are equally positive in general, being able to draw on different styles as a function of the situation could be a strength of those managers who are able to do so.

Managers with strong personality type preferences generally have difficulty accessing their nonpreferred styles. Our research suggests that this makes them more susceptible to biases in their cognitive approach to issues and in the subsequent actions they wish to take. As we discussed in Chapter Seven, managers with different personality type preferences are inclined to pay attention to different types of information, treat it differently, and then make different recommendations. Sensing-Thinking type managers seem to rely on quantitative information and analytical problem-solving methods that lead to greater selective perception biases. Their actions rarely involve radical change and tend to be quick-fix solutions to problems.

Intuition-Thinking type managers exhibit preferences for holistic information, often ignoring disconfirming information, which can lead to greater positivity biases. Their actions tend to be more radical, often seeking opportunities and ignoring the threats involved in implementing their actions.

Sensing-Feeling type managers often place substantial importance on interpersonal relations and social approval, thereby becoming more susceptible to social-desirability biases. Their actions tend to conform to socially accepted norms and values, yield social approval, and satisfy the wants of significant others.

And, Intuitive-Feeling type managers like to use anecdotes, catchy symbols, and vivid imagery to make their points, increasing the likelihood of simplistic views of complex situations. Their actions tend to be novel and are often based on analogies between the present situation and purportedly similar situations.[6]

Suggestion 7: **Determine and become familiar with your personality type preferences. Use this knowledge to develop a sensitivity to the biases inherent in your style and those situations in which your style is not compatible with what is needed by your unit or the organization.**

Having made these suggestions, it is useful to reinforce the need for managers to attend to each of these elements in their day-to-day activities. The difficulties and failures we have observed are easily traced back to shortcomings on one or more of these elements: poor use of concepts, not understanding and influencing the process of creating agendas, lack of skills in dealing with the middle-game challenges, and/or insensitivity to the effect personal style has on cognitions and actions.

BUILD ON YOUR STRENGTHS OR DEVELOP NEW CAPABILITIES?

Managers frequently ask us, "Should we focus more on leveraging our strengths or developing the weaknesses that we have identified?" Since there is a natural tendency for managers to dwell on their weaknesses which generally proves counter-productive, we encourage them to leverage their strengths. By this we mean that managers need to: (1) know what their particular strengths are and in which situations they are really strengths, (2) become aware of when and how each strength can become a weakness, and (3) develop their strengths to their maximum potential. Often managers are not aware of their strengths. Some things have come easily to them for years; they never stopped to reflect on why. Much of the diagnosis suggested above is intended to clarify a manager's strengths. If the diagnosis is conducted thoroughly, it is possible to connect the strengths with the situations in which the strength was exhibited. This is particularly useful in helping managers determine when each of their strengths does *not* deliver for them. It can also suggest how a modest refinement of a strength can enhance its usefulness.

Suggestion 8: **Once you are comfortable with your strengths, use them to their fullest benefit. But be on the lookout for the situations when a strength becomes a weakness.**

But what about managers' developmental needs? How can managers develop a capacity for strategic leadership if they lack critical knowledge, skills, or aspects of personal style? Development is one answer; building effective teams of managers is another. Since development typically requires a change in the way managers think and behave, management development is likely to be a difficult thing to accomplish. Selecting people to work together who compensate for each other's weaknesses may be a more viable approach in some situations.

Consider, for example, the effects of personal style on managers' cognitions and actions. Managers take many actions suggestive of different biases, and there is some tendency for managers with a specific personality type preference to take more actions suggestive of some biases than others. This latter effect on decision-making could be reduced by accurate diagnosis of the decision situation along with selectively involving managers with different personality types to address each issue so as to minimize the risk of any particular bias dominating. Alternatively, individual managers could develop sufficient sensitivity to their predisposed style so as to guard against the bias by exhibiting flexibility in the style they chose to use in a specific situation. The more effective managers would be able to diagnose and understand differences in decision situations so as to involve other managers with styles that were less susceptible to their particular bias and/or modify their approach to complement the situation. This selection approach has its limitations as well as its benefits. The primary limitation is in knowing the strengths of other managers along with which particular strengths are needed in a particular situation.

Suggestion 9: **A great deal of the activity in the middle game involves groups of people working together. Make decisions around group composition that maintains a balance of capabilities—stress the complementarity of individual differences.**

In addition to leveraging strengths and managing team composition, the managers we have worked with want to develop their weaknesses. They want to have as great a capacity to excel as is possible. What they are not as aware of as they might be is the **size** of the challenge of developing a capacity for strategic leadership. Up until this point in many of these managers' lives, they quickly accomplished what they set out to do. It is because they have begun to experience the real challenges of the middle game that they have looked to management development as a way to improve their play. But the challenge is bigger than most realize.

WHAT OBSTACLES HINDERED THE DEVELOPMENT OF STRATEGIC LEADERSHIP?

We questioned many of the participants in our research programs about how they developed their strategic thinking abilities, and why they felt that some of their abilities remained underdeveloped, even though they were in important leadership roles in their organizations. We learned that many managers were not clear on how they developed the abilities that they exhibited effectively, nor were they certain about what to do to further develop their capacity for strategic leadership. Although some work and educational experiences were viewed as contributing to their development, one or more of the following four reasons were frequently mentioned for the abilities that remained underdeveloped:

1. It was difficult to learn strategic leadership while in supervisory and lower-level management positions. The fast-paced, fragmented, and varied activities of a typical work day seemed to focus on solving problems; opportunities to reflect and to think about the longer-term aspects of their units were rare.

2. The time lag between developing ideas, executing them, and measuring observable results was too long for many of the managers to clearly interpret the feedback received on their actions. Because of the large number of people involved in key decisions, it was also difficult to trace a particular outcome to any individual. Both of these factors made it difficult to learn from their successes and failures on the job. This lack of timely and meaningful feedback was accentuated for many managers because they moved on to their next assignment before the results of their prior actions were known.

3. Educational experiences involving lectures and case studies were seen as useful for introducing concepts such as defining what a mission statement might look like, or sharing the visions articulated by some current leaders of organizations. But lectures and case studies were not easily transferred to a manager's day-to-day actions, nor did they communicate how to manage in an ambiguous, frequently changing environment. Lectures and case studies fell short of the experiential dimension necessary for some to emotionally and behaviorally understand how the concepts taught related to their individual and organizational performances.

4. Transferring past learnings to the job was reported to be easiest when the context of the lesson was similar to the situation in which it was to be applied. But most of the work situations confronted that required greater capacity to think strategically were new to the individual; they were unlike previous experiences. When the gap between the past learning experience and the current application was wide, it was difficult to apply the concepts effectively to the new situation.

Suggestion 10: Start early in your career in the development of your capacity for strategic leadership. The opportunities to apply the various concepts and to develop the necessary skills will only be as available as you make them.

When one considers all the obstacles to developing a capacity for strategic leadership, it appears that strategic thinking may not be easily taught. Yet, aspects of strategic leadership are exhibited by many managers. People can develop a capacity for strategic leadership—even if they are not certain of how they developed it. By listening to these managers and then examining management development practices, we were able to identify the kinds of work experiences and educational activities that seem most likely to develop managers' capacities for strategic leadership.

WHICH WORK EXPERIENCES DEVELOP THE CAPACITY FOR STRATEGIC LEADERSHIP?

When interviewed about their careers, many executives have commented about how ill-prepared they were for an executive-level job when they were first offered one. They claimed that their past work assignments, management development activities, and life experiences in general had not prepared them for the challenges of leading a business unit or functional area. These comments have led several researchers to explore the nature of managerial work at senior levels in order to identify the types of assignments, experiences, and activities that develop the capacity for strategic leadership.

Work and Life Events

In a study of the key events in executives' lives, McCall et al. identified 16 types of learning experiences that successful executives believed contributed to their professional development.[7] Through an in-depth interview process, McCall et al. were also able to identify the kinds of management qualities that the various work experiences were believed to develop. Even though many of these experiences seem to focus on the development of managerial core competencies, some of the experiences directly address strategic leadership qualities paralleling the six strategic management skills. Specifically, McCall et al.'s leadership quality of "how the business works" is an element of **Knowing the Business and Markets.** "Dealing with conflict" is an aspect of **Managing Subunit Rivalry.** "Solving and framing problems" is part of **Finding and Overcoming Threats.** Although McCall et al. do not report any specific leadership qualities directed at **Staying on Strategy** or **Being an Entrepreneurial Force,** two of their leadership qualities are components of **Accommodating Adversity:** "comfort with ambiguity, stress, uncertainty" and "persevering under adverse conditions." The strength of the McCall et al. study and the similar studies previously cited is the linkage of specific work experiences to the leadership qualities desired.

Of the various categories of developmental work experiences, six have the potential to develop managers' capacities for strategic leadership. Of these six types of experiences, four involve a change in job assignment that differed from past assignments in one or more meaningful ways: (1) starting a business or project from scratch, (2) fixing or turning around a failing operation, (3) being involved in special projects or temporary assignments that were viewed as central to the organization, and (4) moving from a line operation to a staff position or vice versa. Two additional work experiences, categorized by McCall et al. as hardships, are aspects of accommodating adversity: (1) being demoted, missing a promotion, or getting an undesirable job, and (2) attending to work issues during a personal crisis such as a divorce, illness, or family death. It is through these six types of work experiences that managers develop the capacity to think strategically—to identify the different ways to attain their chosen objectives and to determine what actions are needed to get them into the positions in which they want to be.

Changes in job assignments stretch the managers' capacity for strategic leadership. The stretch associated with starting something from scratch was in the holistic nature of the assignment. Taking on such a task puts managers in charge with full line responsibility. They had to define jobs, identify staff, assign responsibilities, and create a work team. To do this effectively, each aspect of the business had to be learned (i.e., the tasks, how the tasks fit together, how the tasks lead to revenues and costs for the unit) and its markets understood (who the customers, suppliers, and competitors were, and what skills their employees exhibited effectively). Successfully starting something from the beginning forces managers to **know the business and markets.** If managers are also responsible for championing the project or business, including creating a vision of its success several years hence, they may also be developing skill in **being an entrepreneurial force.**

Work experiences that involved fixing or turning around a failing operation forced managers to learn about the business and markets while accommodating the adverse situation. They had to learn how to ask thought-provoking questions, how to diagnose what else could go wrong before it actually did, and how to respond quickly and flexibly to many different situations each day. Without developing and using their capacity for strategic thinking, it was easy to be overcome by the adversity—adversity that took many forms—including union strikes, loss of a large buyer, shutdown of a major supplier, raiding of key employees by a competitor, equipment breakdowns, legal or regulatory interventions, economic downturns, or technological obsolescence. Three strategic management skills can be strengthened through managing turnaround situations: developing **knowledge of the business and markets, finding and overcoming threats,** and **accommodating adversity.**

Involvement in special projects and temporary assignments challenged the managers' abilities to quickly understand a different work situation and perform effectively with people they had not dealt with in the past. Rivalry among members of a project team was common. Learning how to work productively with a group was essential in order to get individuals to make meaningful contributions to the task while respecting the conflicting views presented by others. This challenge increased when some members of the temporary group were not viewed as competent, or when they actively resisted influence attempts made by other members of the group. **Managing rivalry,** particularly when one is not the formal leader of the individuals involved, increases managers' abilities to think broadly about the objectives of the business and stimulates managers to identify and communicate how the different subunit goals are complementary.

The fourth type of job assignment that can enhance managers' strategic leadership is a move from a line operation to a staff position (or vice versa). Line-staff moves afford managers the opportunity to learn how the business works from a different perspective. Such moves often involve a great deal of change for individuals because they must either learn much more about a functional specialty (line to staff moves) or learn how all of the various functions collectively affect the entire business (staff to line moves). The uncertainty, stress, and ambiguity associated with line-staff moves challenges managers' abilities to **accommodate adversity.** It stretches managers' capacities for thinking in more complex ways, including how to **find and overcome threats** before they affect the business adversely.

Suggestion 11: **Seek out the kinds of job assignments and hardship experiences that will develop the specific skills desired. If personal development is not a priority, seek out the job assignments (or hardships) that capitalize on your strengths.**

Management Development Programs

Managerial work assignments and events can develop an ability for strategic leadership. But a number of such experiences will be needed. The size and scope of such events within the managerial workforce suggest that developing strategic leadership abilities on the job can be a lengthy and costly process. Executive development programs have been designed to develop a capacity to manage strategically more quickly and economically.

Course work was identified in the McCall et al. study as an experience that could foster leadership qualities. It was cited by managers as being most beneficial to their ability to gain technical knowledge, understand management models and theories, solve and frame problems, and develop self-confidence and judgment skills. The increasing number of executive development efforts sponsored by organizations certainly demonstrates the perceived value of formal education. But, does course work lead to a greater capacity for strategic leadership? Some experts have concluded that traditional educational methods have not adequately identified and taught strategic leadership.[8] Organizational simulations, including computer simulations and simulated company work experiences, may be able to address this gap.

Each manager's experience in a simulated organizational environment is real for him or her because it provides an opportunity to exercise skills in pursuit of a wide range of goals through different strategies. Each manager determines the mission, vision, and objectives of the firm, which can include expansion or contraction of specific parts of the business, diversification into other lines of business, an increase in customer service, and/or the development of the firm's human resources or community relations. The manager develops strategies for attaining those objectives, which can include finding and targeting a profitable niche, developing a prestigious product offering for the high net worth customer, going after the broad middle market via a differentiation strategy based on service, or becoming a regional low-cost provider of a product or service. Which objectives and strategies are right? It depends on the ability of the managers to think strategically and on their collective ability to assess and respond to lifelike organizational situations.

The power of organizational simulations is that they are comprised of a representative work environment and management issues, just as flight simulators are comprised of a representative airplane environment and flying issues. They are realistic contexts in which managers think, act, and interact in much the same way they do on their real jobs. In contrast to their real jobs, however, they receive quick and rich feedback from self-assessment, peer assessments, and instructors' evaluations on their strategic leadership abilities. Did they have a mission, share a vision, establish realistic objectives? Were they clear on what they wanted, what the key stakeholders wanted, and what they could do? Did they know the business and markets, find and overcome threats, stay on strategy, and accommodate adversity well? Who were the entrepreneurial forces? Who managed subunit rivalry to the benefit of all concerned? Did they take advantage of their personal styles to create an effective work team?

The benefits of such work experiences as tools to develop managers' capacities for strategic leadership are that they can be offered to a large number of people, at relatively low cost, when and as often as is needed. The organization does not need to wait for an appropriate work situation to occur before it can offer someone professional development. Since feedback in management development programs can be timely and directed to the skills of interest, the organization gains some control over the learning that takes place. The organization also avoids the high costs of failure when a skill is not learned effectively. Failing to turn an ailing simulated organization around can provide some of the learning that failing to turn around a real organization provides—with lower costs and less personal trauma.

Suggestion 12: **Seek out management development programs that provide both relevant concepts and opportunities to practice them through participation in realistic work experiences that are observed and that yield both instructor and peer feedback on your performances.**

Mentoring Relationships

Mentoring is developing a meaningful professional relationship with someone other than a boss or subordinate, and generally not someone in the direct line of command. When one develops a mentor relationship with someone in the organizational hierarchy, the other manager is typically referred to as the mentor, and the more junior manager the protege. A "prototypical" mentoring relationship provides several important career and psychosocial functions that can greatly support the protege's development of a capacity for strategic leadership.[9]

The career functions are those aspects of the mentor relationship that support organizational advancement. They include sponsorship, exposure and visibility, coaching, protection, and challenging assignments. Of these, exposure and visibility, coaching, and challenging assignments can lead to a greater capacity for strategic leadership.

Exposure and visibility occur through being provided the opportunity to participate in activities and assignments that require presentations to more senior managers. Because such activities often involve project proposals, business plans, and committee or task force reports, they provide an opportunity for the protege to think more broadly about key business issues and to consider a longer-term perspective in determining the possible resolution of these issues.

The coaching that a mentor can provide often reflects the mentor's more seasoned view of the situations, the organization, and the current issues. Mentors are frequently able to identify and articulate aspects of the organization's culture and habits that more junior managers have yet to diagnose or experience. By sharing this information with a protege, the protege is able to accelerate his or her learning in areas that are key to effective strategic leadership.

Mentors can also facilitate their protege's consideration for challenging assignments. It is often the demands of turning a business unit around, starting up a new operation, or dealing with hardships that lead to the development of one's strategic management skills. Having a mentor support one's nomination for such positions, and having a coach available in one's initial dealings in these situations, can provide the experience base necessary to internalize responses to the many strategic leadership challenges confronted.

Suggestion 13: **Look for opportunities to develop a mentor-protege relationship with more senior managers and executives who have mastered many of the challenges of strategic leadership. Nothing is more valuable to an apprentice than a good master craftsperson.**

BEYOND THE CAPACITY
FOR STRATEGIC LEADERSHIP

The capacity for strategic leadership only defines the potential energy and resources available for the task. Strategic leadership is doing, not just thinking, possessing skills, knowing how the process works, and understanding one's personal style. Like any good craftsperson or artist, the mental preparation is essential to a great performance. But practice, rehearsals, more practice, and trial runs are necessary to translate the mental preparation into excellence in execution. And that is what the audience wants—excellence in execution. The audience is comprised of many people, most of whom have become stakeholders of one type or another. They have a stake in your performance. The mental preparation and physical practice are necessary to meet their wants. This leads us to our final suggestion:

Suggestion 14: **Seek out opportunities to develop and practice strategic leadership. It does not matter whether the context is related to work, to one's personal growth, to one's family, or to one of the many other organizations of which we have selectively become a part. Strategic leadership opportunities are somewhat of a scarce resource, but strategic leadership is even more scarce. Scarcities eventually stimulate more supply. Now is the time to meet the challenge; tomorrow may not be soon enough.**

ENDNOTES

[1]Portions of this chapter are based on the following works: Stephen A. Stumpf, "Towards a Heuristic Model of Career Management." *The International Journal of Career Management,* 1989, *1*(1), 11–20; and Stephen A. Stumpf, "Work Experiences That Stretch Managers' Capacities for Strategic Thinking." *Journal of Management Development,* 1989, *8*(5), 31–39.

[2]See, for example, D. C. Feldman, *Managing Careers in Organizations.* (Glenview, IL: Scott, Foresman and Company, 1988); J. H. Greenhaus, *Career Management* (New York: The Dryden Press, 1987); and M. London and S. A. Stumpf, *Managing Careers* (Reading, MA: Addison-Wesley, 1982).

[3]For more information on where to obtain the Myers-Briggs Type Indicator, contact Consulting Psychologists Press, 577 College Avenue, Palo Alto, California, 94306.

[4]John P. Kotter, *The General Managers* (New York: The Free Press, 1982).

[5]Arkalgud Ramaprasad and Ian I. Mitroff, "On Formulating Strategic Problems." *Academy of Management Review,* 1984, *9*, 597–605.

[6]See also Usha C. V. Haley and Stephen A. Stumpf, "Cognitive Trails in Strategic Decision-Making: Linking Theories of Personalities and Cognitions." *Journal of Management Studies,* 1989, *26*, 477–97; and Stephen A. Stumpf, "The Effects of Personality Type on Choices Made in Strategic Decision Situations." New York University Working Paper #89-93, 1989.

[7]Morgan W. McCall, Jr., Michael M. Lombardo, and Ann M. Morison, *The Lessons of Experience* (Lexington, MA: Lexington Books, 1988); and Esther

Lindsey, Virginia Homes, and Morgan W. McCall, Jr., *Key Events in Executives' Lives* (Technical Report No. 32) (Greensboro, NC: Center for Creative Leadership, 1987).

[8]Lyman Porter and L. McKibbin, *Management Education and Development.* (New York: McGraw-Hill, 1988).

[9]Kathy E. Kram, *Mentoring at Work: Developmental Relationships in Organizational Life* (Glenview, IL: Scott, Foresman and Company, 1985).

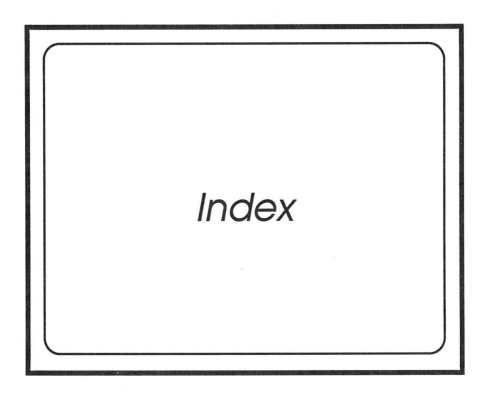

Index